Leo J. Koffeman, Johannes Smit (Eds.)

# Protestant Church Polity in Changing Contexts II

# Church Polity and Ecumenism

## Global Perspectives

edited by

Leo J. Koffeman, Allan J. Janssen
and Johannes Smit

Volume 3

LIT

# Protestant Church Polity in Changing Contexts II

## Case Studies

Proceedings of the International Conference, Utrecht, The Netherlands, 7 – 10 November, 2011

edited by

Leo J. Koffeman and Johannes Smit

LIT

Cover image: Nico Thöne

This publication is sponsored by Kerk in Actie

This book is printed on acid-free paper.

**Bibliographic information published by the Deutsche Nationalbibliothek**
The Deutsche Nationalbibliothek lists this publication in the Deutsche Nationalbibliografie; detailed bibliographic data are available in the Internet at http://dnb.d-nb.de.

ISBN 978-3-643-90311-2

**A catalogue record for this book is available from the British Library**


Klosbachstr. 107
CH-8032 Zürich
Tel. +41 (0) 44-251 75 05
Fax +41 (0) 44-251 75 06
E-Mail: zuerich@lit-verlag.ch
http://www.lit-verlag.ch

LIT VERLAG Dr. W. Hopf
Berlin 2014
Fresnostr. 2
D-48159 Münster
Tel. +49 (0) 2 51-62 03 20
Fax +49 (0) 2 51-23 19 72
E-Mail: lit@lit-verlag.de
http://www.lit-verlag.de

**Distribution:**

In Germany: LIT Verlag Fresnostr. 2, D-48159 Münster
Tel. +49 (0) 2 51-620 32 22, Fax +49 (0) 2 51-922 60 99, E-mail: vertrieb@lit-verlag.de

In Austria: Medienlogistik Pichler-ÖBZ, e-mail: mlo@medien-logistik.at
In the UK: Global Book Marketing, e-mail: mo@centralbooks.com
In North America: International Specialized Book Services, e-mail: orders@isbs.com
e-books are available at www.litwebshop.de

# TABLE OF CONTENTS

# PREFACE

In a globalizing world all churches have to deal with changing contexts. Changes may regard the relation between Christianity and other religions, or the development of new relationships between Christian world families. They may also be a result of political changes, which, in some instances, produce new legal relations between churches and states.

Protestant churches are continuously challenged by such changes. That is why an international conference of church order experts was held in Utrecht, the Netherlands, in early November, 2011. The theme, Protestant Church Polity in Changing Contexts, was chosen in order to further the exchange of experiences and views regarding the contextualisation of Protestant church polity.

This volume offers church polity case studies from different parts of the world. They put some flesh on the bones of the more theoretical contributions that can be found in a companion volume: Volume I: Ecclesiological and Historical Contributions. Narratives like these contribute to a better understanding of the theological questions at stake. Indeed, the distinction between theoretical articles and case studies is quite relative. Many examples of how church order stipulations function in ecclesial practice can be found in the other volume. In this volume the interpretation of the case studies also produces new insights in fundamental issues of church polity as a theological (sub-)discipline. Basically, the articles collected in these volumes can aid in strengthening this discipline both in terms of content and of method. Either explicitly or implicitly, they deal with such fundamental questions as the extent to which it is (still) possible to speak of what has traditionally been understood as 'principles of Reformed polity.' At the same time, they contribute to a better understanding of the theological nature of the discipline of church polity as such.

Most churches as represented at the conference share a Dutch Reformed heritage; historically, their church orders date back to the presbyterial-synodical system of the church order of Dordt (1619). All contributions published in this volume have this tradition in common. Nevertheless, major differences are visible in the way this tradition is valued in light of present contexts.

The contribution of Dries le Roy Du Plooy serves well as an introductory article, particularly for those who are not really acquainted with this specific Reformed branch. It offers a clear presentation of a more traditional approach of church polity, based on classical theological sources.

Three articles present cases of an overall revision of church orders. Zakaria Ngelow was and is actively involved in such processes of church order contextualization of several churches on the Indonesian island of Sulawesi. Wim Dreyer deals with s similar development within the Netherdutch Reformed Church in Africa (South Africa), as a consequence of a missional ecclesiology. His faculty colleague Johan van der Merwe did research with regard to the way migrants from South Africa to New Zealand transcend inherited denominational boundaries in the way they organize church life there.

A more general but no less contextual approach is to be found in the contribution of Roy Alexander Surjanegara; he formulates some major challenges the presbyterial-synodical tradition has to face in his country, Indonesia.

The next five articles focus on particular ecclesial issues, and the way church orders can or should facilitate changing church life from this specific perspective. Robert Vosloo (South Africa) gives an account of the church polity aspects of the reception of the Belhar Confession — born from the anti-apartheid struggle — by the (former 'white') Dutch Reformed Church. Leon van den Broeke (The Netherlands) portrays the development of the interpretation and role of the 'classical assembly', a key aspect of the presbyterial-synodical system, through the centuries, including current challenges. Within the same area, Allan Janssen focuses on the issue of establishing a separate (in this case) Korean-language classis within an majority English-language church, taking the catholicity of the church as his theological standard. The contribution of Godfrey Msiska deals with two major issues challenging his church in Zambia, i.e. church discipline and church unity. Finally, the understanding of diaconate in a church order framework determines the narrative of Hans de Waal (The Netherlands).

It is not only theologians who attended the conference. As a lawyer, Helena van Coller presented — and presents here — a survey of recent developments with regard to the freedom of religion in the context of the Constitution of post-apartheid South Africa.

Finally, two contributions again raise fundamental questions as to central ideas of Protestant church polity. Willie Zeze, from Malawi, deals with authority and leadership in his church from the perspective of the headship of Christ. And Herman Speelman (The Netherlands) argues in favor of flexibility as an important aspect of protestant church polity, drawing upon key features of the Reformation.

An international group of scholars took responsibility in preparing the conference and worked together in evaluating and selecting the essays presented in these volumes: PoHo Huang, Mary-Anne Plaatjies van Huffel, Lazarus Purwanto, Robert Vosloo, and Allan Janssen, together with the editors of this volume.

With gratitude we recognize the role of the Protestant Church in the Netherlands, its department for Mission and World Service 'Kerk in Actie', the Protestant Theological University in the Netherlands, and the Council for World Mission, in organizing and financially facilitating the conference as well as the publication of the Proceedings. They also made it possible to participate in the conference for a number of participants who would not have been able to come without such support.

These volumes are to be among the first in a new series, 'Church Polity and Ecumenism. Global Perspectives', a welcome joint initiative of LIT-Verlag and the editors of the series.

Allan Janssen and the Rev. Joshua Bode (USA) reviewed the English, and the Rev. Gerard van Zanden (The Netherlands) assisted in technical lay-out. Their precision made it possible to present the contributions of participants for whom English is not their native language on an equal footing with those of native English speakers.

The very fact that a new series was set up expresses the hope of the editors that the ecumenical and global theological exchange on church polity will continue.

Leo J. Koffeman
Johannes Smit
*Epiphany, 2014*

# THE FOUNDATION AND RELEVANCE OF REFORMED CHURCH POLITY

## as a Theological Science

Dries le Roy du Plooy

### *1. Introduction*

The title of this article refers explicitly to Reformed church polity, not to Protestant church polity in general. It is clear from some of the referees who commented on my proposal that there is among at least some theologians a desire to be very critical toward Reformed principles and toward what is traditionally known as Reformed church polity. I am therefore aware of a new spirit to change. But often it is change for the sake of change, without convincing criticism addressed to a real and solid reformational approach. I am not implying that one does not have to be well aware of the current discourse, relevant questions, fresh thoughts and new developments. For example, it is indeed important to take into account an emphasis on ecumenical concerns; the character which should be investigated and appreciated (see Koffeman 2009, 26). The most prominent reasons to take an in-depth look at the foundation and relevance of Reformed church polity include the following:

› One can never accept that the final word has been spoken about the best and most effective way the church of Christ could be governed. In theological terms this means that the church has a continuing obligation to assess critically the *status quo*, or the so-called *ius constitutum,* to determine whether changes should be made to get closer to the so-called *ius constituendum.*

› From the angle of scientific theory, it is imperative that church polity as a theological science be able to account for its points of departure, fundamental principles, sources, presuppositions, and function and task (see Vergeer 1993, 563–582). More than two decades ago Nauta, in view of the development of Protestant church polity in Germany, expressed the ardent wish for profound reflection on the foundations of church polity (see Nauta 1971, 38; see also Koffeman 2009, 10).

- Van 't Spijker points out that the spiritual climate of the *Aufklärung* (Enlightenment) had a great impact on the philosophy of church polity, especially at the beginning of the nineteenth century (see Van 't Spijker 1992, 995–997). He maintains that the philosophy of the *Aufklärung* is being revived in our time, largely because people reflect pragmatically according to the needs of the time and present conditions, and from an autonomous humanistic perspective on the church and church polity.
- Tension has developed between the structure and the message of the church, and two extremes have emerged: on the one hand there is a spiritualistic attenuation of church polity, where Spirit and Word are in confrontation with each other in such a way that the work of the Spirit and the charismatic element are the primary focus; on the other hand there is a sociological approach, by which the organization of the church has become the concern of human sciences and the theological view of the church drowned out by a secularized perspective (see Van 't Spijker 1992, 996–997).
- Tremendous interest in practical theology has developed. Spoelstra highlights the dilemma between practical theology and ecclesiology (see Spoelstra 1992, 299–320). He believes that ecclesiology is losing ground since it is allegedly concerned with theory, while practical theology is gaining ground since it allegedly focuses on the practical aspects of the church. It is therefore essential that theologians should have a better understanding of the relevance of Reformed church polity as a science.

I do not intend to enter into a polemic with various approaches and perspectives, but to approach the matter theologically. I shall therefore concentrate on a few key questions:
- Whose responsibility is it to examine and establish the theological foundations of church polity?
- What is church polity, and what is the encyclopaedic place of church polity in theology?
- What are the sources, norms and points of departure of church polity?
- What is the function and task of church polity?
- What are the scriptural principles in church polity?

## 2. *Who must determine the foundation?*

### 2.1 *Scientific theory*

The question of whose responsibility it is to establish the foundations of church polity is linked to the question of what science is, since the essence of science is to examine the foundations, nature, methods and boundaries of science. Reflection on the foundations of a science therefore falls under scientific theory, whose object of study is science *per se.*

2.2 *Philosophy and theology*

Ouweneel, an exponent of the Philosophy of the Idea of Justice, maintains that philosophy is indisputably the science concerned with the foundations of the various sciences. He contends that the lines drawn from Scripture to theological science pass through philosophy (see Ouweneel 1989, 11, 21; Ouweneel 1993, 35). Heyns and Jonker, on the other hand, maintain that philosophy has no right to assume sole jurisdiction over scientific theory, since such jurisdiction belongs to the science in question. According to them, scientific theory is an interscientific discipline in which each science compiles its own theory in conjunction with the philosophy of science (see Heyns and Jonker 1974, 16–17).

The theologian Coertzen wrote several works on the methodology and sources of church polity in which he regards Scripture as the sole determinant of the principles of church polity (see Coertzen 1991, 20–135). Strauss, on the other hand, believes that philosophy plays a crucial part in determining these principles. He regards the Bible and philosophy as co-determinants since his underlying idea is that scientific theory is the exclusive field of philosophy (see Strauss 1991A, 23–34).

Because of the unity of science (see Stoker 1970, 123–180), because of the rejection of pan-philosophism (see Stoker 1961, 240–244), and because we accept that the various sciences assist one another in their own fields of study, we can state unequivocally that tension between theology and philosophy is unnecessary and irrelevant. When theologians are wrestling with fundamental questions of their subject, they are in fact engaged in their subject as theologians while being at the same time receptive to the insights of other sciences, such as philosophy. They do not pretend to have sole insight into the revelation of Scripture, but allow themselves to be predominantly guided by Scripture, which is their particular field of study. When philosophers (especially Christian exponents) study the science of a subject, their particular field of study is the philosophy of that subject, not the subject as such. Since foundations are an integral part of a subject, philosophers in turn should be guided by theology (see Stoker 1940, 293–331).

2.3 *Task of church polity as a theological science*

The answer to the question of who is responsible for establishing the foundations of church polity is that church polity itself as a theological science is primarily responsible for it. Church polity should take note of contributions to its subject from the philosophy of science. It is also important that church polity, which is but one of several theological disciplines, should make good use of the results of biblical and dogmatic research. This does not imply that church polity should not do exegesis on its own or should not be familiar with the dogma and confessions of 'the church.

The tremendous importance that practical theology or diaconiology have come to assume, and the confusion that has developed about the fields of study of practical theology (diaconiology) and ecclesiology (see Spoelstra 1992, 299–320; cf. Te Velde 1989), have made it imperative to enter into discussion with theologians in these fields as well. Koffeman emphasizes the relevance and importance of practical theology, as it addresses and resolves needs and challenges of the church today (see Koffeman 2009, 24). Church polity cannot separate itself from the contribution of practical theology, but has to cooperate and support it with frameworks and outlines of principle.

### 2.4 *Church polity and juridical science*

Another important question concerns the relationship between church polity and juridical science. Should juridical science not have input into the discussion on the foundations of church polity? There is no *fundamental* difference between different kinds of justice (such as those of church polity, constitutional law, criminal law and disciplinary law) since all creation is under the law and reign of God. *All* kingdoms, including those of the world and of the church, are under the jurisdiction of the Word of God and under the reign of Jesus Christ to whom all power in heaven and on earth has been given (see Van Drimmelen 1992, 204–205). Roeleveld points out that the rules of natural justice can be found in Scripture, though not necessarily phrased in the same words (see Roeleveld s.a., 19). Koffeman deals with this and attends to the fact that church polity is an exponent of a law with its own structure, methods and dynamics (see Koffeman 2009, 83–100). I give attention to this issue below where I focus briefly on the hermeneutics of church polity and argue that church polity could benefit from learning from legal science with regard to interpretation of legal texts.

Yet church polity is *sui generis,* since the church has a unique character (see Kuyper 1909, 244). No community other than the church is described as the body of Christ. The Head of this body is Christ, which implies that he himself reigns in it through his Word and Spirit (Eph. 1; *Heidelberg Catechism* [HC], Lord's Day 48). In the church God alone determines what is right. God alone gives the church in his Word and under the guidance of the Spirit the power *(potestas)* and the task *(ministerium)* to study and formulate justice and order in and for the church from the perspective of the Gospel, thus serving the reign of Christ in the church (see Smit 1985, 281–284; Pienaar 1982, 271).

The development of human rights and the important role of official state constitutions have forced churches to position themselves in principle and in practice with regard to the relation of a state constitution to the church order of a given denomination. I will revisit this matter below.

## *3. Church polity as a theological science*

### 3.1 *What is church polity?*

#### *3.1.1 Reformed view*

Haitjema maintains that according to the Reformed Protestant view church polity is undoubtedly a theological subject (see Haitjema 1951, 9). The Reformed viewpoint is that legitimate church polity must be rooted in Holy Scripture and that the confession regarding the church provides the normative guidelines for the church (Haitjema 1951, 9–10). Since theology is a science that studies the Word of God as his particular revelation to people so that they can acquire knowledge of God and of his relationship with all creation (cosmos), church polity is indeed a theological science. Under the guidance of the illuminating working of the Holy Spirit, it studies the inspired Word of God to discover the norms, information, rules and guidelines which God provides for the orderly and uplifting government of his church. This is the viewpoint of Calvin and many other theologians of the Calvinist tradition.

Calvin may be regarded as the architect of the Reformed churches and as the father of Reformed church polity, since he believed that the organization of the church should be based on scriptural data according to which Christ, as the ultimate architect, indicates how he wishes to rule and build up his church. Calvin deals extensively with this matter in Book Four of his *Institutes,* where he frequently makes it clear that church government should not deviate from the precepts set out in Scripture (on Calvin as the architect of the church see Wallace 1988, 133–146). Calvin maintains that even human decrees in church government should be fully divine in character *(prorsus divinae)*, i.e., derived from Scripture (see Calvin 1559, IV, 10, 30; Plomp 1967, 14). Calvin's standpoint that the church should have a true and legitimate constitution (see Calvin 1559, IV, 12, 2) and a well-organized form of government (see Calvin 1559, IV, 10, 27) has a wide range of supporters.

Voetius, in his *Politica ecclesiastica* (1663–1676), describes church polity as 'the sacred science of governing the visible church' (*scientia sacra regendi ecclesiam visibilem*) (see Bouwman 1928, 10). Prominent exponents of Reformed church polity, including Rutgers (see Rullman 1918, 125), Kuyper (see Kuyper 1909, 231–248), Bouwman (see Bouwman 1928, 10–15), Jansen (see Jansen 1947, 6–7) and Nauta (see Nauta 1971, 16), to mention but a few, agree that church polity is not merely a chain of rules and regulations but that it constitutes a theological science which studies the rules for the architecture of the church (as a building) and for people's conduct and existence in the building. It has to study in Scripture the justice of God which obtains — and should obtain — in the church.

In a survey of the viewpoints of Reformed theologians in South Africa, Coertzen shows that no doubt exists among them about the theological nature of church polity (see Coertzen 1991, 156–166). An example to demonstrate this can be found in Heyns and Jonker, who describe church polity as a theological science — a science that studies the following (see Heyns and Jonker 1974, 286–288):

› The fundamental principles of the subject as they are taught in Scripture (the ius constituendum)
› The history of the subject
› The order (ius constitutum) obtaining in a specific church

Pont (see Pont 1981, 6–18), Van der Linde (see Van der Linde 1965, 32; Van der Linde 1978), Spoelstra (see Spoelstra 1989, 1–10), Smit (see Smit 1985, 305), Coertzen (see Coertzen 1991, 152–166), and many other Reformed theologians belong to the school which regards church polity as a theological science. Although Koffeman emphasizes that theology as a science is in principle free, he admits the close relation or connection which exists between church polity and confessing (see Koffeman 2009, 21). The function of the Reformed creeds was and still is crucial. No one practices science without a paradigm or presuppositions, and within Reformed church polity the *disciplina* is part of the *doctrina* (cf. *Belgic Confession, Confessio Belgica,* CB).

### *3.1.2 View of German church polity*

It is important to note that in Germany church polity is regarded as a juridical science. During the twentieth century a juridical theology developed in Germany which concentrates on the theological foundation of church law, even though it still regards church polity as a juridical science (see Coertzen 1991, 155; for an overview of the development of German church polity and of the struggle to escape the traditional two-kingdoms doctrine of Luther and the concomitant tension between church and justice — as typified by Sohm in particular — see Smit 1985, 269–283, Coertzen 1991, 5–166, and Bakker 1992B).

Reformed church polity is sometimes accused of becoming stagnant, since its exponents are inclined to stress well-known principles over and over again. German church polity is then cited as an example of dynamic development (see Botha 1993, 1–7). The problem here is that two totally dissimilar matters are being compared: the Lutheran and the Calvinist traditions. Reformed theologians can indeed be grateful for developments in the church polity of the confessing churches (*Bekennende Kirchen, Evangelische Kirche in Deutschland*), not only because they provide valuable theological contributions but also because they incline toward Calvinist principles wherein Scripture is regarded as the norm for church government (see Coertzen 1991, 157).

In their works on the development of church polity in Germany before, during and after the Second World War, the aforementioned authors point out that Luther's two-kingdoms doctrine and the radical division between the visible and the invisible church result in a dualism between the spiritual and the juridical church. Sohm maintains that since justice has a secular origin and nature it conflicts with the essence of the church. Harnack supports this, and says that justice is not essentially based on religion. He nevertheless regards justice in the church as essential, since the church as an organization must be orderly.

In the field of justice in Germany, a considerable change has occurred since the 1930s, especially after the Second World War, by which attempts have been made to eliminate the tension between church and justice (see Smit 1985, 269–283). Liermann wishes to apply the form of general jurisprudence directly to church polity. Schlaich, on the other hand, believes that church polity should be distinguished from constitutional justice, and that church polity should represent a response to what Christ has given to his church. Heckel, Wolf and Dombois make the most prominent contributions toward reconciling church and justice. Heckel reinterprets, as it were, Luther's doctrine, and maintains that Luther rejected neither justice nor church polity. Heckel's view is basically that church polity is based on love. The spiritual law of love applies in the church. According to Wolf, church polity is confessional justice; in other words, church polity (church order) and the confession are a unity. Church polity is based on the confession or creed and its task is to concretize the confession in the life of the church.

Dombois's view is that church polity is the justice of grace (*Recht der Gnade*). His view implies that this type of justice cannot expect more from the people than what God gives to them. Its precise objective is to enable us to confront God so that God can give his justice to us. For Dombois the foundation of church polity can be found in Jesus Christ's fourfold command regarding mission, baptism, Holy Communion and administration of the keys of the kingdom of God—all of which are God's acts of grace to people on earth. Koffeman points to the important contribution of Dombois with regard to the necessity of ecumenical church polity (see Koffeman 2009, 27–48). An ecumenical approach safeguards the church against exclusivism, stresses the relevance of criticism of fellow churches, and makes churches aware of ecumenical relations and of their participation in the ecumenical environment. Such an approach in church polity allows for ecumenical mutual criticism.

Two important questions among members of the Reformed community are: whether church polity is concerned solely with the church as an institution, and whether church polity concentrates only on the visible side of the church.

### *3.1.3 The church as an institute and organism*

As far as the first question is concerned, we find a variety of opinions. According to Kuyper, church polity is concerned with the church as an institute (see Kuyper 1909, 232–246), and He is supported by Bouwman (see Bouwman 1928, 10), Kleynhans (see Kleynhans 1982, 3–5), and several others. Haitjema disagrees with Kuyper and contends that church polity is also concerned with the church as an organism (see Haitjema 1951, 7–8). Spoelstra warns against church polity focusing too much on the church as an institute, and advocates an approach based on the kingdom of God (see Spoelstra 1989, 2–10). Recently, Velema has also criticized Kuyper's distinction between institute and organism. He suggests that that approach should be abandoned since believers are working in the kingdom of God and are serving their community through their work in the church to the glory of the kingdom (see Velema 1991, 295–309).

In my opinion, church polity is concerned with the church as such and not only with the church as an institute. Although church polity focuses essentially on the foundations — proclaiming the Gospel, administering the sacraments and exercising discipline — so as to equip believers for service in the community, the view that church polity is concerned solely with an institute is too narrow and restrictive.

### *3.1.4 Visible and invisible church*

The question whether church polity is concerned solely with the visible side of the church, as answered in the affirmative by Voetius, Bouwman and others (see Bouwman 1928, 1–10; Bakker 1992A, 13f.), should be approached with care. On one hand, there can be no distinction between the visible and the invisible church. On the other hand, it is true that church polity, in so far as it formulates concrete justice for the church, focuses on the empirical church (see Heyns and Jonker 1974, 286).

### *3.1.5 Kingdom as the point of departure*

When we take the kingdom of God as our point of departure and consider that church polity is primarily concerned with obedience to Christ in his reign as the only Head of the church, it becomes evident that church polity embraces more than the organization of the visible, empirical side of the church. The purpose of church polity is to study in Scripture how Christ can penetrate into the hearts of his children through the administration of the keys of the kingdom so that the church truly becomes the body of Christ.

This implies that church polity is not concerned with the *ius circa sacra*, i.e. the external legal aspects of church life, but with the *ius in sacra*, that is, with conduct, rules and justice in the church as an assembly of believers where the church itself should study these matters in the light of the Word and under the guidance of the Holy Spirit (see Haitjema 1951, 13; Coertzen 1991, 159).

*3.1.6 Definition*

Church polity may be defined as *the theological science which studies and formulates—in the light of the written Word of God and the normative response of the confession to the Word of God, and under the guidance of the Holy Spirit—the justice of God and, consequently, the reign of Christ in the church, and makes all these available to serve and build up the church. It is an ongoing process.*

*3.2 Encyclopaedic place*

I now turn to the encyclopaedic place of church polity. Kuyper and Bouwman indicate that some theologians exclude church polity from theology (see Kuyper 1909, 231f.; Bouwman 1928, 10–15). This is a consequence of canon law which embraces not only the church but also society and the state. In Protestant circles, this is a consequence of church polity being regarded as a practical subject.

Schleiermacher (1768–1834) did not improve matters. He was strongly influenced by pietism, and in turn exerted great influence on the Neo-Protestant model of theology (see Spoelstra 1992, 304). Schleiermacher also felt a strong affinity for Kant's rationalism and his sharp distinction between theory and practice. Schleiermacher therefore divides theology into three subjects: philosophical theology (the root of the theological tree), including philosophy of religion and apologetics; historical theology (the trunk of the tree), including Old and New Testament, church history and dogmatics; and practical theology (the crown of the tree), which is primarily concerned with church practice. The essential part of theology is determined by the philosophical and historical disciplines, and practical theology task is to implement these truths (see Dingemans, 1989, 192). Schleiermacher places church service and church government under practical theology (see Spoelstra 1992, 308). Its field of study is in fact the empirical church, viz., religious practice, in order to provide sound guidance to the practical side of the church (see Dingemans 1989, 195).

In German theology, church polity is sometimes excluded from theology and regarded as a juridical science—or as a juridical-theological subject, although outside the theological encyclopaedia—or even within the science of the New

Testament (see Coertzen 1991, 166–167). In Reformed circles in the Netherlands, particularly since Kuyper (see Kuyper 1909, 217–219, 232–248), church polity has been regarded as an ecclesiological subject (see also Bouwman 1928, 10–15). Haitjema holds that church polity should be placed in the encyclopaedia somewhere on the boundary between the systematic and the historical subjects, since it is concerned with scientific norms (see Haitjema 1951, 13). South African theologians on the whole agree that church polity is an ecclesiological subject, largely following Kuyper's theological encyclopaedia (see Coertzen 1991, 170). There is in South African theology sometimes a tendency to regard church policy encypclopaedically as a subdivision of church history (see Stoop 1982, 25). Spoelstra suggests that the concepts of church polity and practical theology should be replaced by a new diaconiology and a new ecclesiology (see Spoelstra 1992, 316f.).

Because of the close relationship between the various theological subjects, church polity cannot be practiced independently of the other subjects. Koffeman agrees that church polity cannot be seen otherwise than in clear relationship with the other theological subjects (see Koffeman 2009, 23–25).

## 4. *Fundamental markers and relevant matters in Reformed church polity*

### 4.1 *Sources*

Before I consider the sources of church polity, two important points need to be made about the nature of sources. First, sources are important because a source, as an authoritative point of departure, already determines its objects. In other words, the content of a subject is irrevocably determined by the foundation on which it rests. Second, a source is not necessarily concrete or visible at an empirical level. A source can also relate to a presupposition which need not (and in theology should not) derive only from human insight and persuasion; it may exist at a metaphysical level. In turning now to the sources of Reformed church polity specifically, I suffice by stating that its sources are basically threefold: the Word of God, the confession, and church orders in the ecumenical world.

In a concrete sense, the source or basis of Reformed church polity as a theological science is our obedience to and acceptance of the gospel of the kingdom of heaven. Our primary source or point of departure is not something determined by our dulled intellect; we have received it from God through his grace, namely the Word of God as his particular revelation. Scripture is also the *norm* and authoritative standard for assessing, testing, verifying, confirming or rejecting.

In the practice of theology, scientists work both with Scripture as the particular revelation of God and with God's creation in which he makes himself known to us (Rom. 1:20; CB, art. 2) as the general revelation. However, the written Word of God represents the spectacles by means of which we are to understand

and interpret God's revelation in creation, and it constitutes the norm against which we verify scientific results. From its outset, the general Reformed view has accepted the written Word of God as the point of departure for church polity and church government. Bucer and Calvin state explicitly that the church should be governed and ruled solely according to the Gospel (on Bucer. see Van 't Spijker 1972, 2; Calvin 1559, IV,3,1; IV,10,30–32). The Biblische Weisungen (basic principles provided in the Bible) are the only authoritative rules for church government acknowledged by Calvin (see Plomp 1967, 15–16).

This viewpoint obtains throughout the Calvinist tradition. Bouwman (see Bouwman 1928, 31), Haitjema (see Haitjema 1951, 21–22), Jansen (see Jansen 1947, 6–7), and South African exponents of church polity in later years, such as Van der Linde (see Van der Linde 1965, 31), Spoelstra (see Spoelstra 1989, 2–19) and Coertzen (see Coertzen 1991, 117–141), to mention but a few, agree that Scripture constitutes the primary source and point of departure for church polity. The strong emphasis on Scripture as the source and norm of church polity should be seen against the background of the Roman Catholic view. For Rome, the *ius divinum* (divine law) consists of two main components: Scripture and tradition, and natural law. In addition, it also accepts church legislation as an authoritative source of church polity. This whole system is incorporated in the *Corpus Iuris Canonici* (known since 1918 as the *Codex Iuris Canonici*; for a survey see Smit 1985, 15–21).

In addition to Scripture, the Reformed view accepts the creeds as an important source of church polity. I shall not deal extensively with the relationship between Scripture, confession and church polity in this article (but see Hovius 1962; Du Plooy 1988; Coertzen 1991, 141–148). During the Reformation of the sixteenth century, the guidelines provided in Scripture for church government were embodied in creeds (see, e.g., CB, art. 27–32. The development of church polity during the Reformation of the sixteenth and seventeenth centuries ran parallel to that of the creeds, since *doctrina* (doctrine) and *disciplina* (discipline) were recognized as inextricably linked (see Van 't Spijker 1993, 178–201).

It follows that the historical church orders are a source of church polity since they all at some stage represent the fruit of the study of the *ius constituendum*. In addition, contemporary church orders other than those used in specific church communities are a source of church polity (see Coertzen 1991, 148).

### 4.2 *Function and task of church polity*

Since theology is a science which has to speak about God *(theos)* by means of a word *(logos)* (see Spoelstra 1992, 316), or, more specifically, which is a response to the Word of God (see Heyns and Jonker 1974, 132), church polity as a theological science is concerned not with the church as a sociological or juridical phenomenon but with the church as the body of Christ as revealed in the Word of God. In the light of Scripture, then, the field of study proper to church polity as an ecclesiological subject is the church, bearing in mind that the church is unique since only the church can be known as the body of Christ. Among the ecclesiological subjects, church history focuses on the church of the past, whereas church polity concentrates on the church of the present and future.

We can make a distinction between the internal and external tasks and functions of church polity. The internal side concentrates on scientific activities and justifications regarding the science of church polity, while the external activity focuses on service in the church and on promoting the interests of the church (see Heyns and Jonker 1974, 187–198). This distinction does not mean that the internal and external functions may be separated, since science and faith, or theology and church, should not be in conflict.

The internal task and function of church polity is to justify its classification as a theological science. Particular attention should be paid to such factors as the foundation of the subject, its unique nature and its relationship with other theological disciplines, its points of departure, and its purpose and function. The external task of church polity is concerned with the church, yet the approach must remain scientific. The particular aim of church polity is to promote the building up of the church. It has at least three distinct, not necessarily equal, functions (see Kuyper 1909, 248; Heyns and Jonker 1974, 187–188; Coertzen 1991, 172–174):

› *Study of the* ius constituendum

  The main task of church polity lies in the field of the *ius constituendum.* This is ultimately the aspect which makes church polity a theological science, since it concentrates on the justice or rules of conduct laid down in Scripture as fundamental and normative for church government.

  When a theological subject neglects to examine the Word of God as its particular field of study, we are fully justified in questioning whether it is in fact theology. Hence research on the *ius constituendum*—that is, justice as set out in Scripture—is of profound significance for the theological nature of church polity.

› Study of the history of church polity

  The second logical task of church polity is to study the history of the church and church government through the ages. The element that distinguishes this function from the task of church history is that it concentrates on evaluation rather than on description of facts. It conducts its evaluation using the norms and standards laid out by Scripture. In this regard church polity has to consider factors such as the following: God's promise as the Head of the church that he himself will reign over the church, that he will be with the church until the end of the world, and that the Holy Spirit has been sent to guide the church. God also reveals himself in history, but this (general) revelation should be tested against the Gospel as God's particular revelation and understood in its light (CB, art. 2).

› *Creating the* ius constitutum
The third task of church polity, utilizing the results of the two aforementioned functions, is to create a detailed and well-formulated method of church government; in other words, to create a legitimate church order (known as the *ius constitutum).* This implies that church polity has a special function regarding the justice which obtains in the church. Apart from creating a church order, it is also the task of church polity to approach the *ius constitutum* from the scientific and critical perspective of the *ius constituendum,* so that the *ius constitutum* increasingly comes to resemble the *ius constituendum.* In other words, the task of church polity is not complete once it has determined the justice which obtains in the church. The *ius constitutum* must be regularly tested against Scripture. Its relevance to the church must be examined. And it should be evaluated as to whether it promotes order and the building up of the church.

### 4.3 *Important concepts for church polity*

When we study Scripture we find clear guidelines provided by God regarding the fact and the method both of justice and of government in his church. It is not sufficient merely to identify these guidelines; genuine understanding of them — of their meaning and of their function — is of crucial importance to church polity. To that end, and as examples, I will now consider the concepts *kingdom, offices, church,* and the *authority* granted by God to his church to administer the keys of the kingdom.

#### 4.3.1 *The kingdom of God*

A very important key to understanding the church and to establishing a foundation for church polity is to start with the kingdom of God (see Van der Linde 1978; Spoelstra 1989, 4–5). In an earlier exhaustive discussion of mine on this matter, the following emerged (see Du Plooy 1982, 1–63).

The idea of the kingdom of God occupies a pivotal place in Scripture. The New Testament explicitly describes the course from kingdom to church and the particular relationship between them. The concept *kingdom* deals specifically with the fact, domain and method of God's reign through Christ. The kingdom of God points to God's dynamic reign in and through Jesus Christ — a reign to which his children or subjects have to submit. We see the advent of the kingdom wherever the Word and the Spirit are obeyed, and the community of obedient believers is known as the church. Thus the church is the fruit of the kingdom and, in turn, the instrument through which the kingdom has to be proclaimed. In addition, the church itself has to grow until the manifestation of the kingdom at the end of the world. The church is charged with the mission to administer the keys of the kingdom, precisely to unlock the kingdom of heaven to believers and to lock it against unbelievers.

Where people obey the Word and the Spirit, God creates a new order in an imperfect world—an order known as a new creation or church of Jesus Christ. Those who regard the kingdom of God as their point of departure acknowledge and confess that Christ is the only Head of the church, and that true church government should be nothing less than the reign of Christ. In his view of the concept *justice,* Smit uses the kingdom of God as his point of departure. He states that Christ as the Head of the church, i.e., the reign of God through Christ, is crucial to the question of who determines justice in the church. Neither the pope, nor the statutes of a country, nor the churches in a synod, nor a local church, nor a majority of votes determine justice in the church (see Smit 1985). Rather, Christ as the Head reveals in his Word what is right. Christ is the Legislator, and the church is taught through his Spirit and Word how to behave with regard to doctrine and life, as well as what the order in the church should be. God's justice relates directly to love, grace and judgment, and to the will of God. We see then, that the kingdom of God is the only basis on which to build church polity. The headship of Christ is naturally the most important principle of church polity. For this reason church polity should start its study and research on the church with the kingdom of God and not with the church.

#### *4.3.2 The offices*

Even before the church of the New Testament acquired concrete and visible status with the outpouring of the Holy Spirit (Acts 2), we find Jesus Christ's command to the apostles to administer the keys of the kingdom (Matt. 16:17–19, 18:18; HC, Lord's Day 31). The church to which Matthew 16:17–19 refers is already, and will be in the future, the outcome of the *administration* of the keys of the kingdom of God. Snyman and Floor state that since the beginning the proclamation of the Word of God effected the formation of the church (see Snyman and Floor 1969, 41).

Fundamentally, the offices precede the church (see Spoelstra 1989, 27–28). Through the preaching of the Word and the Spirit, Christ the King summons a congregation for himself and leads his people out of the darkness into the light. It is interesting to note that where Calvin writes specifically about the church in his *Institutes* he starts by referring to Ephesians 4:11f., where we read about the office-bearers who have to proclaim the gospel (see Calvin 1559, IV, 1, 1). It is therefore obviously correct that Reformed church orders, such as the one from Dordt (1618/19), do not proceed from the church as an institution but from the offices. This approach differs from that of other exponents of church polity who are inclined to do just that (see Roijaards 1834, 5; Kuyper 1909, 232f.).

Exponents of church polity who bear in mind that Christ's main aim is to assemble his chosen children in a church through the proclamation of the Word and the Spirit so as to enable them to enter the kingdom of God will dissociate themselves from the trend to approach church polity from the perspectives of institutionalism and structuralism which focus exclusively on the church, and also from a one-sided juridical perspective. This point of departure will also prevent exponents from either overemphasizing or underemphasizing the spiritual gifts *(charismata)*. There can be no conflict between *diakonia* and *charisma*; the one cannot be understood without the other, and both are gifts from God in and to his church (see Ridderbos 1966, 479–514). Church polity is concerned with much more than the church. It focuses primarily on service in the church and is ultimately directed to the kingdom of God. This implies that practical theology (diaconiology) and church polity should reflect intensively and encyclopaedically on identical elements and fields of study. Spoelstra deals extensively and aptly with this matter (see Spoelstra 1993, 299–320).

#### *4.3.3 The church*

The various schools of thought on the meaning and use of the word *church* in the Word of God have given rise to different systems of church government. A study of the history of church polity, which concentrates on the key aspects of various systems or models of church government, highlights the fact that widely differing concepts of church is the main reason for the wide variety of systems that exists. Although one of the tasks of church polity is to study models of church government critically and scientifically, my present aim in dealing with the foundations of the subject is to stress the importance of a scriptural concept of church. In an earlier study I dealt exhaustively with this subject (see Du Plooy 1982, 64–120). I will look now at a few points relevant to this article.

The church of Jesus Christ is a unique community of believers, and it is the fruit of the grace of God in Christ who created the church through the proclamation of the Word and the Spirit and who is still assembling, protecting and maintaining it. This is why the church is unique: it is the body of Christ, the congregation of God and the temple of the Holy Spirit. Christ alone is the Head of this church and, hence, the One who reigns over his church.

In the New Testament we find important information related to the meaning and use of the word *church*. When this word refers to the assembly of believers it can be used in two senses only: the local and the general. In church polity it is important to note that the New Testament never refers to a collection of churches as a *church*, despite those who argue Acts 9:31 seems to imply just that (see Coertzen 1991, 78–86). The co-existence of churches and the concrete experience of their unity on the basis of a common doctrine, such as we encounter in the New Testament, have never led to a structure next to or above the local churches. Calvin states explicitly that a synod or council is not the church; it is an assembly of a number of local churches in order to promote the building up of the churches, in so far as that assembly acknowledges Christ as the chairman and adheres to the Word of God in matters of government (see Calvin 1559, IV, 9, 1–3).

It is obvious that a pure or scriptural concept of church is indispensable for the practice of church polity. Throughout the history of the church, different concepts of *church* have led to different views on church polity and government. Koffeman deals with the concept *church* and its important role in church polity (see Koffeman 2009, 115–136). He refers to the tension among the Reformed churches in The Netherlands of the nineteenth and twentieth centuries with regard to the relation between *ecclesia localis* and *ecclesia universalis*. In his analysis he wrongly says that one cannot speak of the 'independence of the local congregation' (see Koffeman 2009, 133). It is clear from Scripture that the local church is a complete church, but not the only church, and that there must be fellowship among local churches and ties between them. This unity does not however create a permanent structure alongside the local churches. In Reformed church polity this point remains important. It is crucial for how the church should be governed (see Du Plooy 1982, 64–120).

#### *4.3.4 Authority to administer the keys, and the building up of the church*

Continuing this train of thought, it is significant for church polity to read in Scripture that Christ himself, as the Head of the church, has the authority to administer the keys (Is. 22:22; Rev. 3:7). Yet he vests the church with the authority to administer the keys through the ministry (Matt. 16:17–19). Calvin believes that the keys are the proclamation of the gospel and church discipline (see also HC, Lord's Day 31), and that the authority to administer the keys does not represent authority but implies a service performed by the office-bearers in the interests of the church (see Calvin 1559, IV, 11, 1, 5–6). The church is built up through the administration of the keys of the kingdom of God, and this is possible because the Holy Spirit has been given to the church (John 20:22–23).

The ministerial authority or potency of the church is threefold; it regards the authority regarding doctrine as well as judiciary and legislative powers (*potestas doctrinae, potestas iurisdictionis* and *potestas in legibus ferendis*).

During the Reformation in the sixteenth century, people such as Bucer and Calvin stressed the fact that the church must be built up, and that this should be done through the proclamation of the gospel of Jesus Christ and the exercise of church government (church discipline) (see Van 't Spijker 1993, 317–323; Calvin 1559, III, 4,10–14; IV,11,1). For the purposes of this article it is important to note Bucer's belief that there are three essential elements in the church; namely, the proclamation of the Word, the administration of the sacraments, and the exercise of discipline (see Van 't Spijker 1993, 192). According to Bucer, these elements function not merely as the marks of the church (*notae ecclesiae*), but, according to divine law (*ius divinum*),also as a basis for the classification and content of a church order (see Van 't Spijker 1972, 35–37).

From a Reformed point of view, church polity should therefore concern itself with this explicit information regarding administration of the keys and with the marks of the true church. Church polity must lead to a system of church government which provides the channel for true doctrine through which the church can be built up (see Van 't Spijker 1990, 331–332). It is therefore significant that the classification and content of Reformed church orders (such as that of Dordt 1618/19) must correspond to the kingdom of God, and thus to the marks of the true church. The focus must be on the proclamation of the Word, administration of the sacraments, and the exercise of discipline in the church.

### 4.4 *Church order and Constitution*

A church order is an ecclesiastical document containing stipulations and prescriptions agreed to by a group of churches. It is juridical in nature. It is closely related to and derived from Scripture and the application of confessional principles regarding the government and upbuilding of the church. A church order's authority lies in its relationship to the Word of God and in the mutual agreement (*mutuo consensu*) it enjoys among the group of churches subscribing to it.

The constitution of a country is to be distinguished from a church order. It should not apply in the internal matters of a church, but should respect and allow for the right and authority of a church to govern itself according to its own nature and character (which is *sui generis*) (see Du Plooy 2008, 248–251).

### 4.5 *Hermeneutics of Reformed church polity*

In church polity the time has come to pay more attention to the hermeneutics of church polity. Much can be learned from the common law and from legal topics such as the interpretation of legal texts and documents. I have dealt with this matter in another article (see Du Plooy 2012). Church polity should clearly define the presuppositions of the hermeneutics of church polity. It should give attention to aspects such as grammatical interpretation, systematic (or contextual) interpretation, teleological interpretation, and historical interpretation. And it should elaborate on matters such as rationality, legality and legitimacy.

If the hermeneutics of church polity were taken seriously, little danger would exist that the church—both locally and ecumenically—will tend to view church orders as canonical documents forever unchangeable. Efforts would be made to read and apply church orders with respect, and they would be used for their real purposes: honoring God and building up his church in the world.

### *Abbreviations and bibliography*

CB: Confessio Belgica (Belgic Confession) (1561).
HC: Heidelberg Catechism.

Bakker, Wim. 1992A. Wat is kerkrecht? In: Van 't Spijker and Van Drimmelen 1992,13–19.

Bakker, Wim. 1992B. Geschiedenis van de wetenschap van het kerkrecht. In: Van 't Spijker and Van Drimmelen 1992, 20–31.

Botha, Christoffel J. 1993. Die stand van die gereformeerde kerkreg. Skrif en Kerk 14(1993)/1, 1–7.

Bouwman, Harm. 1928. Gereformeerd kerkrecht. Kampen: Kok.

Calvin, John. 1559. Institutes of the Christian Religion. Two volumes. Edited by John T. McNeill. Translation Ford Lewis Battles 1960. Philadelphia: The Westminster Press—London: SCM.

Coertzen, Pieter. 1991. Gepas en ordelik. Pretoria: RGN.

Dingemans, Gijs D.J. 1989. Praktische theologie als een academische discipline. In: Nederlands Theologisch Tijdschrift 43(1989)/3, 192–211.

Du Plooy, A. (Dries) le R. 1982. Kerkverband: 'n Gereformeerd-kerkregtelike studie. PhD diss., University of Potchefstroom. Potchefstroom: PU cir CHO.

Du Plooy, A. (Dries) le R. 1988. Die verband tussen die Skrif, konfessie en kerkorde volgens gereformeerde kerkreg. Potchefstroom: PU vir CHO.

Du Plooy, A. (Dries) le R. 2012. Die hermeneutiek van die gereformeerde kerkreg. In: In die Skriflig/In Luce Verbi 46(2012)/1, Art #36, 8 pp. http://dx.doi.org/10.4102/ ids.v46i1.36.

Du Toit, Stefanus, et al. (ed.). 1969. Die koninkryk van God. Potchefstroom: Herald.

Eybers, Ian H., Adrio Konig, and Jan A. Stoop (eds). 1982. Inleiding in die teologie. Pretoria: NG Kerkboekhandel.

Haitjema, Theodorus L. 1951. Nederlands hervormd kerkrecht. Nijkerk: Callenbach.

Heyns, Johan A., and Willem D. Jonker. 1974. Op weg met die teologie. Pretoria: NG Kerkboekhandel.

Hovius, Jan. 1962. Het verband tussen onze belijdenis en onze kerkorde. Sneek: Weissenbach.

Jansen, Johannes. 1947. Handleiding gereformeerd kerkrecht. Kampen: Kok.

Kleynhans, Ewert P. 1982. Gereformeerde kerkreg. Pretoria: NG Kerkboekhandel.

Koffeman, Leo J. 2009. Het goed recht van de kerk: Een theologische inleiding op het kerkrecht. Kampen: Kok.

Kuyper, Abraham. 1909. Encyclopaedie der heilige godgeleerdheid. Derde deel. Kampen: Kok.

Nauta, Doede. 1971. Verklaring van de kerkorde van de Gereformeerde Kerken in Nederland. Kampen: Kok.

Ouweneel, Willem J. 1989. Die Bybel in die wetenskap. Department Wetenskapsleer, Studiestuk 21. Potchefstroom: PU vir CHO.

Ouweneel, Willem J. 1993. A critical analysis of the external and internal prolegomena of systematic theology. PhD diss., University of Bloemfontein. Bloemfontein: UOFS.

Pienaar, Gerrit J. 1982. Die gemeenregtelike regspersoon in die Suid-Afrikaanse privaatreg. PhD diss., University of Potchefstroom. Potchefstroom: PU vir CHO.

Plomp, Johannes. 1967. Beginselen van reformatorisch kerkrecht. Kampen: Kok.

Pont, Adrianus D. 1981. Die historiese agtergronde van ons kerklike reg. Pretoria: HAUM.

Ridderbos, Herman. 1966. Paulus: Ontwerp van zijn theologie. Kampen: Kok.

Roeleveld, Leendert. s.a. [1958]. Gereformeerde kerken in het privaatrecht. Zeist: Steenbergen.

Roijaards, Herman J. 1834. Hedendaagsch kerkregt bij de hervormden in Nederland. Utrecht: Altheer.

Rullmann, Johan C. 1918. Dr. F.L. Rutgers in zijn leven en werken geschetst. Rotterdam: Libertas.

Smit, Cornelis J. 1985. Kerkreg en kerkorde in die lig van God se reg en orde vir sy kerk. PhD diss., University of Potchefstroom Potchefstroom: PU vir CHO.

Snyman, Willie J., and Lambertus Floor. 1969. Die koninkryk van God in die Nuwe Testament. In: Du Toit et al. 1969, 34–58.

Spoelstra, Bouke. 1989. Gereformeerde kerkreg en kerkregering. Hammanskraal: HTS.

Spoelstra, Bouke. 1992. Dilemma tussen praktiese teologie en ekklesiologie. In: Theologia Reformata 35(1992)/4, 299–320.

Spoelstra, Bouke. 1993. Besinning oor die teologiese ensiklopedie van Kuyper met kerkreg en diakoniologie as parameters. In: In die Skriflig 27(1993)/1, 69–89.
Stoker, Hendrik G. 1940. Beginsels van 'n Christelike wetenskapsleer. In: Koers in die krisis 2(1940), 293–331.
Stoker, Hendrik G. 1961. Beginsels en metodes van die wetenskap. Potchefstroom: Pro Rege.
Stoker, Hendrik G. 1970. Oorsprong en rigting. Band 2. Kaapstad: Tafelberg.
Stoop, Jan A. 1982. Kerkgeskiedenis. In: Eybers et al. 1982, 121–154.
Strauss, Piet J. (ed.). 1991. Byderwets en gereformeerd. Kerkregtelike opstelle opgedra aan P.B. van der Walt. Bloemfontein: Pro-Christo-Publikasies.
Strauss, Piet J. 1991A. Vanwaar gereformeerde kerkregtelike beginsels? In: Strauss 1991, 23–34.
Te Velde, Mees. 1989. Gereformeerde gemeenteopbouw. Barneveld: De Vuurbaak.
Van der Linde, Gert P.L. 1965. Die grondbeginsels van die presbiteriale kerkregeringstelsel. Potchefstroom: Pro Rege.
Van der Linde, Gert P.L. 1978. Die betekenis van die verhouding tussen die koninkryk van die hemele en die kerk vir die kerkreg. Potchefstroom: PU vir CHO.
Van Drimmelen, Leen C. 1992. Kerk en staat. In: Van 't Spijker and Van Drimmelen 1992, 196–206.
Van 't Spijker, Willem. 1972. Goddelijk recht en kerkelijke orde bij Martin Bucer. Kampen: Kok.
Van 't Spijker, Willem. 1990. Aspecten van gemeenteopbouw in de reformatie. In: Theologia Reformata 33(1990)/4, 309–332.
Van 't Spijker, Willem. 1992. Rechtvaardiging en recht in de kerk: Over de theologische achtergronden van het gereformeerde kerkrecht. In: Hervormde Teologiese Studies 48(1992)/3 and 4, 995–1011.
Van't Spijker, Willem. 1993. Reformatie en kerkorde. In: Theologia Reformata 36(1993)/3, 78–201.
Van't Spijker, Willem, and Leen C. van Drimmelen (eds). 1992. Inleiding tot de studie van het kerkrecht. Kampen: Kok. 2nd edition.
Velema, Willem H. 1991. Kuypers conceptie van de kerk als organisme kritisch bekeken. In: Theologia Reformata 34(1991), 295–309.
Vergeer, Wim. 1993. Teologie en kenteorie. 'n Reaksie op die artikels van Gerrie Snyman. In: In die Skriflig 27(1993)/4, 563–582.
Wallace, Ronald S. 1988. Calvin, Geneva and the Reformation. Grand Rapids: Baker Book House.

# SOME NOTES ON THE REVISION OF CHURCH ORDERS

## in Sulawesi, Indonesia

Zakaria J. Ngelow

### *Introduction*

Protestantism according to the Calvinist tradition was introduced into Indonesia since the early 17th century. But the doctrines and the church polity of Calvinism were not applied accordingly. Distortion with respect to church polity was the case, as the Protestant church was integrated into the colonial government system. Churches with a mission board background in eastern Indonesia developed a church polity which was heavily influenced by secular polity. In the last decade, some churches have revised their respective church orders in order to be grounded in solid Reformed traditions and ecclesiology.

This short paper is intended to share some information on the revision of church orders of some churches in Sulawesi, Indonesia. In the past, revisions were done mostly in an *ad hoc* way, in response to particular problems, but over the last few years this been done in a more comprehensive way. Revision programs began by initiating consulations on contextual ecclesiology, and on a renewed understanding of the character and function of church orders. Pastors and elders were invited to share their experiences concerning the application of the church order in their ministries. From the consultations and the revision process we have learned about some specific aspects of the church orders, as they had developed in the churches. Then the revision committee drew a new revised draft, to be introduced and evaluated in a conference with leaders of the church. It was also significant to introduce the draft in the classis or in congregation meetings, to get more feedback.

Before sharing more information on the scope of the revision, the next paragraphs will present a short introduction into the background of Calvinist Protestant churches in Indonesia, i.e. the 'Indies Church' and the churches that were founded by missionaryorganizations (see Aritonang and Steenbrink 2008; Bigalke 2005; Cooley 1981; Purwanto 1997; Schröter 2010), followed by a decription of the main churches present in Sulawesi.

*'Indies Church'*

Protestant Christianity was introduced into Indonesia by Dutch clergy working in the Dutch East Indian Company (DEIC; *Verenigde Oostindische Compagnie*, VOC) since the early 17th century: the first Protestant church service was held in Ambon in 1605. Roman Catholic congregations in the archipelago were left by the Portuguese, and were converted to Calvinism the DEIC, following the tradition of the European rulers at the time, according to the principle *cuius regio eius religio* (i.e.: the religion of the ruler dictates the religion of the ruled). Congregations were mainly present in the eastern part of the Indonesia archipelago, and some were scattered in main cities of Java and Sumatra. After the DEIC dissolved (1799), the congregations in Indonesia were united in 1815 into the 'Indies Church' (Dutch: *De Indische Kerk*, or formally *Protestantsche Kerk in Nederlandsch-Indië*) by the Dutch government. In 1815, the church had only about 70,000 members (some 50,000 Indonesians); but in 1938 the number had increased to 700,000, as more and more Indonesians were converted. Church services were in the Dutch or the Malay language.

There was no clear doctrinal foundation of the Indies Church. In 1854 a vague formulation was put into a regulation, stating that the Indies Church doctrine was 'the Gospel doctrine according to Protestant foundations'. In the Netherlands, a committee for colonial affairs—the *Haagsche Commissie*—was commissioned by the King in 1815, in order to supervise the Indies Church, while in Batavia (now Jakarta) a committee (*Kerkbestuur*, the Church Board) was appointed, consisting of representatives of the colonial government and church officers, as an executive board for the Indies Church. But it was the colonial Gouvernor General of Netherlands-Indie who held the strings, and who even appointed elders in the congregations. The church was governed by and was part of the colonial government. Ministry of the church was under the authority of a group of hierarchical ministers which were appointed, assigned and paid by the government. The hierarchical character of the ministry office implied the subordination of one to the other offices. At the top of the hierarchy were Dutch ministers; their number was fixed to only 35 ministers in 1867, but there were 43 of them in the 20th century. Then at the second level there were 10 Assistant Ministers (*hulppredikers*; since 1881 they were also called *Indisch predikant*, Indonesian ministers, and their number increased to 31 persons). The next level was that of the indigenous ministers (*inlands leraar*). There were 347 indigenous ministers in 1935. Then at the lowest, there was the congregational teacher (in 1935 they were about 900). In some Moluccan areas, the teacher was helped by an evangelist (*utusan Injil*) or by elders (*tuagama*). The assistant minister was limited in his powers and ministry. He was allowed to administer the sacraments only to indigenous (Indonesian) church members. That right was not granted to an Indonesian minister if he was not appointed as an assistant minister; but he was allowed to bless weddings. Prior to 1850, church councils were only there in towns, in order to supervise some congregations in the region, and later such councils were founded where assistant ministers were assigned. Elders were appointed by a minister. It was not until 1924 that male congregation members had the right to choose their elders (female members were granted the same right soon afterwards, in 1930). The first female minister was ordained in 1936. Elders were Dutch, and only in Batavia and Ambon they had indigenous elders, and much later in other places as well. In some congregations the members of the church council were divided into Dutch and indigenous elders, in order to take care of their respective members according to the language lines (Dutch and Malay speaking members). Pastoral care and church discipline was rarely applied among the Dutch speaking members, and among the indigenous members eucharist was limited to few: often adult baptized members were not allowed to participate in eucharist, due to moral considerations.

Since 1848, there was a move to separate the church from the colonial government, but resistance came from the church leaders. It was only in 1913 that a committee was assigned to draw proposals and in 1916 a church assembly (the first since 1605) gathered, where only one Indonesian was present among the delegates. Eventually, in the second general assembly in 1933 (with a significant number of Indonesians), the Indies Church was separated from the state. The Indies Church was reorganized into three regional-ethnic churches, of Minahasa (1934), the Moluccas (1935), and Timor (1947); and the rest as the Western Indonesia Protestant Church (1948).

The reorganization resulted in the creation of four churches out of the Indies Church, but the Indies Church itself as an institution was not dissolved. It became a synod with an executive board, but without church members, as all her members belonged to the four churches after the reorganization. It became an umbrella for the new churches. In the course of time, some ethnic churches in Sulawesi and Papua with historical links joined the family of the Protestant Church in Indonesia (Indonesian: *Gereja Protestan di Indonesia*, GPI, the new name of the Indies Church after Indonesian independence).

### *Churches founded by Missions Organizations*

Since the early 19th century, missionaries of various mission boards were sent to work in different parts of Indonesia. They worked mostly outside of Java island, as the colonial government prohibited mission among the Muslim population in the island (and also later in Hinduism Bali). Mission of Lutheran background worked in Sumatra, Nias and Kalimantan, while Dutch mission with a Calvinist background worked the in eastern Indonesia islands. Dutch missionaries were helped by Indonesian teachers from an Indies Church background. They graduated at a theological school, that was founded to provide indigenous ministers (STOVIL, *School tot Opleiding voor Inlands Leraars*; School to educate indigenous teachers) which provided education in some places in eastern Indonesia since the 1880s. Eventually, missionaries managed to plant the Gospel; congregations and churches were formed according to the Dutch Calvinist ecclesiology of Dordt. The Synod of Dordt (1618–19) decided the famous contra Remonstrant articles (*Canons of Dordt*), and a *Church Order* (DCO), and commissioned a new Dutch translation of the Bible. The churches were instituted according to the DCO; a church/congregation should preserve the true Calvinist doctrines (following the *Belgic Confession*, the *Canons of Dordt*, and the *Heidelberg Catechism*); it had four equal church offices, of minister, elder, deacon and teacher; it should maintain church discipline; and it had periodic ecclesial assemblies. For various reasons these ideals were not fully applied in Indonesian churches. For a relative long period, the congregations in the mission fields were taken care of by missionaries. It was in 1930s that Indonesian congregations were organized into independent churches along the ethnic lines.

At the same time a new kinds of Protestant Christianity was introduced into the country; they were the 'American Denominations' of the Pentecostal movement, Gospel Tabernacle, Seventh-Day Adventism, the Salvation Army, etc.

### *Churches in South, Southwest and West Sulawesi*

There are six churches whose synods are located in South, West, and South East Sulawesi, but this paper will deal only with four churches, namely the Toraja Church, the Toraja Mamasa Church, the West Sulawesi Christian Church and the Protestant Church of South East Sulawesi.

In the early 20th century, the Dutch colonial government subjugated the regions of south, southeast and central Sulawesi and developed the port of Makassar as the main capital city in the region. This opened the chance for Muslim traders to disseminate Islam among the natives in the hinterlands. Christian missions also acquired government permission to work among the indigenous peoples. A Dutch congregation of the Indies Protestant Church was founded in the city of Makassar in the 17th century. Some small congregations of colonial civil and military personnel were also found in several places. Since 1908 the Indies Protestant Church of Makassar opened schools in some places in the Toraja and Toraja Mamasa regions, and eventually baptized the students and the people without proper Christian education. Systematic Christian mission works were taken over by the GZB (*Gereformeerde Zendingsbond*, Reformed Mission Alliance) in the Toraja area of South Sulawesi in 1913, by the NZV (*Nederlandse Zendingsvereeniging*, Dutch Missionary Society ) among the Tolaki and the Moronene of Southeast Sulawesi in 1916, and by the ZCGK (*Zending voor Christelijke Gereformeerde Kerken*, Mission of Christian Reformed Churches) in Toraja Mamasa (West Sulawesi) in 1928.

The GZB divided its mission work in Toraja into four regions, i.e. Rantepao, Makale, Palopo and Rongkong-Seko. In terms of church polity, progress was significant in the Rongkong-Seko region. Elders were elected and congregations were organized into a classis, and a simple church order was introduced, with a strong emphasis on church discipline. The life of the congregations in the mission fields was mainly under administrative and pastoral authority of the missionary with his helpers (mostly school teachers from other ethnic groups of Maluku, Minahasa and Timor). An annual meeting of missionaries (also attended by missionary helpers) was held in order to exchange information from the mission fields, to develop general policies and to decide on controversial matters concerning customary law of the people. In Toraja (and other churches) the paternalistic character of the missionaries' role was continued after the Toraja Church was established as an independent synod in 1947. A kind of paternalistic character of leadership was attached to the chairperson of the church. This was complicated, as he was also elected as the chairperson of the local branch of a Christian political party. Transformation to a more collegial character of leadership emerged much later.

ZCGK was a conservative Dutch Calvinist mission organization. This mission board took over the Toraja Mamasa region from the Indies Church in 1928. Thousands of people had been mass baptized without proper education by the Indies Church, and most of them returned to their ancestral belief when they realized that baptism was not ordered by the colonial government. ZCGK recognized their baptismal status but had to educate the people in the basic teachings of Christianity. ZCGK also took care of the schools and employed them both as tools for Christianization and for social transformation. As with GZB in Toraja, the Dutch missionaries were helped by Indonesian teachers from Maluku, Minahasa, and Timor. Local teachers emerged, as modern education was developed. They worked as school teachers but also as community teachers. Eventually a Christian community emerged. The local communities were organized into congregations and classis (in Mamasa there was one in 1931, but there were three in 1938). Local congregations were first lead by the community teacher. Then the teacher selected some male members to be appointed as elders. They joined in the work of the community teacher as trainees. According to recent estimates, the Toraja

Mamasa Church (*Gereja Toraja Mamasa*, GTM), has about 350 congregations with a total of more than 100 thousand members, served by about 200 pastors, with a small number of women pastors, as the church recognized the ordination of women only in the 1990s.

In early 1942, in response to the advance of the Japanese military campaign into Indonesia, missionaries ordained J.E. Latuihamallo and some other community teachers as pastors. In terms of church independence from foreign missions, the Japanese military occupation in Indonesia had a bright side. As the Dutch missionaries were put into prison camps, the young congregations in the mission field had to survive with their own leadership and financial support.

After the war a process to establish local churches was put in place. Delegations from congregations agreed to establish the Toraja Church (1947) and then the GTM, in 1948. The Christian Church of Southeast Sulawesi was established much later, in 1957.

Gtm covers several Torajan sub–ethnic groups. One of them is the Toraja of Kalumpang in the Karama river valley, West Sulawesi. For their own reasons, the Kalumpang people decided to have their own church, and on 31 October 1977 they established the Protestant Church of South Sulawesi (Gereja Protestan Sulawesi Selatan, gpss), a break away from gtm. In the year 2000 the church was renamed the Christian Church of West Sulawesi (Gereja Kristen Sulawesi Barat, gksb), after the formation of the West Sulawesi Province. At present this church has 101 congregations with about 20 thousand members and 46 pastors (including five women). Gksb's main problem is human resources, but finances is also one of the crucial points for this church with mainly rural congregations in one of the economically poorest areas with limited transportation. Most of the congregations cannot afford to provide the minimum salary for a pastor and therefore some congregations join together to be served by one pastor. Contributions from congregations to classis and synod do not cover the annual budget of the synod.

The Protestant Church of Southeast Sulawesi (*Gereja Protestan di Sulawesi Tenggara*, GEPSULTRA) was established on 20 February 1957, as an outcome of mission works of NZV since 1916 among the Tolaki and Moronene in the southeast peninsula of Sulawesi island. Since the 1970's this church became a multiethnic church, as Christian migrants and transmigrations from different ethnic groups — of Toraja, Java, Bali, and others — increased the membership. They came from different churches or denominations. While the church consists of different ethnic groups, individual congregations — notably in the rural areas — were of the same ethnic group. There is thus a strong influence of ethnic traditions in the life of the congregations. The church has 124 congregations (of about 36,000 total members) ministered by 100 active pastors (about 45% women). GEPSULTRA tried to set up a church structure consisting of two levels, congregations and synod, with a synod representative as regional coordinator. This structure did not work well, as regional congregations needed a forum of their own. The last revision made the classis revive. One crucial problem is the management of the placement and rotation of the congregational pastors. This church vests authority in the synod board to decide where a pastor will be moved after her/his term of ministry is over. This church also employs a centralized budget (especially for the payment of pastors' salaries).

*Why a revision of the church order?*

From the beginning, Calvinistic church polity was introduced to these churches, following their Calvinistic mother churches in the Netherlands. Elders were appointed and classes were formed. But leadership of the Dutch missionaries, and also of the community teachers, set an example of a kind of paternalistic leadership — a familiar characteristic of leadership in traditional society. The missionary was the one who held power over his helpers as well as over the council of the congregation.

Another influential factor to the church order was the Indies Church. While the background of this Protestant Church of the Netherlands-Indies was the Dutch Calvinist tradition, the Indies Church was a colonial government institution which applied the hierarchical structure and order of the government administration in church life. There was a hierarchy with the pastor at the top, then assistant minister, evangelist, and then elders and deacon at the lowest level. This hierarchical character was preserved in the church by the first generation church leaders. A younger generation of church leaders emerged in the late 1960s or 1970s. They imitated the paternalistic example of their predecessors, while they were also heavily influenced by the paternalistic character of Suharto's New Order regime.

Revision of the church order was proposed from time to time, mostly related to administrative matters, such as the number of representatives to the general assembly or the qualifications of synod personnel, and limits on their term of service. All the churches mentioned above did some revision of their respective church order in the last five years. The most recent revisions were significant in terms of process and substance. A committee was appointed to draft the revisions. They began their work with a consultation on the character and basis of a church order and its contextual relation to the life of the church. Experts were invited to enlighten participants on ecclesiology and church order. The consultations underlined the close relation between ecclesiology, contextual setting and the church order. It was a relevant approach as most of the church leaders needed to improve their understanding of the basics of church order.

The biggest church in the region is the Toraja Church, with more than one thousand congregations and half a million members. Congregations are mostly located in Toraja and neighboring regions in Sulawesi, but also in Java, Kalimantan, Batam and Kuala Lumpur. As the Torajans migrate to different places, congregations of the Toraja church will be founded in these new locations. Bilateral agreements with local churches prevent the Toraja Church from establishing congregations in Papua and Maluku. The revision of its church order addressed some problems of structure, of categorical ministries (children, youth, women) and of the status of a pastor's spouse. This ethnic church was divided into four regional synods consisting of classes in the region. In the past there were four levels of ecclesial structure: congregations, classis, regional synod, and synod. Revision was made to establish only three spheres: congregation, classis and synod with their respective meeting/assembly and executive council. The regional synod was dissolved, but a member of the synod executive committee was appointed as a regional coordinator. Categorical ministries to children, youth and women are organized as specific ministries in the congregation with their own management alongside the congregational council, but they also have an executive committee at classis and synodlevels. They have their own respective synod congress and their statutes. Another concern was with the status and role of the pastor's spouse. Many church pastors are ordained couples. Eventually it was regulated that if one is called to serve a congregation, then her/his spouse will serve in general ministry (meaning they will not be placed in a congregation). This controversial regulation was revised in the last General Assembly in order to enable one's spouse to serve as a pastor in (neighboring) congregations. In the Toraja Church, recruitment of a pastor is done by the synod board, but it is a congregational council's privilege to call a pastor to ministry in the congregation for one or two periods of four years.

Another controversial matter is the 'deviation' of a pastor from her/his main assignment. In the past few years some Indonesian churches have faced the problem of pastors' activity in political parties, while others have taken fulltime jobs as civil servants (most of them as Christian religious teachers). The Toraja church denies recognition to such double functions among her pastors. A pastor has to decide whether to be a full time pastor or to leave her/his call for another occupation. Some other churches recognize and maintain the ordained status of the deviated pastor.

The Toraja Mamasa Church cancelled the process of revising its church order. The last General Assembly did not extend the revision process. In the past GTM employed four levels of the presbyterial-synodical structure. Then the regional synod was dissolved to have only three levels: congregations, classis, and synod. It seems that the main reason for revision concerned the improvement of communication between synod and congregations. The issue is actually not directly related to structure, but it concerns the leadership character. Another concern is how to accommodate sub-ethnic communities in the church organizational structure. There are now 66 classes, which is too many and irrelevant to the setting of traditional communities. There is a discussion on the possibility of reducing the number of classes to less than half the current total and appoint a fulltime ordained pastor to chair the classis council, so as to empower the function of the classis. Communication and transportation availability and ethnic or traditional relations between neighboring congregations should be considered in establishing a classis. Another crucial problem is financial stewardship. This church with mainly rural congregations needs a regulation on the subject, notably of transparency and accountability and fidelity to pay monthly contributions to the synod.

*Some remarks*

As mentioned before, the paternalistic character of church office is a product of the churches' history. The paternalistic character of the missionaries' traditional leadership culture and the hierarchical structure of the Indies Protestant Church shaped the development of the organizational culture. While in theory churches acknowledge the equivalence of the three offices, the deacon is seen as the lowest office after that of elder, and they are both beneath the pastor. In the liturgy, when elders and deacons lead the service, they are not allowed to raise their hands as they pronounce the blessings, and are required to change the blessing formulation of Num 6: 24ff. -"The LORD bless *you* and keep *you*; the LORD make his face shine upon *you* and be gracious to *you*; the LORD turn his face toward *you* and give *you* peace" — or 2 Corinthians 13:14 — "May the grace of the Lord Jesus Christ, and the love of God, and the fellowship of the Holy Spirit be with *you* all" — saying 'you' to instead of 'us'.

The deacon is seen as a candidate for the office of elder. This perception corresponds with the absence of *diakonia* as one of the main vocations of the church. The diaconate is practiced as a ceremonial event on Christmas or Easter, and limited to a small gift for widows in the congregation. Revision of the church order makes the understanding of church mission revive, as including the diaconate in its holistic character, and its relation to the specific office of deacons.

Most Indonesian churches acknowledge three major aspects of church mission, namely *koinonia* (communion), *martyria* (witness) and *diakonia* (social ministry). In the ecclesiology consultation we have introduced broader aspects such as *leitourgia* (worship), *oikonomia* (stewardship), and *didache* (teaching).

Churches are also exposed to problems regarding the presbyterial-synodical structure. The Toraja Church, GTM and GKSB allocate relatively greater power to local congregational councils; while GEPSULTRA tends to centralize power in the synod, including centralized finances (for the payment of pastors' salaries). It is interesting to know that some churches in Indonesia, such as *Kalimantan Evangelis Church* (GKE) and Christian Church of Gospel Lighthouse (*Gereja Kristen Pemancar Injil*; GKPI) employ the term synodical-presbyterial (*sinodal-presbiterial*) in their church order in order to underline the greater power at the synod level!

Churches generally employ a three-levels structure of congregation, classis and synod. But bigger churches like Toraja and GTM had four in the past, as some classis were united in a regional synod. In most cases, churches have developed top-down relationships in their church structure, with the synod on the top, then classis and then congregations at the bottom. In the consultation on ecclesiology a reversed understanding was developed, meaning that the local congregation is central as it is the full expression of the Lord's church in the world. Normally a classis or a synod was formed by the local congregations to serve their common needs. But in Indonesia churches were formed to unite congregations founded by missionaries. The synod executive committee was regarded as a replacement of missionaries

Churches employ different organizational structures for the categorical ministries of children, youth and women. These are independent organizations in the congregation, and they function more as close partners rather than working in sub-ordination to the presbyters council. While the church has its church order, these organizations have their own respective statutes. Youth and women's organizations then become a strategic factor in terms of both church ministry and socio-political leadership.

Regarding the role of the General Assembly, the Toraja church with its big membership and strong human resources recently managed to conduct a relative successful General Assembly. Other churches in the region need to develop a better quality of their respective General Assemblies. In the General Assembly, participants seem to spend most of their time promoting their respective candidates for the new Synod Executive Committee.

There are some aspects that need to be addressed to have a good General Assembly: well prepared documents, an organizing committee with a qualified steering committee, a team of qualified General Assembly moderators, and also well informed and disciplined participants. In general, General Assembly documents consist of (a) the report (including financial report) of the outgoing Synod Executive Committee with all its attachments; (b) a draft of the programs for the coming period; (c) other draft documents to be evaluated or decided; and (d) other documents for the General Assembly: agenda, list and address of participants, daily liturgy, rules of order, etc. Steering committees and moderators should be well aware of the process and progress of the meeting and the substance of the ongoing session. They also should lead every session toward achieving well-conceived goals for the assembly.

One area of development of church order that is often neglected is that of the pastoral offices: church discipline and the ministries of baptism, communion, marriage, and funerals. Several of the churches surveyed here maintain largely outdated practices of barring church members from communion (and often refusing baptism to their children), mostly for violating sexual and marital norms, while other serious moral failings such as domestic violence and corruption are routinely ignored. There is also a tension between the practice of church discipline and local traditions for the resolution of conflicts and disputes by means of councils of traditional elders to levy fines on those determined to be in the wrong. This is one area in which the contextualization of church order needs further development based on a more contextual theology of ministry. The same applies to the integration of baptism with rituals celebrating the birth of a child, and the integration of marriage and funerals with local ritual practices relating to these important rites of passage.

Finally, we should note the difficulty faced by the churches in producing regulations that are equally applicable to both rural and urban congregations, and also providing structures that enable continuing fellowship between urban and rural members. As the process of urbanization progresses in Indonesia, this will become a more urgent problem.

### *Conclusion*

A church order needs to be contextualized. The revision of church orders, therefore, should also consider historic aspects of Reformed traditions in which the collegial and equivalent character of different offices is preserved in the spirit of Christocracy. But church orders should also consider local traditions of communal fellowship, to both strengthen and transform those traditions. The wisdom of traditional leadership should also be adopted in the church, rather than a rigid application of church regulations. Pastoral ministries need to be emphasized more than organizational management. Most of all, the prospects for contextualizing church order require the foundation provided by a fully developed contextual ecclesiology and a contextual theology of ministry.

*Abbreviations and bibliography*

DCO: Dordt Church Order; Church Order. Drawn up in the National Synod [of Dordt] (held in 1618 and 1619) and accepted as a concord of ecclesiastic community by the Reformed Churches in the Netherlands. Accessed August 10, 2010. http://www.sacred-texts.com/chr/nethord.htm.

DEIC: Dutch East Indian Company.

GEPSULTRA: Gereja Protestan di Sulawesi Tenggara (Protestant Church of Southeast Sulawesi).

GKE: Kalimantan Evangelis Church (Evangelical Church of Kalimantan).

GKPI: Gereja Kristen Pemancar Injil (Christian Church of Gospel Lighthouse.

GKSB: Gereja Kristen Sulawesi Barat (Christian Church of West Sulawesi).

GPI: Gereja Protestan di Indonesia (Protestant Church in Indonesia).

GPSS: Protestant Church of South Sulawesi (Gereja Protestan Sulawesi Selatan).

GTM: Gereja Toraja Mamasa (Toraja Mamasa Church).

GZB: Gereformeerde Zendingsbond (Reformed Mission Alliance).

NZV: Nederlandse Zendingsvereeniging (Dutch Missionary Society).

VOC: Verenigde Oostindische Compagnie (= DEIC: Dutch East Indian Company).

ZCGK: Zending voor Christelijke Gereformeerde Kerken (Mission of Christian Reformed Churches).

Aritonang, Jan S., and Karel Steenbrink (eds). 2008. A History of Christianity in Indonesia. Leiden — Boston: Brill.

Bigalke, Terance W. 2005.Tana Toraja: A Social History of an Indonesian People. Leiden: KITLV Press.

Cooley, Frank L. 1981.The Growing Seed: The Christian Church in Indonesia. NCCUSA: Division of Overseas Ministries.

Purwanto, Lazarus H. 1997. Indonesian Church Orders Under Scrutiny: The Relation between the Church Members and the Church Office-Bearers: How It Is and How It Should Be. PhD diss., Theologische Universiteit Kampen. Kampen: Van den Berg.

Schröter, Susanne (ed). 2010. Christianity in Indonesia: Perspectives of Power. Berlin: LIT-Verlag.

# NEW CONTEXT, NEW CHURCH ORDER

Wim Dreyer

## *1. Introduction*

During the 68th General Assembly (2007) of the *Nederduitsch Hervormde Kerk van Afrika* (NHKA) the Mission Board offered a proposal that the NHKA should consider rewriting its church order. The NHKA is one of the Afrikaans speaking Reformed churches in South Africa with historical and theological roots in the Nederlands Hervormde Kerk. It is not to be confused with the Nederduitsch Gereformeerde Kerk (Dutch Reformed Church, DRC). NHKA is officially translated as Netherdutch Reformed Church in Africa. The proposal to consider rewriting the church order was accepted unanimously. A commission was appointed, charged with the responsibility to outline an ecclesiology which could form the basis of a new church order (see NHKA 2007, 196). This decision was reaffirmed by the 69th General Assembly (2010), when the report of the commission was again unanimously accepted and a new commission was appointed to start rewriting the church order (see NHKA 2010B, 224).

These decisions were remarkable when we consider that the NHKA adopted a new church order as recently as 1997 after years of extensive preparation (see CO-NHKA). Within one decade, delegates to the General Assembly came to realize that a new church order was (again) necessary. What would be the reason for this remarkable situation? I am of the opinion that within a decade fundamental shifts in our understanding of the church, ministry and context took place. It was the realization that the Reformed maxim *ecclesia reformata, semper reformanda* is of the utmost relevance to the church of the 21st century that led to the decision that a new church order was necessary.

This contribution is presented as a case study. It is argued that a new approach to ecclesiology and ministry as well as changes in context exposed the shortcomings of the NHKA church order and made the development of a new church order absolutely necessary.

*2. A traditional approach to ecclesiology*

Internationally, after the Second World War, ecclesiology received more and more attention (see Kärkkäinen 2002, 7). This was not different in South Africa. Many scientific and popular articles had the church as their focal point. Official publications of the NHKA carried articles on church order, ecumenical relations, church unity, indigenisation, church and state, and many more. They included a discussion on the concept of 'volkskerk': a Dutch/Afrikaans word meaning a church which is not primarily a state church or national church, but rather a church with membership consisting of a particular population group. Theologically this concept is based on the ecclesiologies of P.J. Hoedemaker, A.A. van Ruler and others (see Dreyer 2006 for more detailed discussion). In the case of the NHKA its primary membership consisted of white, Afrikaans speaking South Africans. It could be regarded as an indigenous church. Theological reflection on the nature and calling of the church regularly appeared in popular magazines as well as scientific journals.

The reason for the growing interest in ecclesiology was the world-wide crisis churches experienced in terms of dwindling membership, poor Sunday service attendance and loss of stature in post-christendom society. At the same time, severe criticism levelled against Afrikaans churches within the context of their support to Apartheid made a debate on ecclesiology essential. Initially, the debate in the NHKA was dominated by an exposition of traditional ecclesiological maxims:

› The church is one, holy and catholic;
› The true church is to be found where the gospel is preached and the sacraments are administered in accordance with the Word of God;
› Church order and congregational ministry must be based on the typical Calvinist presbyterial-synodal ecclesiology;
› The NHKA is historically and essentially a volkskerk, called to minister to the Afrikaans-speaking community in South Africa.
› One of the important exponents of this traditional approach to ecclesiology and church polity in the NHKA was A.D. Pont. Pont was professor of Church History and Church Polity from 1957 to 1992 at the University of Pretoria. He produced two volumes on the history of church polity: *Historiese Agtergronde van ons Kerklike Reg* (see Pont 1981; Pont 1991). Included were the complete texts of church orders, general principles of church polity as well as an exposition of the most important church orders of the Dutch and South African churches of Calvinist origin. As a result of his endeavours the presbyterial-synodal ecclesiology, church order and congregational ministry became even more dominant and entrenched in the NHKA than in the past.

Pont was of the opinion that the NHKA could not be church in any other way than in terms of a Calvinist ecclesiology (see Pont 1995, 772). Calvin (following Luther) maintained that the true church can be found wherever the gospel and the sacraments are ministered in accordance with the Word of God. This understanding of the church leads to congregational ministry which places a lot of emphasis on the functioning of the minister, elder and deacon as well as the Sunday service and preaching. This approach to ministry could be described as a 'pastoral ministry'. The traditional Reformed ecclesiology, pastoral ministry and presbyterial-synodal structure were entrenched in the church order accepted by the General Assembly in 1997. Almost 80% of the pages of the CO-NHKA give a detailed exposition of what the official duties of the minister, elder and deacon entail.

### 3. *In search of a relevant ecclesiology*

By the early 1990s more and more voices were heard in the NHKA, criticizing the traditional approach to ecclesiology and church polity. As L.J. Koffeman correctly points out, church polity and church order are fundamentally based on ecclesiology, on our understanding of what the church is and should be (see Koffeman 2009, 16–21). With the ecclesiological paradigm shift which took place in the NHKA, the CO-NHKA lost some of its relevance and functionality. The traditional presbyterial-synodal understanding and functioning of the church is progressively coming under more pressure. The following examples demonstrate a new approach to ecclesiology in the NHKA during the last two decades, making it abundantly clear why the General Assembly in 2007 took the decision that a new church order was necessary just ten years after the current church order was implemented.

One of the important critics was J.P. Oberholzer who had been professor of Old Testament Studies, Dean of the Faculty of Theology (University of Pretoria) and Moderator of the General Assembly. In his opening address at a national convention of ministers Oberholzer made the remark that the growing interest in ecclesiology and the church is something of a confession, an acknowledgement that the church had been busy with lots of things without really listening to the Word of God (see Oberholzer 1995, 852). In his address, Oberholzer pleaded for a new understanding of what it means to be church. His words reflect a growing impatience with an outdated church model. He pointed out that for several years there had been a pervasive sense that a more contemporary approach to ecclesiology was needed — one which could lead to the transformation of the NHKA and to a simplified approach to ecclesiology and ministry (see Oberholzer 1995, 851). His criticism became even sharper when he wrote in 1999: "The new millennium confronts us with the failures of almost everything that kept the church occupied. The church is getting smaller; it struggles to survive economically; its theology became unusable and its political history lies shattered" (Oberholzer 1999, 449, translated by WAD).

At more or less the same time, G.M.M. Pelser, Professor of New Testament Studies (University of Pretoria) started an extensive research program on the various ecclesiologies to be found in the New Testament (see Pelser 1995). His research has shown that the New Testament accommodates a wide-ranging diversity in ecclesiology and that it is impossible to speak of "the church in the New Testament" (see Pelser 1995). In his research the following key concepts are developed:

› Being church implies discipleship.
› Being church implies a continuing laying down of particularistic interests in favor of God's kingdom.
› The church is an eschatological community which will always remain pilgrims through history and will never have permanent dwelling in this world.
› Unity with Christ and the indwelling of the Holy Spirit is fundamental to being church.
› The church is a community of believers who in Christ become friends, brothers, sisters, servants of God and disciples of Jesus willing and able to learn from him.
› To be church means to be 'in Christ': to be one with Him in His death and resurrection.
› Poverty and loss of family were real problems in the early Christian communities, which led to the understanding of the church as a caring community or the 'household of God'.
› The church lives as the body of Christ under his governance. In this way the church became a reflection of the kingdom of God.
› The church is the sphere where salvation in and through Christ is realized. This leads to reconciliation between God and his people, as well as reconciliation between people.
› The church is the temple of the Holy Spirit.

Pelser's research on New Testament ecclesiology indicates some development in the New Testament from an early charismatic ministry to a more institutionalized form of ministry. In the pastoral letters the household of God includes members with certain gifts, which meant that they became leaders in the early communities. The eschatological second coming of Christ moved to the background. As a result, the building up and maintenance of the church became important. The focus shifted, from missional outreach to pastoral care. It is clear that a gradual shift took place: The church evolved from a spiritual movement into a structure with certain rules, offices and traditions.

Another NHKA theologian, G.C. Velthuysen, propagated a move away from the generally accepted presbyterial-synodal ecclesiology prevalent in the NHKA. Velthuysen was Professor of Systematic Theology at the University of Pretoria. As early as 1988, Velthuysen proposed an "experimental approach to ecclesiology" (Velthuysen 1988, 489). Following H. Ott and H-J. Kraus, Velthuysen builds his ecclesiology on Christology, according to which the church can be understood only in relation to Jesus Christ and an unbreakable and essential unity exists between Christ and his church. Velthuysen also agrees with Karl Barth, who referred to the congregation as the earthly and historical existence of Christ (see Barth 1953, 738). This does not mean that Barth understood the church as *Christus prolongatus*, because in his typically dialectical approach he distinguished sharply between Christ and the church: Christ and the church are one, but not in such a way that the church becomes deified. The unity of Christ and the church implies a radical identification of the church with Christ.

Velthuysen also refers to D. Bonhoeffer who spoke of the congregation as *Christus existierend als Gemeinde* (see Velthuysen 1988, 501). Thus the congregation is *a priori* a form of revelation. The church makes Christ visible on earth. To be church is to be one with Christ, to be *in Christ*. At the same time, Bonhoeffer distinguished between Christ as the head of the body and the church as his body. Velthuysen comes to the conclusion that the church is not *Christus prolongatus*, but at the same time the church could never be without Christ (see Velthuysen 1988, 502). The unity between Christ and the church is a reality which can only be experienced through faith.

In 1995, L.J.S. Steenkamp proposed a paradigm shift in our understanding of the church (see Steenkamp 1995, 604–622). The paradigm of Christendom is dead, he writes. A new paradigm needs to be developed which would be relevant to the 21st century. After a discussion of biblical metaphors such as the church as God's family, the church as a building of which Christ is the cornerstone, the church as God's people, the church as the body of Christ, and others, Steenkamp reiterates the necessity of conversion and a radical reformation of the church as we approached the 21st century (see Steenkamp 1995, 619). Steenkamp defines the new paradigm in terms of the missio Dei. The heart of being church should be a missional and diaconal presence in the world which flows from a living faith in Jesus Christ (see Steenkamp 1995, 620).

Since 2000, when J. Buitendag became Professor of Systematic Theology at the University of Pretoria, ecclesiology has received particular attention in his lectures and published work (see for example Buitendag 2008). As Moderator of the NHKA and also Dean of the Faculty of Theology, he has been deliberately promoting a new understanding of the church. His ecclesiology reflects influences from theologians such as Berkhof, Dingemans, Küng (see Küng 1976), Moltmann, Pannenberg and Zizioulas. He also accentuates an ecumenical approach to ecclesiology, specifically the work done by *Faith and Order* (see NPC, NMC). His ecumenical understanding of the church became even more visible in his efforts to restore the NHKA's membership of the then World Alliance of Reformed Churches (WARC). Under his leadership the moderature of the NHKA hosted a National Colloquium from 27 to 29 April 2006. The theme of the colloquium was "Identity and relevance of the NHKA in the 21st century". In his opening address at the National Colloquium, Buitendag confronted the NHKA with a clear and unequivocal challenge: The church must enter a process of transformation or it will become totally irrelevant in the 21st century (see Buitendag 2006). One of the authors he referred to was Pete Ward, with his concept of a 'liquid church' (see Ward 2002). Buitendag envisioned a church which could become more adaptable, like water which flows in a clear and life-giving stream. The church needs to become a dynamic, communicative network, distinguished by its participatory nature under the direction of the Holy Spirit and the Word. The church can only exist in a living relationship to Jesus Christ, as part of the one body of Christ (see Buitendag 2006, 8).

Another influential figure in the NHKA is T.F.J. Dreyer. Dreyer served several terms as moderator of the NHKA. Under his leadership, during 2001, the NHKA adopted a vision: "Our dream is that all people will believe in Jesus Christ as the only hope for the world". This speaks of a more open, missional and inclusive ecclesiology. As the first decade of the 21st century passed, Dreyer became more outspoken in his criticism of a traditional approach to ecclesiology (see Dreyer 2009, 427–431). As Professor of Practical Theology, he developed a practical ecclesiology very much influenced by the thoughts of Gerben Heitink (see Heitink 2007). Dreyer used Heitink's ecclesiological matrix, which indicated a high level of stagnation in the NHKA and its inability to adapt to a new context. He came, as did Heitink, to the conclusion that the church should enter a process of 'radical reformation'.

### *4. Missional ecclesiology as a matrix for a new church order*

The most recent development in the NHKA in terms of ecclesiology could be described as a movement toward 'missional ecclesiology'. But how should we define missional ecclesiology? One of the best definitions was formulated by Paul Hooker: "Missional ecclesiology demands more of the church than deciding which community service projects to undertake or setting congregational priorities for the coming year. Missional ecclesiology is a way of understanding the church. It begins with the Missio Dei — God's own 'self-sending' in Christ by the Spirit to redeem and transform creation. In a missional ecclesiology, the Church is not a building or an institution but a community of witness, called into being and equipped by God, and sent into the world to testify to and participate in Christ's work. The Church does not have missions; instead, the mission of God creates the Church. The Church serves God's call to mission through its work in three broadly defined categories: the proclamation of the Word of God, the administration of the sacraments of Baptism and the Lord's Supper, and the nurture of the covenant community of disciples. It undertakes this mission without regard for its own agenda or survival" (Hooker 2008, 1–2).

Missional ecclesiology emphasises the continuing conversion of the church (see Guder 2000, 150) and congregational praxis. Fundamental to transformation is a shift in focus from congregational maintenance to openness to the world and participation in God's mission and God's kingdom. Central to missional ecclesiology is the theological concept of the *missio Dei*: the essence of being church is to be found in its participation in God's mission to the world. As such, the *missio Dei* is the basis and point of departure for congregational ministry (see Bosch 1991, 467f.).

The moderature of the NHKA, in accordance with the decisions made by the 68th General Assembly in 2007, appointed a commission to develop an ecclesiology which could form the basis of a new church order. The commission presented the 69th General Assembly with its report, which was accepted unanimously. The complete text of the commission's report on a new ecclesiological approach can be found in the agenda of the 69th General Assembly, under the heading *Ekklesiologiese kontoere met die oog op die herskryf van die kerkorde* (see NHKA 2010A, 522–534). When the text of the report on ecclesiology is examined, the principles on which it is based become clear:

› There is no reference to any specific theologian's contribution to ecclesiology. At the same time, it is quite clear that the leading ecclesiologists of the 20th century influenced the document.
› The focus is very much on the local congregation as the living community of believers, not on the church as an institutional entity.
› The report is based on a missional ecclesiology.
› The report uses only biblical metaphors in its ecclesiological exposition. The report presented the church with a biblical, systematic and well-structured ecclesiology which is easy to understand and accessible to every member of the church.
› The biblical metaphors were structured in accordance with the Trinity: The one God who revealed Himself as the Father, the Son and the Holy Spirit.

- The basic principle reflected in this approach is the conviction that our understanding of God is fundamental to our understanding of the church. The way we speak about the church reflects our understanding of God. The implication of this approach is that theology influences ecclesiology, ecclesiology influences church polity and church order. As such, church polity and church order in essence reflect our relationship with God the Father, the Son and the Holy Spirit.

The report on ecclesiology discussed the biblical metaphors under the following headings:

*The congregation as God's people*
- We are God's people
- We are part of the covenant
- We are God's people in this world
- We are God's people on a pilgrim's journey

*The congregation as the family of the Father*
- We are the household of the Father
- We are a family
- We care for each other
- We eat at the same table

*The congregation as the Body of Christ*
- We are the body of Christ
- We are one in Christ
- We are called and equipped for service
- We are baptized into the body of Christ

*The congregation as the temple of the Holy Spirit*
- We are the temple of the Holy Spirit
- We received the Holy Spirit
- We are guided and equipped by the Holy Spirit
- We worship God under the guidance of the Holy Spirit

By accepting this ecclesiological approach, the General Assembly of the NHKA made a fundamental shift in its understanding of the church—from a traditional presbyterial-synodal ecclesiology to a missial ecclesiology based on the key concept *missio Dei.* The challenge remains, however, to translate a missional ecclesiology into a functional church order and relevant congregational ministry.

### 5. *A new approach to ministry*

What would be the effect of a missional ecclesiology on ministry? Ministry in the NHKA could be described as fundamentally *pastoral*. The current church order creates *de jure* a situation where 90% of congregational activities are centred on pastoral ministry (see CO-NHKA, ord. 2.1.5, 2.3 and 2.4). This reflects the normal Reformed type of ministry which centres on the activities of the minister, elder and deacon. Characteristics of a pastoral ministry are the following:

› Pastoral ministry has a strong focus on church members attending the Sunday service. A 'good' church member is one who regularly attends the Sunday service. Over centuries Sunday service became the undisputed focal point of ministry. The world must come to church on Sunday — but does the church go to the world on weekdays?
› Ministry is the responsibility of the minister, elder and deacon.
› Ordinary church members have a very limited role in congregational ministry. There is a clear distinction between the responsibilities of ordinary church members and those holding office in the church.
› Pastoral ministry is to a large extent dependant on the efficacy of the pastor loci.
› Pastoral ministry is focused inward, giving high priority to pastoral care and the maintenance of congregational structures.
› Pastoral ministry has an inherent weakness in terms of missional ministry. Missional ministry, as research had shown, receives very little attention in traditional Reformed congregations with a strong focus on pastoral care (see Dreyer 2011, 109–115).

The 68th General Assembly came to the conclusion that missional ministry should be emphasised. Ministers were encouraged to facilitate a shift from pastoral ministry to missional ministry, without compromising pastoral care in congregations:

› The General Assembly confirms that missional ministry is an important part of congregational ministry and enough time should be devoted to it.
› The General Assembly encourages congregations to start with a process of transformation and development, of which missional ministry should be the primary focus (see NHKA 2007, 36–38 as translated by WAD).

The debate on missional ministry was continued during the 69th General Assembly (2010). During this debate terminology was clarified and a distinction was made between *missionary and missional*:

› The first identifies mission as an external activity with a strong focus on missionary work done elsewhere and in the format of support to specific projects or missionary endeavours.

› The second indicates a missional mode of existence and paradigm, where a missional approach is part of the daily functioning of a congregation. The DNA of the congregation should become missional, which determines the way in which a congregation (as the people of God, the family of the Father, the body of Christ and the temple of the Holy Spirit) is present in the world (see NHKA 2010A, 235).

The General Assembly clearly stated that missional ministry has as its point of departure the great commission of Jesus Christ (Matt. 28) and came to the conclusion that missional ministry should form an essential part of Reformed ministry. According to the 69th General Assembly of the NHKA, missional ministry is the result of our understanding of the nature, purpose and mission of the church (see NHKA 2010A, 236). Missional ministry emphasises a living relationship with God, real faith, a focus on the kingdom of God, a relevant ministry, discernment through the Holy Spirit, a systemic approach of congegrational development, a focus on people and relationships, and discipleship. Congregations should understand that they exist for, and are sent to, the world. The current church order already makes limited provision for the establishment of unique forms of ministry and communities (see CO-NHKA, art. 68). This is especially important in a situation where a typically Reformed, pastoral approach to ministry is not suitable. The question remains how this could be extended in a new church order.

These few remarks on pastoral and missional ministry are sufficient to show that a new church order became necessary. Not only did the NHKA experience fundamental changes in terms of its understanding of the church (ecclesiology), but also in its understanding of the *missio Dei* and the implications for ministry.

### *6. Changes in context*

A third reason why a new church order became necessary was the significant changes in context. Many of these changes are universal to all churches. So much has been published on this topic; it needs very little further discussion. Some of these changes are globalization, secularization, loss of credibility and the status of the church, post-christendom culture, post-modernity, post-apartheid South Africa, loss of members, and changes in the way people communicate. In light of these changes, the 69th General Assembly came to the conclusion that extensive research must be done on ministry in small congregations and on how ordinary church members could be utilized in congregational ministry (see NHKA 2010B, 87).

It is self-evident that incorporating congregants into ministry will require a clear understanding of the challenges the church is facing, including the transformation of the traditional functioning of the church in terms of official ministry. A new synergy between discipleship, general priesthood and official ministry needs to develop.

### *7. Concluding remarks: a new church order*

The radical reformation of the church which is needed in the 21st century leaves nothing untouched and requires changes on the deepest levels of the church (see Niemandt 2007, 52). Adaptive change begins with a new understanding of what it means to be church. Adaptive change is about changing the hearts and minds of individual congregants as well as the church collectively.

In this regard, we must consider what Alan Hirsch wrote: "Restructure the organization and leave the system story in place and nothing changes in the organization. It's futile trying to revitalize the church, or a denomination, without changing the system" (Hirsch 2006, 54). Hirsch defines a systems story as "the set of core beliefs which result from the multiplicity of conversations and which maintains the unity of culture" (Hirsch 2006, 53). This becomes evident in the way in which theology is taught and functions in the church, and in myths, symbols, rituals, church structures and systems of control. In applying Hirsch's analyses and definitions to the NHKA as the present case study does, it is my contention that the dominant system story of recent decades could be described as a traditional presbyterial-synodal ecclesiology and church order resulting in an inwardly focused pastoral ministry.

I believe the NHKA should continually embrace a process of transformation (as an internal process) as well as reformation (as a structural process). This will only be possible if the dominant system story migrates to a missional understanding of the church and of ministry. This is an extremely complex process that needs to be facilitated with extreme care, part of which will be the writing of a new church order. Writing a new church order is therefore not a question of superficial and cosmetic changes, but of radical renewal in our understanding of the church, in its mission and in the way ministry should be structured. Koffeman points out that church polity and a church order is always dependant on the ecclesiological understanding of the church, as it manifests in a certain time and certain place within a certain community (see Koffeman 2009, 11). In other words, a church order needs to be contextual. When a church order is written for a specific church in a specific context, it implies making choices based on fundamental ecclesiological insights (see Koffeman 2009, 12). It reflects a certain theological position. Even more important than our understanding of ecclesiology, ministry and context is our understanding of the relationship between the visible and invisible church (see Koffeman 2009, 19). How do we, in a church order, give expression to what we believe of the one, holy and catholic church? How is it possible to make visible the people of God, the family of the Father, the body of Christ or the temple of the Holy Spirit?

These are some of the questions the NHKA will grapple with in the next decade. The challenge will be to write a church order which is less institutional and more organic, focused on what we discern as God's will for his church within the South African context.

### *Abbreviations and bibliography*

CO-NHKA: Kerkorde van die Nederduitsch Hervormde Kerk van Afrika. Pretoria: NHKA Church Archives (1997).

DRC: Dutch Reformed Church.

NHKA 2007. Besluitebundel van die 68e Algemene Kerkvergaderingbundel. Pretoria: NHKA Church Archives.

NHKA 2010A. Agenda van die 69e Algemene Kerkvergadering. Pretoria: NHKA Church Archives.

NHKA 2010B. Besluitebundel van die 69e Algemene Kerkvergadering. Pretoria: NHKA Church Archives.

NMC: Faith and Order Commission. 2005. The Nature and Mission of the Church: A Stage on the Way to a Common Statement. Faith and Order Paper 198. Geneva: WCC.

NPC: Faith and Order Commission. 1998. The Nature and Purpse of the Church: A Stage on the Way to a Common Statement. Faith and Order Paper 181. Geneva: WCC.

WARC: World Alliance of Reformed Churches, since 2010: World Communion of Reformed Churches.

Barth, Karl. 1953. Kirchliche Dogmatik, IV/1. Zürich: EVZ.

Bosch, David J. 1991. Transforming Mission. New York: Orbis Books. 22nd Edition 2006.

Buitendag, Johan. 2006. Openingsrede, Nasionale Colloquium 27 April 2006. Pretoria: Church Archives.

Buitendag, Johan. 2008. Ecclesia reformata semper reformanda—die ongemaklike eis. In: HTS Theological Studies 64(2008)/1, 122–138.

Dreyer, Theunis F.J. 2009, 'n Kerk met karakter: Die perspektief van Gerben Heitink. In: HTS Theological Studies 65(2009)/1, Art. #315, 5 pages. DOI: 10.4102/hts.v65i.315.

Dreyer, Wim A. 2006. Die Nederduitsch Hervormde Kerk van Afrika as volkskerk—oorsig en herbesinning. In: HTS Theological Studies 62(2006)/4, 1337–1368.

Dreyer, Wim A. 2011. Praktiese Ekklesiologie en Bedieningspraktyk met verwysing na die Nederduitsch Hervormde Kerk van Afrika. PhD diss., University of Pretoria.

Guder, Darrell L. 2000. The Continuing Conversion of the Church. The Gospel and our Culture Series. Grand Rapids: Eerdmans.

Heitink, Gerben. 2007. Een kerk met karakter: Tijd voor heroriëntatie. Kampen: Kok.

Hirsch, Alan. 2006. The forgotten ways: Reactivating the missional church. Grand Rapids: Brazos.

Hooker, Paul. 2008. Missional Ecclesiology. Accessed November 28, 2012. http://www.negapby.org/missionalecc.pdf.

Kärkkäinen, Veli-Matti. 2002. An Introduction to Ecclesiology: Ecumenical, Historical and Global Perspectives. Downers Grove: InterVarsity Press.

Koffeman, Leo J. 2009. Het goed recht van de kerk: Een theologische inleiding op het kerkrecht. Kampen: Kok.

Küng, Hans. 1976. The Church. London: Search Press.

Niemandt, C.J.P. (Nelus). 2007. Nuwe drome in nuwe werklikhede: Geloofsgemeenskappe in pas met 'n postmoderne wêreld. Wellington: Lux Verbi BM.

Oberholzer, Johannes P. 1995. Die kerk. In: HTS Teologiese Studies 51(1995)/3, 851–857.

Oberholzer, Johannes P. 1999. Terug op die pad. In: Van Wyk 1999, 449–462.

Pelser, Gerhardus M.M. 1995. Die kerk in die Nuwe Testament. In: HTS Theological Studies 51(1995)/3, p. 645–676.

Pont, Adrianus D. 1981. Historiese agtergronde van ons kerklike reg, Deel 1. Pretoria: HAUM.

Pont, Adrianus D. 1991. Die historiese agtergronde van ons kerklike reg, Deel 2. Pretoria: Kital.

Pont, Adrianus D. 1995. Die reformatoriese kerkbegrip: Enkele groot lyne op grond van Calvyn se uiteensetting. In: HTS Theological Studies 51(1995)/3, 771–791.

Steenkamp, Lourens J.S. 1995. Die kerk onderweg na die 21e eeu: 'n Kritiese besinning oor kerkwees in 'n veranderende konteks in Suid-Afrika. In: HTS Theological Studies 51(1995)/3, 604–622.

Van Wyk, Daniel J.C. (ed.). 1999. 20ste Eeu Hervormde Teologie. Pretoria: Sentik.

Velthuysen, Gerrit C. 1988. Die wese van die kerk: 'n Teologiese antwoord op 'n filosofiese vraag. In: HTS Theological Studies 44(1991)/2, 489–513.

Ward, Pete. 2002. Liquid Church. Carlisle: Paternoster Press.

# THE CHURCH ORDER OF THE AFRIKAANSE CHRISTEN KERK VAN NIEU SEELAND

## Does the Glove Fit the Hand?

Johan Van der Merwe

### *1. Historical background*

With the advent of democratic change in South Africa at the end of the previous century, numerous white Afrikaans speaking South Africans decided to leave the country. Many of them immigrated to New Zealand. Statistics confirm this. According to Statistics of The New Zealand department of Home affairs, there were 3840 South African born citizens in New Zealand in 1976, 26061 by 2001 and 41676 by 2006. The people that left South Africa for New Zealand stated the high crime rate, crumbling infrastructure, corruption, affirmative action and a lack of faith in African leadership as reasons for their decision (see Marais 2009).

Like in 1652, when Jan van Riebeeck arrived in the Cape to establish a refreshment post for Dutch ships en route to India and also brought the Reformed church with him (see Van der Watt 1975, 4), many of the emigrants that went to New Zealand were devoted Christians and took their faith with them. Although they initially tried to become members of the different Reformed churches in New Zealand, the need for an own church became more apparent as more and more emigrants arrived (see ACKNS 1998).

Ds Dawie Kriel, formerly from the Nederduitsch Hervormde kerk in South Africa, and at that time minister of the Presbyterian Church in Te Kauwhata was approached for an Afrikaans church service once a month in North Shore, Auckland. Due to the demand, once a month soon became every Sunday. On the 1st of November 1998 the Afrikaanse Christen Kerk van Nieu Seeland (ACKNS) was established. A name with any connotation to the Afrikaans sister churches in South Africa was deliberately avoided so that all Afrikaans speaking Christians from the Reformed faith would feel at home. Church council meetings were held once a week to monitor the progress of the new church. Besides practical ministry issues such as worship and catechesis, the Church council gave attention to setting up a church order, policy making and the registration of the Afrikaanse Christen Kerk van Nieu Seeland as an official church in New Zealand (see ACKNS n.d.).

Approximately at the same time as the establishment of the ACKNS, Dr Stanley Theron began with worship services for a group of Afrikaans speaking Christians in The Howick area, in the south eastern suburbs of Auckland. Due to commitments in his own congregation, Rev. Kriel did not see his way open to continue with the Afrikaans services. He however made contact with Rev. Gawie Cloete who lived in Hamilton and worked as a salesman. Cloete agreed to conduct a worship service in Auckland once a month. In June 1999 the church council asked Rev. Cloete to become the first full time minister of the church in Auckland. He accepted and became the first full time minister of the ACKNS on the 12th of July 1999 (see ACKNS 2005, 14). By 2005 the congregation had more than a thousand members. As more and more emigrants arrived in New Zealand, more congregations were established: Hamilton 2003, Rotorua and Wellington 2006. The church kept growing and at the moment consists of 11 congregations, 10 on the North Island and 2 on the South Island (see ACKNS 2012, 1). What makes the ACKNS unique is the fact that its members come from all the different Afrikaans speaking churches in South Africa, not only Reformed, but also charismatic and even Roman Catholic. To my mind, this makes the ACKNS a truly ecumenical church. This being said, the question can rightfully be asked if a church consisting of mainly Afrikaans speaking members can be ecumenical. My understanding of ecumenical is not qualified by Christians from different colour or race groups coming together in one church, but rather by Christians from different denominations and traditions joining hands to become one church. This is what the *una sancta* is all about and this is what happened in New Zealand. The congregation in Hamilton serves as a perfect example where the second minister of the congregation is a pastor coming from the Apostolic Faith Mission in South Africa. Members of the congregation consist of previous members of the Dutch Reformed Church, the Nederduitsch Hervormde Kerk, the Gereformeerde Kerk, the Apostolic Faith Mission and other charismatic churches like Lewende Woord and Hatfield Christian Church. There are even members coming from the Roman Catholic Church (Hendriks 2012).

It is precisely this ecumenical nature of the ACKNS that challenged the leadership to write a church order that serves the very specific needs and features of the church. Because the church is ecumenical in its composition, the church order had to serve the ecumenical nature of the church (Reynecke 2012).

*2. An ecumenical church order for an ecumenical church?*

The question that poses itself is if the church order of the ACKNS serves the ecumenical character of the church. In order to answer this question we must take a few steps back and first ask the question: What attributes must a church order have in order to be of service to an ecumenical church? Coertzen helps us on our way when he writes: "As such, a church order is not a mere neutral manuscript for order. Important principal viewpoints are fundamental to such a document. Therefore, a church order, itself is also an object of reflection by Church Law" (Coertzen 2004, 187).

If we want to take this statement seriously we must revisit the church polity behind a specific church order. This means that the foundation of an ecumenical church order can be nothing else than ecumenical Church Polity. The question we must answer then is: what is meant by ecumenical church polity and is ecumenical church polity even possible?

Koffeman, in his book *Het Goed Recht van de Kerk*, reflects on this when he writes: "The concept of ecumenical church polity seems strange. It seems like a contradiction in terminis" (Koffeman 2009, 27). This is most probably the general point of view of many students of church polity. He then however argues with Dombois that there are two important principles when considering the nature of church polity. The first principle is the fact that the unity of the church is embedded in Christ himself and that this makes the unity of the church in the first place an indicative and an imperative. It also makes the objective ecumenical nature of church polity a historical given (see Koffeman 2009, 28). Koffeman builds on this when he clearly states: "Church polity must serve the unity of the church" (Koffeman 2009, 29) This point of view also makes it important to take note of the other characteristics of the church namely holiness, catholicity and apostolicity. Heyns is correct when he states that although it is possible to differentiate between the four characteristics of the church, it would be wrong to separate then from each other. "They are different aspects of the same matter. They flow into each other and build on one another" (Heyns 1977, 114). This means, that not only must church polity serve the unity of the church, but flowing forth from the *una sancta*, it must also serve the holiness, apostolicity and catholicity of the church. If this is true of the church polity which is practised in a specific church, then it must be reflected in the church order of the church. This will be taken into account when assessing the church order of the ACKNS.

The second important principle according to Dombois, is the fact that the church lives in the sphere of the power of the Holy Spirit and like the Spirit worked in history, it is still working today to create the church. This gives the church open-endedness directed to the future (Dombois 1979, 235f., as quoted by

Koffeman 2009, 29). The church is continually moving from the mission given to it by the Lord to the Kingdom of God. This implies two movements which are related to one another: ecumenism as a movement and church polity as a movement. Koffeman describes this process as follows: "It is exactly in the combination of the two movements—Ecumenism as porcess of unity and church polity as process of law where we find the foundation of ecumenical church polity. The two movements call for each other. In the ecumenical movement, identified as movement of the Spirit, churches know that they are called to give shape to structures and inter church relations so that the the unity of the church of Christ becomes more recognisable. The ecumenical movement has in this sense a legal dimension". Koffeman continues: "the contrary is also true: in the development of church polity, churces are busy creating visible unity—beside the holiness, catholicity and apostolicity... By doing that, church polity has an ecumenical dimension". Koffeman then makes an important conclusion: "It is in the connection between these two movements, namely the process of legislation and the process of growing visible unity where the foundation of ecumenical church polity lies" (Koffeman 2009, 36).

This means that the process of expressing this 'one holy catholic apostolic church' in the structures, governance and relations of the church is the very essence of church polity. The above statement has far reaching consequences for the church. In so far as a local church, whether it is a particular denomination or a congregation, is regarded as a manifestation of the one holy catholic Church, regarding itself as part of the universal church, and recognizes the same in other churches, its polity can be nothing else as ecumenical in nature. In this regard, church polity and the church order of a specific church become the way in which it gives practical and structural expression to the fact that it is a local manifestation of the universal church. This kind of ecumenical church polity contains within itself the invitation to other churches or members of other churches which are also considered to be a local manifestation of the one, holy, catholic, apostolic church to join in one another's mutual recognition, witness, service and worship. Most important: There will always be an element of deliberate non-exclusive language. It is not within the scope of this article to discuss this matter in detail. What is important is to recognise that these basic principles confirm that the very nature of church polity can't be anything else than ecumenical. The unity of the church, founded in Christ himself and the work of the Holy Spirit guiding the church through history defines the church and if church polity wants to serve the church, as it is supposed to do, it also has to be ecumenical in its very nature. If we take Coertzen seriously, this must then be reflected in the church order of a church which claims to be ecumenical.

The question which must be answered is: How should this be done? Some direction can be found in paragraph 53 of the Faith and Order Document *The nature and Mission of the Church* (NMC) which reads as follows: "The essential oneness which belongs to the very nature of the Church, and is already given to it in Jesus Christ, stands in contrast to the actual divisions within and between the churches. Yet in spite of all divisions the unity given to the Church is already manifest in the one Gospel present in all churches, and appears in many features of their lives (cf. Eph. 4:4–5; 1Tim. 2:5; Acts 4:12). The unfortunate divisions among the churches are due partly to sin, and partly to a sincere attempt of Christians to be faithful to the truth. Working for the unity of the Church means working for fuller visible embodiment of the oneness that belongs to its nature" (NMC, § 53).

It also corresponds to paragraph 34 of the *Leuenberg agreement* which clearly states that the unity of the church, "the essential oneness ... belongs to the very nature of the church, and is given to the church in Jesus Christ" (LA, § 34). A good example of how this kind of Church polity reflects in a church order can also be found in the opening paragraph of the church order of the Protestant Church in the Netherlands (PCN).

> Article I
> 1. In accordance with its confession the Protestant Church in the Netherlands is manifestation of the one holy apostolic and catholic or universal Christian Church which, sharing in the expectation granted to Israel, looks forward to the arrival of the Kingdom of God.
> 2. Living by God's grace in Jesus Christ, the church carries out the mandate of its Lord to hear and to proclaim the Word.
> 3. Involved in God's turning towards the world, the church, in obedience to Holy Scripture as the one source and norm of the church's proclamation and ministry, confesses the triune God, Father, Son, and Holy Spirit.
> 4. The confession of the church takes place in communion with the confession of our ancestors as Formulated in the *Apostles' Creed*, the *Nicene Creed* and the *Athanasian Creed*—by which the church is joined to the universal Christian church –, in the *Unaltered Confession of Augsburg* and the *Catechism of Luther*—by which the church is joined to the Lutheran tradition –, in the *Heidelberg Catechism*, the *Catechism of Geneva* and the *Belgic Confession* with the *Canons of Dordt*—by which the church is joined to the Reformed tradition.
> 5. The church acknowledges the significance of the *Barmen Theological Declaration* for its confession today.
> With the *Leuenberg Agreement* the church acknowledges that the Lutheran and Reformed traditions come together through a common understanding of the Gospel (CO-PCN, art. I).

I believe that it is clear, from the above excerpt, that although the church defines itself, on the one hand, as a particular denomination which has as its confessional basis certain confessional documents as stated in Art. I, § 4, of the church order, it positions itself within the broader theological concept of the Universal church which transcends all those who confess Christ is Lord, the Church which is called into being by God himself which has come through the ages in history under the guidance of the Holy Spirit and the Word, and continues to be guided in this manner

It is also clear from the above paragraph that the church order itself, as a juridical document, that regulates the life of the broader denomination and the local congregations, is based on a polity which has its point of departure in the Universal church and practices its polity with the view that the local church is part or a local embodiment of the universal church.

### *3. An Overview of the Church order of the ACKNS*

The question at hand is if the same can be said of the church order of the ACKNS. The current Church order of the ACKNS was approved on the 9th of September 2006. It was revised on the 18th of September 2009 and valid from March 2010. The revised church order was compiled after a long consultation process which was facilitated by Rev. Johan Hendriks who was chairman of the general assembly of the church (Hendriks 2012). This became necessary because the original church order, composed from the different church orders of the Dutch Reformed Church, the Nederduitsch Hervormde kerk van Afrika, the Gereformeerde Kerk and the Afrikaanse Protestantse kerk no longer served the ecumenical nature of the church as it grew and more congregations were established. The ecumenical composition of the church forced the leadership to rewrite the church order. The revised church order consists of 13 chapters and 1 regiment which are divided as follows:

> Chapter 1: The Church
> This chapter states the confession of faith of the church, membership, church governance and relationships with other churches
>
> Chapter 2: The Congregation
> The first paragraph of this chapter defines what is meant by a congregation. Secondly it describes the process of founding new congregations and concludes by the incorporation of current congregations into other churches.
>
> Chapter 3: The Offices
> The church acknowledges, apart from the general office of the believer, three special offices to which Jesus entrusted the work of his Church, namely that of the teaching elder (minister), ruling/governing elder and deacon. These three offices are equal, but are differentiated on the grounds of commission and work.

Chapter 4: Meetings of the congregation
In this chapter the church order distinguishes between two different meetings namely a Congregational meeting and a session. The compilation of the different meetings as well as their functions is described.

Chapter 5: The General assembly
The compilation, meetings and functions of the General assembly are described.

Chapter 6: Majority in decision making
The church order states that an ordinary majority that is half of the members eligible to vote plus one who are present, are required for decision making purposes except where the contrary is clearly stated otherwise.

Chapter 7: Preaching of the Word
This chapter describes the participation and leading of worship services, liturgy, different formularies, music and singing, Christian days of celebration and special services. The worship service is described as a meeting between God triune and His congregation gathered at a specific place and time as determined by the session.

Chapter 8: The Sacraments
The Church acknowledges two sacraments namely, Baptism and Communion. The church order describes the administering of the sacraments

Chapter 9: Teaching
This chapter describes faith teaching to children in the church as well as to non churched adults. It also states that teachings of members of the congregation as well as the leaders are of utmost importance for the spreading of the gospel

Chapter 10: External relationships
Any formal contact or statements, as well as the formalising of ecumenical relationships and external contacts on behalf of the Church, are considered and approved by the General Assembly.

Chapter 11: Church supervision and discipline
Supervision and discipline are practised to maintain the honour of God, to reconcile the sinner with God and his neighbour and to remove offence from the congregation. The church order differentiates between members, offices and ministers. Every member has the right to appeal to the General assembly

Chapter 12: Property and other assets of the church.
The principle that each congregation is wholly church implies that congregations retain complete ownership of properties and assets of that congregation. In the event of a congregation closing down, all assets and property will be given to another congregation of the church.

Chapter 13 Alternation of the Church order
The revision of the church order can only be done by the General Assembly (see CO-ACKNS).

### 4. *The Church order of the ackns: Ecumenical or not?*

As I already mentioned, the members of the ACKNS come from many different denominations in South Africa. The church truly demonstrates this oneness in its constitution. In discussions with the ministers of the church it became clear that ecumenical theology is their point of departure. This influences the way in which they think about church polity. Does this however reflect in the church order of the church? In order to assess this, the four characteristics of the church as mentioned elsewhere in this article can be used. I choose however to turn to Koffeman once again. In his ground breaking work: *Het Goed Recht van de Kerk*, Koffeman recognises the importance of the four characteristics in ecumenical church polity but then proceeds to identify four quality markers which to my mind is a better way to assess the ecumenical nature of the church order of the ACKNS. Koffeman himself says: "Inclusivity, authenticity, conciliarity, and integrity are pivotal in terms of the possibilities of any church to 'manifest the *una sancta*', in daily church life, and, therefore, also in church polity" (Koffeman 2009, 165). He then proceeds to define inclusivity as follows: "When a church tries to live up to its destination, it cannot accept any limitation beforehand", and further: "A church even knows of the relativity of its own historical limitations: it reaches out, beyond borders, and it is missionary and diaconal in nature" (Koffeman 2009, 164). The second marker is the authenticity of the church. Koffeman defines this marker as: "the churches' connection with tradition, and more specifically with Holy Scripture, which is decisive" (Koffeman 2009, 164). The third marker is the conciliarty of the church which is described as follows: "In its institutional life the church further sustain mutual relations between people, groups, as well as between ecclesial communities, in order to let the gifts of each of them serve the vocation that all share" (Koffeman 2009, 165). The fourth marker is the integrity of the church. Koffeman says: "Although (as we saw above) no limitation can be accepted beforehand, it is, therefore, true also that not 'everything goes' within the church" (Koffeman 2009, 165).

Because it is impossible to assess the whole church order I choose to use two examples that assess the ecumenical nature of the church order.

#### Example *1*

In chapter 1 of the Church order the church order reads as follows: "The mission of the ACKNS is as follows: 'As Gods children we want to create a spiritual home mainly for Afrikaans speaking people where we can serve and care for all people and in doing so, obey the command of Christ to make disciples of all people'" (CO-ACKNS, ch. 1)

The confessional foundation of the church is then stated as follows: "The Bible as the holy and infallible Word of God is the foundation of the church. The teachings of the Church in accordance with the Word of God are expressed in the Forms of Unity as appointed by the Synod of Dordrecht in 1618–1619, namely the thirty seven articles of the *Belgic Confession of Faith*, the *Heidelberg Catechism* and the five *Canons of Dordt*" (CO-ACKNS, ch. 1).

Although the mission statement of the church seems to be exclusive by declaring that it is a church for *mainly Afrikaans speaking people*, the inclusivity is defined by the word *mainly*. Being a church which was founded by Afrikaans speaking immigrants for Afrikaans speaking immigrants it could easily have become an Afrikaans only church which would have made it totally exclusive. The fact that the church order states clearly that it is *mainly* for Afrikaans speaking members, confirms the ecumenical nature of the church order. The second quality attribute identified by Koffeman, namely authenticity, becomes clear from the confessional foundation of the church which confirms that the Bible as the holy and infallible Word of God is the foundation of the church. The third attribute, namely conciliarity is evident from the rest of the mission statement which reads: "where we can serve and care for all people and in doing so, obey the command of Christ to make disciples of all people" (CO-ACKNS, ch. 1). This also underlines the missionary character of the church which is critical for the ecumenical character of the church. The fourth quality attribute comes to fore in the rest of article one where the boundaries of the church are drawn. The church order states that: "The teachings of the Church in accordance with the Word of God are expressed in the Forms of Unity as appointed by the Synod of Dordrecht in 1618–1619, namely the thirty seven articles of the *Belgic Confession of Faith*, the *Heidelberg Catechism* and the five *Canons of Dordt*" (CO-ACKNS, ch. 1). This defines the Reformed character of the church and prepares the way for the church's understanding of the *notae ecclesiae* namely the preaching of the gospel, the understanding of the sacraments and discipline. It is clear that the quality markers identified by Koffeman (see Koffeman 2009, 164) confirm the ecumenical nature of the church and that this also becomes evident in the church order. This is also confirmed by what happens in practice in the different congregations (see ACKNS 2008). Although the main aim of the church is being an Afrikaans church with a Reformed character, nobody is excluded from worship, participation in church activities or even the sacraments. However, to become a member of the church, adherence to the confessional foundation is required. This confirms the movement Dombois is talking about (see Dombois 1979), and to my mind shows that the glove does fit the hand.

Example 2

A second example is that of the sacraments, and especially baptism. The church order states in chapter 8 on baptism: "The symbol of water at the Holy Baptism

(Math 28:18–20) is a sign of the cleansing of sin and of the new life in Christ and of the inauguration in the body of Christ" (CO–ACKNS, ch. 8). Par 8.2 reads as follows: "A minister administers baptism with water in the name of the Father and the Son and the Holy Spirit. The Church acknowledges both the covenant baptism (infant baptism) and believer's baptism (credo baptism) as substances of the sacrament" (CO–ACKNS, ch. 8). How is this applied in the congregations? On the webpage of the congregation in Rotorua it is explained as follows: "This means that parents have the responsibility to decide if their children will be baptised as infants or as adults when they confess their faith. Infant baptism means that babies are baptized and then escorted and taught by their parents and the church on their way to confirmation. The babies of parents who decide that their children must rather be baptised as adults with the confession of their faith, will be dedicated to the Lord. This dedication is also done by a minister. There after parents accompany and guide their children on the road to confession of faith and baptism" (ACKR n.d.).

This is a much more inclusive way of handling a very complicated matter and clearly shows the inclusivity of the church. The authenticity is underlined by the fact that the church's understanding of the sacrament is directly related to the Bible. The conciliarity becomes clear from the fact that members or groups of members don't have to baptise their children as infants but that they can guide their children on the road of faith to credo baptism. This is important because many of the church's members come from more charismatic churches in South Africa where infant baptism is not practised. This once again confirms the open-endedness and to my mind the ecumenical character of the church as stated in the church order. The importance of the fourth attribute, integrity is underlined by what happened at the General Assembly of the church form 7–9 September 2012. The minister and the elders who represented the congregation of Wellington challenged the General assembly with a declaration which stated that infant baptism was unbiblical and that they would no longer administer infant baptism in the congregation. After a long discussion the General assembly distanced itself from the statement by clearly reconfirming what is written in article 8 of the church order. The General assembly also told the representatives of the congregation that their decision would separate them formally from the ACKNS. After the delegation from Wellington confirmed their decision, their status in the meeting was changed from representatives to visitors. The General assembly also decided to send the moderature to the congregation to inform them about the consequences of the decision of the church council (see Van der Merwe 2012). This clearly underlines the fact that although the church is open-ended and ecumenically orientated, it takes its boundaries very seriously.

Adherence to the confessional foundation of the church is important. Although both the *Belgic Confession* article 36 as wells as the *Catechism of Heidelberg* in question and answer 74 clearly states that children must be baptised (see NGK 1988, 179), the church has an openness towards credo baptism and the dedication of children. This once again confirms the church is doing its utmost to make the glove fit the hand.

### 5. *Conclusion*

The founding of the ACKNS was a direct result of many Afrikaans speaking Christians who immigrated to New Zealand during the past fifteen years. Although many of these people found a spiritual home in local churches in New Zealand, the need for an Afrikaans church gradually grew. The church was officially established in November 1998. What drew attention to this church was the ecumenical composition of the church. Members came from most of the denominations in South Africa, ranging from Reformed and charismatic to Roman Catholic. This posed a special challenge to the leadership of the church when a church order was written. The big question was: How can members form different denominations be accommodated in one church? The answer was found in ecumenical church polity, similar to what is defined by Koffeman. This was in line with the ecumenical mission of the church. The fact that the initial church order was inadequate emphasised the need for a truly ecumenical church order. After a long consultation between church leaders, a revised church order was accepted in 2009. Did this new church order fulfil the purpose and the mission of the church? Does the glove really fit the hand? Although no church order will ever be complete, to my mind, the revised church order indeed helps the church to fulfil its ecumenical calling, namely to be a spiritual home to members who come from all the different denominations in South Africa. The glove indeed fits the hand.

### *Abbreviations and bibliography*

ACKNS: Afrikaanse Christen Kerk van Nieu Seeland.

ACKNS n.d.: Afrikaanse Christen Kerk van Nieu Seeland n.d.. Accessed October 27, 2011. http://www.africhristenkerk.co.nz.

ACKNS 1998: Afrikaanse Christen Kerk van Nieu Seeland (Minutes: Founding commission 9 September 1998.

ACKNS 2005: Acta Algemene Vergadering (General Assembly) Afrikaanse Christen Kerk van Nieu Seeland 2005.

ACKNS 2008: Acta Algemene Vergadering (General Assembly) Afrikaanse Christen Kerk van Nieu Seeland 2008.

| | |
|---|---|
| ACKNS 2011: | Acta Algemene Vergadering (General Assembly) Afrikaanse Christen Kerk van Nieu Seeland 2011. |
| ACKNS 2012: | Agenda Algemene Vergadering (General Assembly) Afrikaanse Christen Kerk van Nieu Seeland, 2012. |
| ACKR n.d.: | Afrikaanse Christen Kerk van Rotarua n.d. Accessed September 20, 2011. http://www.ackrotorua.co.nz. |
| CO-ACKNS: | Church Order of the Afrikaanse Christen Kerk van Nieu Seeland (2009). |
| CO-PCN: | Church order of the Protestant Church in the Netherlands |
| LA: | Leuenberg Agreement (1973). Accessed October 19, 2011. http://www.leuenberg.net. |
| NGK 1988: | Nederduitse Gereformeerde Kerk. 1988. Handboek vir die Erediens. Kaapstad: NG Kerk-Uitgewers. |
| NMC: | The Nature and Mission of the Church: A Stage on the Way to a Common Statement. Faith and Order paper 198. Geneva: WCC (2005). |
| PCN: | Protestant Church in the Netherlands. |

Coertzen, Pieter. 2004. Decently and in Order: A Theological Reflection on the Order for, and the Order in, the Church. Leuven: Peeters.

Dombois, Hans. 1979. Ökumenisches Kirchenrecht heute. In: Zeitschrift für Evangelisches Kirchenrecht 24(1979), 225-249.

Hendriks, Johan. 2012. E-mail message to author, Augustus 12, 2012.

Heyns, Johan A. 1977. Die Kerk. Pretoria: NG Kerkboekhandel.

Info: SA immigration to New Zealand n.d. Accessed October 14, 2011. http://www.scatterlinks.info/sa-born-migrants-in-new-Zealand-xidc46728.html

Koffeman, Leo J. 2009. Het goed recht van de kerk: Een theologische inleiding op het kerkrecht. Kampen: Kok.

Marais, Danie. 2009. As almal ver is: Suid Afrikaners skryf huis toe. Kaapstad: Tafelberg.

Reynecke, Jaco. 2012. E-mail message to author, July 27, 2012.

Van der Merwe, Johan M. 2012. Report of attendance of the 9de Algemene Vergadering van die Afrikaanse Christen Kerk van Nieu Seeland, Universiteit van Pretoria, Pretoria.

Van der Watt, Philip B. 1975. Die Ned Geref Kerk 1652-1795. Pretoria: NG Kerkboekhandel.

Volschenk, Gert J. 2012. E-mail message to author, April 20, 2012.

# BEING PRESBYTERIAL-SYNODICAL IN THE CHANGING LANDSCAPE OF THE REFORMED CHURCHES IN INDONESIA

## Responses to a Problematic Past and Present

Roy Alexander Surjanegara

Many Reformed churches in Indonesia are still struggling to find their place in the society. They have, sad to say, become irrelevant and unaware of the changes happening around them. In many cases, the Reformed churches in Indonesia still preserve the 'faulty software' handed down from their predecessors, mainly just for the sake of keeping the 'tradition' alive.

The churches need to reflect on their own being as part of the Indonesian society, shaped by the country's history, and aware of its faults and mistakes it has made. There are patterns of separation between the churches, hierarchy within them, and subordination in relation to the state. This is no way for the churches to be relevant to Indonesian challenges. I think the churches should respond by being aware of the history that shaped them, critical of the factors contributing to that history, true to their principles as churches, and by taking corrective measures accordingly. In this contribution I relate the problems facing the Reformed churches in Indonesia today to their historical backgrounds, and then suggest some healthy responses.

### *1. Indonesia: A Brief Observation of the Present Socio-Political Condition*

Present day Indonesia is a vast archipelagic entity that is home to 220 million people according to the 2010 survey by the Indonesian Board of Statistics (*Badan Pusat Statistik* 2010). Home to almost 200 million Muslims, Indonesia has the largest Muslim population in the world. The 2005 census conducted by the Indonesian Ministry of Religious Affairs (*Kementrian Agama Republik Indonesia*) counted the Christian population to be about eight percent, nearly 20 million, in the whole country. The figure is certainly debatable, with the reported Christian population being stagnant at eight percent for the past few decades. That sort of limiting statistic could hint at the prevailing tension between Muslim and Christian in the political discourse of Indonesia.

Frank L. Cooley made the following interesting connection between that tense situation and the unique geographic traits of the Indonesian archipelago: "Indonesia is made up of many diverse ethnic and language groups, which have been relatively isolated from one another until quite recently. This isolation resulted from the country's marked geographic traits: deep straits and wide seas separating islands, high volcanic mountain ranges, heavy tropical rain forests and wide swampy sea coasts. These have led to differences in history, regional development, traditions, customs and religion, which accentuate the difficulty of binding these diverse groups into a unified nation. Indonesia's present condition and her main problem are symbolized by the national motto: *Bhinneka Tunggal Ika*, (Diversity Becoming Unity)" (Cooley 1968, 11).

Although Indonesia's expanse is formally divided into three different time zones (Western, Central, and Eastern Indonesia time), it is more common to distinguish the regions of Indonesia according to the socio-political division between western and eastern Indonesia. One will not find a formal statement regulating the division, but almost all discourse about Indonesia cannot avoid using the distinction between 'western and eastern' Indonesia.

And at the 'center' of it all lies Java. Although never officially stated as the center of Indonesia, it is home to Jakarta, the country's capital. One cannot avoid recognizing that the tendency of Indonesian policy is to favor Java. Is it because the ancient kingdoms in Java once had a prominent position in the political constellation? Or is it because the Dutch East India Company (DEIC; *Vereenigde Oost-Indische Compagnie*, VOC) and later the Dutch East Indies Government used Jakarta — then called Batavia — as their center for distribution during their occupations?

SarDesai writes about this in his book *South East Asia*: "Two kinds of states developed in the Indonesia archipelago: those based on maritime commerce and those capable of large-scale cultivation of agricultural products for consumption and export. While Srivijaya in southeastern Sumatra belonged to the first category, most of the Javanese states, particularly those in the volcanic and *sawah* (rice field)-cultivating central and eastern parts of the island, belonged to the latter kind. Sumatra's only advantage was topographic, deriving from its location on the shortest sea route through the Strait of Malacca. Java's strong points were a central location among the myriads of islands; access to and control of the products of the archipelago...and finally, its control over an alternate trade route between the East and West through the Sunda Strait" (SarDesai 1997, 44).

Relating this dominant role of Java for the Indonesian context to Cooley's observation of how geographic traits shaped the people, we should not understand Java by limiting it to people of Javanese ethnicity only; rather, Java should be understood as the whole people who are situated in (and shaped by) Java. This paper ventures not into this discourse, but it bears mentioning that the prevailing emphasis on Java is still a fact worth noting, regardless of one's evaluation of it.

I would like to emphasize two basic characteristics of Indonesian society. First, Indonesia's geographic traits by default provide its people more gaps and walls than bridges and doors. Therefore even though Indonesia is a pluralistic country, encountering and dealing with diversity is a relatively new experience for the majority of the Indonesian people. Second, Java and Islam have been the dominant political forces in society since the nation's conception. These characteristics serve as a background for the next part of this paper, in which I will give a description of the place and shape of Christianity in general, and of the (Dutch) Reformed Churches in particular, in Indonesian history.

## 2. *A Brief Historical Background of Reformed Churches in Indonesia Prior to Independence*

Christianity was first introduced to the islands that now comprise eastern Indonesia by Portuguese expeditions in the early sixteenth century. However there was neither enough sovereignty nor motivation for the Portuguese Catholic missions to make a lasting impact during that period. At the turn of the seventeenth century, Protestantism came along with the settlements of the DEIC and soon absorbed many of the remaining Catholics in the region into Dutch Protestantism—with a major twist.

By 'major twist' I mean to say that, as opposed to the commonly accepted presbyterial-synodical practice of 'no lording over' in the Reformed polity, the Protestant churches in Indonesia of that time (and plausibly until today) did have 'lords' all over the place. It was a measure to preserve power among the Dutch rulers during the DEIC period, and later during the colonization period. But the practice still exists nowadays perhaps because of the churches' unawareness. Or are there other motives? I will return to this question at a later stage of this paper where I will examine the general structure of the (Dutch) Reformed Churches in Indonesia.

Already in 1605, the first church that in the future would become *De Protestantsche Kerk in Nederlandsch-Indie* (also known as *Indische Kerk*; Indian Church) was founded in Ambon, during the transition of power from the Portuguese. The church was founded to take care for the religious needs of the Dutch people there. However, the DEIC in general had little interest in missionary activities; as long as the Christians did not disturb the DEIC's business activity and avoided conflict with the Muslims in the area, they were given room to grow. In 1799 the DEIC was dismissed due to bankruptcy, and in 1800 its role in the archipelago was replaced by the Dutch East Indies Government, which continued the same policy for maintaining order. Meanwhile during these three centuries, Islam, which in 1500 was professed only in some parts of Sumatera and Java, had grown to cover the majority of the Indonesian region by 1800 (Van den End 2009, 137).

The nineteenth century introduced different influences into Indonesian church history. Pietism and revivalism had influenced the previous generations of Christians in Europe, nurturing in them fresh optimism and an interest for overseas missions and missionaries. These developments, together with technological progress as a direct result of the Enlightenment in European society, provided a new generation of missionaries and the bodies they formed with incentive and freedom to explore the 'outside world', as well as with a feeling of superiority toward the indigenous peoples (Van den End 2009, 139–143). During the nineteenth century the Dutch government's political power over the region was expanding enormously. In 1817 the Dutch retook their position in Indonesia, after a brief transfer of power to the British (1811–1816). After the Dutch returned, the *Gereja Protestan Indonesia* (*Indische Kerk;* GPI) still remained to serve the Christians the DEIC had left behind. But, because it was a state-governed and state-funded church, it lacked missionary interest. Another theory explaining this lack of missionary interest was the thought that the Reformed tradition from the time of John Calvin did not really stimulate foreign mission (Aritonang and Steenbrink 2008, 101).

From 1816–1864 the 'East Indies' was under direct control of the Dutch Kingdom without any intervention from the Dutch parliament. Only after 1864 was the Dutch Parliament involved in determining political decisions in Indonesia. By 1910 there were no longer any independent states in the Indonesian archipelago. Unlike the Portuguese and the DEIC, both of which specifically endorsed only a single version of Christianity, the Dutch East Indies Government of the nineteenth century allowed different denominations of Christianity to enter Indonesia, although in reality it was never that simple as political and religious activities overlapped more often than not. This chain of events directly influenced the spread of Christianity in Indonesia as waves of missions and missionaries came to the archipelago.

In line with its priority to maintain order within the Dutch East Indies, the government enacted the *Regeringsreglement* (Government Regulations) in 1854 that stipulated the freedom of religious expression. However, its final article stated that all religious workers had to obtain a special permit from the Governor

General, and that the permit could be retracted. In reality, the government used this regulation to limit missionary activities to only those areas where Islam was absent or to regions where traditional religions were strong. In addition to maintaining order, the motive behind this was to ensure that the followers of traditional religions would become Christians rather than converting into Islam because Indonesian Muslims were more hostile toward the Dutch government than the Indonesian Christians were. Hence, the government became the designator of missionary activities, specifically allocating different mission bodies to appointed regions. With most of Indonesia's population centers already being Islamized, this meant that the missionaries were working in relatively isolated areas, surrounded by Muslim areas. This situation forced the missionaries to cooperate with the interests of the government in exchange for security.

Another dimension of the situation was that most of the missionaries did not have adequate knowledge and understanding of the local cultures. This in turn resulted in a generally favorable attitude among both the Dutch government and missionaries toward the DEIC's policy of strict control over the church and mission fields.

Indeed, from the seventeenth to late nineteenth centuries, Christian activity in general was restricted to two circles: the GPI and the mission bodies. The relationship between the two was characterized by mixed feelings and ups-and downs, usually with the political interest of the Dutch authorities being the deciding factor. This prevented any actual progress by Indonesian Christianity apart from geographical expansion allowed by the Dutch ruler.

Even inside the church, there were not any native Indonesian church officials until 1881 when the GPI introduced the office of 'indigenous minister' (*Pendeta Pribumi/inlands leraar*) who had no authority to administer the sacraments until 1916. It is also worth noting that until 1942 the GPI was still supported by government funding even though it was no longer a state church after 1935 (Van den End and Weitjens 2008, 56). On the mission side, not a single church was declared independent by its mission body until 1930. And even after becoming independent churches, many of the formal or informal leaders in those churches were Europeans.

Churches and mission activities changed drastically after the Japanese occupation in 1942 (until 1945). The Japanese were very serious in trying to wipe out any Dutch influence in the region, and this had direct impact on church life as many Dutch (and other European) political and religious leaders were sent into prison camps and many others left the country. From that moment, and later with Indonesian independence, Indonesian churches started to become independent. In May 1950, the Communion of Churches in Indonesia (*Dewan Gereja-gereja di Indonesia*, now *Persekutuan Gereja-gereja di Indonesia*; PGI) was born.

I will end the historical description here, as it is intended to give a general picture of the forces at play in shaping what would become the Reformed churches in Indonesia. In terms of church polity, the resulting effect of this historical process proved to be critical. With respect to church governance, Van den End points out three complications that arose after Indonesian Reformed churches gained their independence:

1. While the official polity of these Reformed churches was Presbyterian, in reality the Indonesian Christians were not trained in this new system. Throughout the previous centuries the churches were governed in a very hierarchical manner.
2. In some areas with feudalistic cultures, this hierarchical pattern of governing the church was easily welcomed and preserved, rather than developing the Presbyterian nature of the church.
3. The geographical barriers and economic gaps between many congregations were so wide that it became a major challenge promoting a wider level of Presbyterian life in the churches (see Van den End 2008, 358).

### 3. *Portraying the Latent Problems of Reformed Churches in Present-Day Indonesia*

I will briefly summarize the points I would like to describe below with this sentence: from their problematic past the Reformed churches in Indonesia have inherited a dilemmatic self-understanding, which in turn has shaped their dilemmatic positioning and functioning in society.

First of all, from the Indonesian Reformed churches' history, briefly described above, the churches were handed down a major dilemma in terms of articulating the presbyterial-synodical nature of Reformed church governance: the meaning of being both presbyterial and synodical (the wider assembly of presbyters) is always colored with conflicting connotations — often literally conflicting, as a matter of power struggle.

This is evident from the structure of all churches from the (Dutch) Reformed tradition in Indonesia, putting as they do a stronger emphasis on the role of the synod (and its board) than on the role of the presbytery (or as it is commonly termed in Indonesia, *Klasis*), and even more again than on the role of the congregation. When it comes to church polity discourse, synodical identity is determined by the language of control and order, and that language is dominant over the language of freedom of expression by, and autonomy of, the minor assemblies. Thus the local congregations are made to serve as outlets of the synod's identity rather than synod being an expression of the whole community.

The presbyterial-synodical system is nevertheless a system that performs well when certain requirements are met. I believe one of those requirements is the functioning of democratic capability in the communal life of the wider Indonesian society. A 1977 Faith and Order document entitled *How Does the Church Teach Authoritatively Today?* made this interesting conclusion: "Styles, ways, and modes of teaching in the Church are influenced by patterns of authority in society....Sometimes structures of authority in the Church are a conscious or unconscious reflection of the structures of authority prevailing in society. For instance, in many churches the emphasis on the role of synods is partly due to the rise of democracy; in many African Independent churches the role of the leader corresponds closely to that of the local chief" (Gassman 1993, 248).

This relation between how leadership functions in the church and in society I believe explains the preservation of hierarchical characteristics in the presbyterial-synodical churches by ethnic (although not necessarily limited to those) groups that already have hierarchical tendencies.

Second, as a direct result of the geographic factors affecting missionary activities, Indonesia now has many new independent churches that are closely-knitted to Indonesian ethnic groups, some even knitted to sub-ethnic groups. Because of the rise of mobilization within the country, migrations have created new settlements of 'domestic foreigners', bringing their versions of Reformed churches to their new places instead of joining the local ethnic churches, and vice versa. The problem lies not in being an ethnic church in itself, but in the lack of effort and incentives to redefine the church's identity in this changing landscape of the Indonesian society.

One could find for example in Java many ethnic churches from different backgrounds among the Reformed tradition itself. The same is true of many bigger cities throughout Indonesia. Although the nation's settings have changed drastically, very little has changed in terms of church polity for the Reformed churches in Indonesia.

General observation of the Indonesian settings tells us that Reformed churches there still preserve the tendency to be ethnic-based ghettoes living amidst their Muslim neighbors. Is this a situation that simply echoes past missionary policies? If so, should it not be a worrying sign of the churches' inability to appropriately respond to the plurality of Indonesia?

Third, in terms of church and state relationship the church has had a long history of being subordinate in the relationship. After the national independence, Reformed churches in Indonesia are living life with different state actors than before. They are no longer the DEIC, nor the Dutch Indies Government. The state is now the Indonesian people, with the church and her members as an integral part of it. Have the churches made serious efforts to re-find their position in this new political constellation?

The church–state relationship has typically become dichotomized in situations where both the church and the state find themselves either in contrasting differences or in blind obedience to each other. Have the churches assessed the current situation between the church and the state and come to a realization about where they stand in this relationship? If this is not done, chances are that discourses on the church–state relationship could be based on outdated assumptions.

Another way of seeing this church–state relationship is that all this time the churches have probably somehow neglected another dominant force at play since the beginning: the power of the corporation. Looking at Indonesian history, the DEIC was, after all, a major corporation. In the past most of the financial power and state authority — and in many cases also religious authorities — were interwoven into a single entity. And as we have witnessed throughout history, it is the financial motive that moves the other two, relating primarily to one or the other depending on which could provide the most benefit

Today, too, we are seeing this financial power in the form of major corporations, sometimes moving beyond the rigid borders of states and religions, making transactions with and between, within and in the name of both. I think it is precisely this manifestation of power politics that deserves intense attention and responses from churches in Indonesia. The church should make a contribution to Indonesian society by helping it discern the constructive and destructive forces that are at play and all the faces those forces could be showing, whether as the state, as the corporation, or as the church itself.

### *4. Healthy Responses*

How could the Reformed churches in Indonesia respond to the dilemmas they are facing? Furthermore, how could they do it without betraying their identity as church?

I think the key to answering these questions lies in the understanding of what it means to be a Reformed church in the Indonesian context. Let me explain it.

One of the prominent characteristics of the presbyterial–synodical system is that it is representational. Church governance is entrusted to an assembly of elders, consisting of elected church members together with the church's ordained minister. However, this representative conciliarity does not automatically grant the elected representatives authority. They are perceived as authoritative to the extent that they adhere to God and his Word. It is not the process of election alone that grants them that authority, but the binding of those offices to the whole of Scripture.

Therefore it is possible retrospectively to review and weigh our church history and its polity in that light: did church authorities bind the churches to the Scripture? Or were they representing something else? This should not mean that the churches today simply choose to avoid taking the blame for what has happened in the past; rather this would help them to clearly identify their past mistakes as churches, to confess their sins, and to guide them into not continuing to re-live them. This, I believe, is the first healthy response Reformed churches in Indonesia could make.

The second response has to do with inter-relatedness. Local congregations in the same region entrust the governance of their being together as a church to a wider level of assembly (i.e., the *Klasis* or the Presbytery), consisting of elected elders from the local congregations. This process is repeated again, usually until an assembly on the national level is reached. Thus, in general a church will have three layers of assemblies: the local assembly (*Jemaat*), the wider assembly (Presbyteries or *Klasis*), and the general assembly (*Sinode*). This way, local churches in their essence are always in close relation with one another and they regard the general assembly as the widest expression of their congregations.

The difficulty in such a system lies in dealing with differences between local contexts without falling into over-simplified generalizations about those contexts and without making uniformalized policies for the whole. What usually happens in Indonesian churches is that synods take a certain position that is regarded as a one-fix-solution for all conditions inside the church, and they do not hesitate to enforce that position for the sake of order and stability. The synod board believes that its function is to become the shepherd, the guardian of the 'truth' for the whole church. While romantic, this idea usually only leads to subordination of the presbyteries and the local congregations to the synod.

The problem lies in the somewhat commonly accepted pattern of centralization in Indonesia. In its sixty-eight years of independence, the development and the pattern of governing the society in Indonesia have been very centralized, with Java as the center. Uniformity was a kind of accepted norm in most Indonesian communities. The center designed a pattern, and the whole had to use it. That is the norm in almost every setting in Indonesian government. From my observation, this behavior did not arise as a reaction out of fear of differences, but rather as a result of euphoric desire for unity. But it has not been clearly developed.

Therefore, a kind of communal movement toward decentralization is needed. Even in its ecumenical structures, all the church's human resources are located in Jakarta where the head office of the PGI is situated. I do not encourage separatism, as so often been the reality among the Reformed churches in Indonesia. By 'decentralization' I mean the ability for the churches in their own context to discern and decide with conviction what is best for their specific contexts while at the same time still respecting the wider context. We need to develop a kind of post-colonial paradigm of being a church. This kind of paradigm would be beneficial not only for the churches, but also for the whole of Indonesian society. This is precisely the role the churches could take as pioneers. This is the second response I suggest.

These two responses are in principle efforts necessary to give new meaning to the notions of representation and inter-relatedness in the presbyterial-synodical churches. Yusak Soleiman, a minister of the *Gereja Kristen Indonesia* who teaches church history in the Jakarta Theological Seminary, shared with me an idea he is working on at the moment. In short, he described three important milestones that Indonesian churches should have in their ecclesial journey: 'starting point, turning point, and ecumenical awareness'. I believe that the historical description I provide in this paper could serve as a *starting point* for many Reformed churches in Indonesia. This is where they came from. Bad or good, it is a part of the churches' being, including the many factors that have contributed to making them who they are now. Nevertheless, the churches are not without the ability to change for the better. As they recognize their tendency to preserve the past paradigm of being church, their unawareness of their ecumenical calling, and their need to be more relevant to Indonesian contextual challenges, they need to create their own *turning point* in the present. This is a homework assignment that all Indonesian churches must do. My hope is that the simple thoughts I have shared in this short contribution could resonate with the churches toward that goal.

### *Abbreviations and bibliography*

GPI: *Gereja Protestan Indonesia* (*Indische Kerk;* Indian Church).

PGI: *Persekutuan Gereja-gereja di Indonesia* (Communion of Churches in Indonesia).

Aritonang, Jan S., and Karel Steenbrink (ed.). 2008. A History of Christianity in Indonesia. Leiden: Brill.

Badan Pusat Statistik. n.d. Penduduk Indonesia menurut provisinsi 1971, 1980, 1990, 1995, 2000 dan 2010. Accessed February 22, 2012. http://www.bps.go.id/tab_sub/view.php?tabel=1and daftar=1and id_subyek=12and notab=1

Cooley, Frank L. 1968. Indonesia: Church and Society. New York: Friendship Press.

Gassman, Gunther (ed.). 1993. Documentary History of Faith and Order 1963–1993. Geneva: WCC.

Kementrian Agama Republik Indonesia. n.d. Penduduk Menurut Agama. Accessed May 7, 2012.

http://www.kemenag.go.id/index.php?a=artikeland id2=data2009rev.

SarDesai, Damodar R. 1997. South East Asia: Past and Present. Colorado: Westview Press.

Van den End, Thomas. 2009. Ragi Carita 1—Sejarah Gereja di Indonesia 1500—1860. Jakarta: BPK Gunung Mulia.

Van den End, Thomas, and Jan A.Th. Weitjens. 2008. Ragi Carita 2: Sejarah Gereja di Indonesia 1860-sekarang. Jakarta: BPK Gunung Mulia.

# THE RECEPTION OF THE BELHAR CONFESSION IN THE DUTCH REFORMED CHURCH AND CHURCH POLITY DISCOURSE

Robert Vosloo

## 1. *Introduction*

The tenth of May is the day on which we commemorate the birthday of Karl Barth, the great Swiss Reformed theologian who contributed much to the discourse in the twentieth century on the nature and meaning of Reformed confessions. The tenth of May is, incidentally, also the birthday of Beyers Naudé, the controversial South African church leader who played such a prominent and decisive role in the struggle against apartheid and who, already in the mid-1960s, had made an influential plea for the need for a confessing church in South Africa. It is therefore quite fitting that on 10 May 2011 the Synod of the Dutch Reformed Church of South Africa, viz., the Western Cape regional synod, discussed at their meeting at Goudini an important proposal concerning the *Belhar Confession*, a Reformed confessional document that developed out of struggles within church and theological circles in apartheid South Africa.

Much has been written on the *Belhar Confession* (BC) since it was accepted in draft form nearly three decades ago in 1982: on its pre-history; on the socio-political contexts in which it developed and was received; on the link to the Bible and the Reformed confessing tradition; on its continuity and discontinuity with the *Barmen Theological Declaration* of 1934; on its local and international reception; and on its promise for dealing on a theological level with some contemporary challenges (see for instance Cloete and Smit 1984; Van Niekerk 1996; Botha and Naudé 1998; Strauss 2005; Adonis 2006; Botman 2006; Koopman 2007, 2011; Boesak 2008; Naudé 2010; Botha and Naudé 2011; Horn 2011; Theron, 2012; Smit 2012). It is also important to remember that from the beginning the draft confession was supported by an accompanying letter ('begeleidende brief'), and that this letter serves as an important source for understanding the confession's origin and theological content. After a period of consultation and some minor changes to the draft confession, the BC was officially adopted in 1986 as a fourth confession by the Dutch Reformed Mission Church, one of the churches in the family of Dutch Reformed Churches in South(ern) Africa. For many years, until 1994, the 'family of Dutch Reformed Churches' consisted of the Dutch Reformed Church (DRC, the so-called 'mother church' or 'white church'), the Dutch Reformed Mission Church (DRMC, the so-called 'colored church'), the Dutch Reformed Church in Africa (DRCA, the so-called 'black church'), and the Reformed Church in Africa (the so-called 'Indian church'). The BC was also included as part of the confessional base when the DRMC and a large part of the DRCA united to form the Uniting Reformed Church in Southern Africa (URCSA) in 1994. In the church order of the newly established church, in an article on 'The Confession of the Church', we read: "The Uniting Reformed Church in Southern Africa accepts the ecumenical creeds, viz., the *Apostles' Creed*, the *Nicene* and *Athanasian Creeds*, and by virtue of its own origins believes that the *Confessio Belgica* (*Netherlands Confession of Faith*), the *Heidelberg Catechism* and the *Canons of Dordt*, as handed down in history, give pure expression to its faith. It furthermore accepts the *Confession of Belhar* (1986), as demanded of the church in the Southern African situation" (CO-URCSA, 15).

Recently the Uniting Reformed Church in Southern Africa celebrated the 25th anniversary of the official acceptance of the BC. In a sermon preached at a thanksgiving service at these celebrations (on 26 September 2011), Dirkie Smit alluded to the reception history of the BC and its continuing challenge to churches. Using 1 Peter 3:15–16 as text, Smit said: "For confessional documents 25 years is a very brief period and reception of such documents takes place in many different ways, but already the list speaks for itself–Braamfontein and Bloemfontein; Kitwe, Debrecen, Buenos Aires, Accra and Grand Rapids; Belgium, Germany and Palestine; the Reformed Church in America, the Presbyterian Church USA, the Christian Reformed Church, Goudini. In gratitude we celebrate this tradition and this community–present with us in spirit, represented among us by brothers and sisters....Gathered here tonight, in gratitude, facing old and new challenges, we owe it to our mothers and fathers to *ask ourselves* to what extent we have indeed given account of our hope in this spirit to which they committed themselves that evening, in this spirit of gentleness and reverence" (see Smit 2011).

The reception history of the BC in the relatively brief period of its existence demands thorough and careful (church historical) analysis. And serious theological engagement is needed to assess the promise and pitfalls of using the BC in the light of some of the challenges facing the church today. Although it falls outside of the scope of this article to comment extensively on the reception history of the BC, I do want to make a few brief remarks on some important episodes in the reception history of the BC in the Dutch Reformed church, especially as it took shape in some official decisions taken by the General Synod. It should be kept in mind, moreover, that the reception history of the BC should not be equated merely with discussions and decisions at synod meeting and other official church gatherings. The story of the reception of the BC is also in some ways the story of the 'non-reception' of the confession. In an interesting newspaper article that points to this aspect, Duvenhage recalls an incident in which he interviewed Allan Boesak, then the moderator of the Synod of the DRMC, for national television in 1986, but that this interview was not broadcasted as a result of government 'orders from higher up' (see Duvenhage 2011).

From the outset it must be said that within the Dutch Reformed Church the BC has had an emotional and contested reception ever since it was accepted in draft form in 1982. It is within the context of such a controversial history of reception that one should place the discussion on the BC that took place at the meeting of the Western Cape Synod on 10 May 2011. On that day Synod discussed the following motion put forward by the Moderamen: "The Synod is convinced that the Biblical call for justice for all people, reconciliation between people, and the unity of the church are at the heart of the gospel. The BC gives expression to the call of the gospel in a different way than the other confessions of the church. The Synod, as a church meeting, accepts the *Belhar Confession* and calls on the General Synod of the Dutch Reformed Church to make the *Belhar Confession* in a church-orderly way part of the confessional base of the Dutch Reformed Church" (DRC 2011, 7).

Given the long history of controversy surrounding the BC, it came as quite a surprise when the Western Cape synod accepted this proposal with a large majority (around 80%). Although there were also some strong and passionate dissenting voices speaking against the proposal, this decision reflects an important development regarding the discourse on the BC at synod meetings in the DRC. It should be noted, however, that since 1982 there has always also been a minor, but nevertheless theologically significant and influential, strand that unequivocally supports the acceptance of the BC as a fourth confession. Even so, this meeting in 2011 was the first time that a synod actually voted in favor of a proposal regarding the acceptance of the BC as part of the confessional base of the Dutch Reformed Church. This decision by the Western Cape Synod in May 2011 also meant that at its meeting in October 2011 the General Synod had to discuss the call by one of its regional synods to make the BC part of the confessional base of the Dutch Reformed Church in a church-orderly (i.e., in accordance with the church order, 'kerkordelike') way.

In addition to the reference to some episodes regarding the reception of the BC in the Dutch Reformed Church leading up to 2011, this article seeks to address some questions and proposals concerning what it means to make the BC part of the confessional base of the Dutch Reformed Church *in a church-orderly way*. In the process I will argue for the importance of placing church polity discourse on the BC within the context of continual *theological* reflection on the nature and significance of Reformed confessions, as well as within the context of a theological engagement with questions regarding the optimal way to express Reformed theological and ecclesiological convictions in Reformed church polity documents, including church orders.

## 2. *The General Synod of the Dutch Reformed and the* Belhar Confession

Also in 2011 the fourteenth session of the General Synod of the Dutch Reformed Church took place in Boksburg. The proposal of the Western Cape Synod regarding the acceptance of the BC was taken up and, again to the surprise of many, Synod decided with an overwhelming majority (of around 90%) to support the proposal. The official decision taken by the General Synod reads: "The General Synod decides to make the *Belhar Confession* in a church-orderly manner part of the church's confessional base and commissions the Moderamen to start the necessary church order(ly) processes ('kerkorderlike prosesse") that are required in this regard".

According to *Die Kerkbode*, the official DRC newspaper, delegates described the synod, in the light of the decisions regarding the BC and church unity, as 'a ground-breaking synod' (*Die Kerkbode*, 21 October 2011, 1). The moderator of URCSA, Prof. Thias Kgatla, who attended the synod, is also quoted as saying that he was overwhelmed with joy and that he had to pinch himself to make sure that he was not dreaming (*Die Kerkbode*, 21 October 2011, 1). Shortly after the meeting of the DRC General Synod, the Moderature of URCSA issued a 'Pastoral Letter to URCSA Congregations on the Decision of the Dutch Reformed Church General Synod's Acceptance of the *Belhar Confession*'. In this letter we read the following description and comments: "After two hours of a thorough debate the delegates were asked to vote and indicate where the General Synod stands concerning the BC for the Dutch Reformed Church. They needed to decide to accept the BC as part of the confessional basis and to request the Moderamen to put into place the process to achieve it. Our hearts were pounding and before our eyes a miracle happened when we saw that more than 90% of the delegates showed that they wanted the *Belhar Confession* as part of the Dutch Reformed Church confessional basis.... The emotions were high and tears of joy rolled. We could not speak to one another. We hugged and cried. The Spirit of God moved like a tsunami to wash away the fears and to bring courage and hope to people. For us from URCSA it was indeed an awesome moment. We witnessed God at work".

The decision of the DRC General Synod on the BC indeed seems to hold much promise for re-energizing the discussion on church reunification in the Dutch

Reformed family of churches, including between the DRC and URCSA where discussions came to a halt in recent years, even leading to the point that URCSA declared a moratorium on church reunification talks. It is therefore quite telling that the URCSA pastoral letter not only praises the new leadership, and thanked the "ministers and members of the DRC who never gave up their hope to work for the acceptance of Belhar through word and deed, many times at great cost", but even states: "The Dutch Reformed Church took the first step in accepting Belhar by showing the way to regional synods and congregations....Their leadership has committed themselves to assist and gave us the assurance that they will ask URCSA to be part of this journey. In the light of what happened at Boksburg URCSA is now challenged to look again at the relationship with the Dutch Reformed Church that is guided by the moratorium on Church unity talks".

Time will tell in what way the recent decision by the Dutch Reformed Church General Synod regarding the BC will contribute to church reunification within the Dutch Reformed family of churches, but it can be said that this decision represents a decisive shift from earlier positions of the General Synod of the DRC regarding the BC.

The first official response of the DRC after the declaration of a *status confessionis* and the acceptance of the draft BC had a strong critical tone. At the DRC General Synod in Pretoria in October 1982 it was stated: "Synod has with great sorrow took note that, as a result of the *status confessionis,* a confession has come into being that stands in conflict with the DR Church and on the same footing as our other confessions" (DRC 1982, 1403).

In the stormy years that followed the draft confession, relations between the DRC and the DRMC became more strained. In 1984 the Broad Moderature ('Bree moderatuur') of the DRC formulated a response to several important documents regarding church unity, including the draft confession, and this response was sent to the DRMC on 23 March 1984. Again the response to the draft confession was mostly negative. Although the Broad Moderature acknowledged the principal right of a church to accept a confession under certain circumstance, it did state that "your envisaged confession does not do justice to the legitimate pluriformity ['regmatige pluriformiteit'] of the church" (cf. DRC 1986, 26). In addition to some other points of critique, the report further suggested that the idea "that the church as property of God must stand...by the oppressed" is too one-sided: "Your point of departure is, however, different from ours, since you seemingly reach this conclusion based on an unacceptable horizontalistic exegesis ["n onaanvaarbare horisontalistiese eksegese'] typical of liberation theology" (DRC 1986, 27). The report of the Broad Moderature concluded that they want to declare emphatically that the DRMC must seriously consider whether they want to continue with this new confession, since it can lead to new polarization. The report further expressed an openness to continuing conversation in the light of the joint history of these churches. The DRMC's response to this report also makes for interesting reading (DRC 1986, 27–29). Suffice it to say for our purposes here that at this stage there was strong official antagonism from the side of the DRC against the draft confession. The official correspondence and discussions between the DRC and the DRMC also reveal underlying theological tensions and conflicting paradigms. Jaap Durand, at that stage a professor in Systematic Theology at the theological school of the DRMC at the University of Western Cape, has made some telling comments in this regard: "The DRC's first reaction — from its general synod of October 1982 in Pretoria — gives the impression that a parting of ways is inevitable. This reaction can be understood in more ways than one. On the face of it, the synod's reaction was an unmistakable attempt to render the urgent appeal of the DRMC fruitless for all practical purposes by expressing the synod's 'sadness and dismay' over the 'unreasonable accusation of theological heresy' without, however, addressing the theological merit of the situation....It would be a fair judgment to say that the DRC was not theologically strong enough to cope with the event. The sterility of the particular theology of creation orders with which the DRC equipped itself in the difficult area of race relations rendered it incapable of responding sensibly" (Cloete and Smit 1984, 119f.).

In the years that followed these early reactions to the draft confession, voices critical of the church's official criticism of the BC (also from within the Dutch Reformed Church) became more vociferous and influential. These theological responses to the critique against the BC (drawing also on insights from Reformed sources), together with important changes in the South African socio-political landscape, contributed, at least to some extent, to an important proposal brought before the General Synod of 1990 by the General Synodical Commission (the executive committee, 'Algemene Sinodale Kommissie', or ASK). This proposal was accepted, with some minor changes, by Synod. Point 5 of this decision reads: "The General Synodical Commission (ASK) is of the opinion that the *Belhar Confession*, taken by itself, is not in contradiction to the *Three Formulae of Unity*, and that it need not bring separation between the churches". Moreover, the commission was also of the opinion (see point 8 of the decision) that "certain statements could have been formulated differently, such as paragraph 4 of the *Belhar Confession*, and that the description in *Church and Society* [an important reformist document for the DRC accepted in 1986 and further amended in 1990] regarding the Lord as God of the 'the poor and the oppressed' states the matter in a more sound biblical way" (DRC 1990, 30).

What is significant in the 1990 decision is that the DRC accepted that the BC viewed on its own (i.e., divorced from any possible ideological setting and motivation) is, in effect, in accordance with the other confessions, and thus by implication in accordance with Scripture. It is, of course, an important question whether the BC, and also other confessions, can in fact be viewed in isolation in this way, and whether one should not judge a confession in terms of its theological content, and–at the same time–should place it in its social and historical context (see Smit 2012, 185). Notwithstanding the acceptance of the BC 'viewed on its own', some reservations were still emphasised (as seen in point 8). Some commentators on the reception of the BC in the DRC have noted that the 1990 decision points to the need for the full acceptance of the BC, as well as that point 8 of the decision reveals a theological deficiency in the DRC. Piet Naudé, for instance, writes: "As early as 1990, the DRC was of the opinion that Belhar passed all possible tests for new confessions. The time has now come that we as church should realize that, since then, no valid Biblical or confessional objection could be brought against Belhar. The DRC leadership should state this clearly" (Botha and Naudé 2011, 110). And Russel Botman has stated in a comment on the 1990 decision: "Centrally, the DRC stands against the *Confession of Belhar* 1986, with specific reference to the fourth clause, because it lacks the universe of theological discourse that is required for a real understanding of the *Confession of Belhar*" (Botman 2001, 39). Although the 1990 decision was viewed by many as an insufficient response to the BC, it did mark an important milestone on the road to the decision of October 2011. The 1990 decision that Belhar, taken on its own, is not in contradiction to the *Three Formulae of Unity*, was again affirmed in 1998. In addition the executive committee ('Dagbestuur') was of the opinion that the church should look anew, in consultation with other conversation partners, to ways in which the BC can be incorporated into the confessional base of the newly unified denomination (see DRC 1998, 305).

Between 1998 and 2011 the General Synod of the DRC met three times (in 2002, 2004 and 2007). The way in which Synod dealt with the important matter of church reunification and the BC during this period, as well as with the broader processes in the church, deserves a fuller account than I am able to give in this article (see Botha and Naudé 2011, 125–159). Suffice it to say that it seemed to be the case that the process of reunification (including discussions on the acceptance of the BC) was, as Piet Naudé has observed, "still continuing with strides of both hope and despair" (Naudé 2010, 138). Before 2011 there were several attempts to test the views of church members and congregations on the BC. One such process produced varied results in 1998, but the received commentary was nevertheless mainly negative about the acceptance of the BC (DRC 1998, 305). A later process of testing the congregations (that started after the 2007 General Synod) also had a negative impact on unity talks. Although there were some significant joint meetings between members of the DRC and URCSA, no new principles regarding the BC and church unity were accepted at the meeting of the General Synod in 2002. At the synod of 2004 more than a quarter of the delegates expressed their commitment to church unity by signing the BC in a symbolic gesture, even though this gesture had no legal status. The period between 2004 and 2011 can be seen as a road with many highs and lows regarding church unity and the reception of the BC, and this history certainly warrants further church historical and theological inquiry.

In essence the decision of 1998 was confirmed by the synods of 2002 and 2004. And in 2007 no specific decision was taken on the BC. This means that the decision still stood that accepted the content of the BC, without actually accepting the BC as a fourth confession. Even the above broad cursory overview of some important synod decisions reveals an important development from the initial official reactions in 1982. Although we should not equate the DRC with the sum total of decisions and discussions at official meetings, these developments nevertheless represent an important aspect of the reception of the BC within the Dutch Reformed Church. It is furthermore clear that the decision of October 2011 marks an important new stage in the reception history of the BC in the DRC. What is important to note, also within the context of the theme of this conference, is that the acceptance of Belhar is qualified with the phrase that it should be done in 'a church-orderly way'. We now turn to the meaning and implications of this phrase.

### 3. *The BC, the DRC Church Order, and Church Polity Discourse*

Article 43 of the *Church Order of the Dutch Reformed Church* (CO-DRC) deals with the tasks of the General Synod. Among these tasks are included "the stipulation of the confessions according to article 44" (CO-DRC, art. 43.1.4.). But what does article 44 say? The first two parts of this article are of crucial importance for the process of accepting the BC 'in a church-orderly way'.

› Article 44.1: The amendment of the confession can only take place after each synod separately decides with a two-third majority in favor thereof *and* two-thirds of all church councils each with a two-thirds majority decide in favor of it as well.
› Article 44.2: Articles 44.1 and 44.2 are amended after each synod separately decide in favor of this with a two-thirds majority and after that the General Synod decides in favor thereof with a two-thirds majority.

The CO-DRC therefore points towards an elaborate process when it comes to amending the confessions of the church. Two thirds of all church councils must approve such a decision with a two-thirds majority, as must all the regional synods, again with a two-thirds majority. It is important to note, furthermore, that this current formulation, as is found in the two most recent DRC Church Orders (2004, 2007), was the result of an amendment based on a decision at the Synod of 2004. The 2002 Church Order, for instance, still states that the Confession can only be changed "after each synod decides separately with a two-thirds majority in favor thereof" (CO-DRC 2002, art. 44.1). Why was this article amended to include the provision that not only the regional synods but also two thirds of all congregations must approve the change with a two-thirds majority? Was this an attempt to put in place more hurdles in order to delay or stifle church reunification and the acceptance of the BC?

In a recent article in *Die Kerkbode,* entitled "Tweederdebesluit hou kerk nie gevange" ("The two-thirds majority decision does not hold the church captive"), Dr Johann Ernst, the current registrar (or actuarius, 'aktuarius') of the Synod of the Dutch Reformed Church argues that some good and honest reasons can be given for these changes to article 44. For our purposes here, let me recall the first two—and in my view most important—reasons that he mentions. Ernst points, firstly, to the fact that URCSA has a similar church order article. This is indeed the case, since article 11 of the CO-URCSA states, among other things, that General Synod shall deal with all matters pertaining to " (CO-URCSA, art. 11.1) the doctrinal standards of the church, on condition that any change to the doctrinal standards of the church can only be made after two-thirds of all the congregations have decided in favor thereof". The CO-URCSA therefore also requires that two thirds of the congregations decide in favour of the change to the doctrinal standards (although this specific article does not mention that a further decision is required by the regional synods or specify the size of the majority needed within congregations for the change to come into effect). It should be added, though, that there is still a difference between the requirements of the DRC and URCSA (as seen in the relevant articles in their church orders). The second reason that Ernst mentions why changes were made to article 44 in the CO-DRC is of special importance. He refers to a ruling by the Appeal Court in 1998 that suggested that each congregation (via its representation in the regional synod) should have a say in the possible change of the confession by the General Synod. General Synod does not have the authority to change a congregation's nature or identity. During this case Judge W. Viviers then made an important side remark (*obiter dictum*): "That one remaining congregation member can form the congregation, must be taken into account in the current situation, given the stipulations of the church order according to which the church council is the authoritative body that acts on behalf of the congregation" (quoted by Ernst 2011, 19). In the light of this remark by Judge Viviers the General Task Group for Legal Affairs ('Algemene Taakspan Regte', or ATR) obtained some legal advice that suggested that if the church order does not make provision for majority decisions, then unanimity ('eenstemmigheid') might be required for making changes. In order therefore to avoid a situation in which one remaining church member can have a right to the church's assets, the church order was changed in 2004 to read as it currently stands.

This decision has indeed made it harder to amend the confession of the church and has complicated the process for the DRC to accept the BC as part of its confessional base. This longer route is, however, not necessarily less desirable. As Ernst argues in the conclusion of his article in *Die Kerkbode*: "It cannot be viewed as unfair that the a large majority of church councils be in favor of weighty matters.... After the Dutch Reformed Church family is united, there must be only one church denomination with a legitimate common confessional base. In this regard the church order, with sensitivity to both sides, points towards the responsible path" (Ernst 2011, 19). It needs to be said, as also pointed out by Ernst, that neither the majority nor the minority is necessarily right, hence the need for the majority and the minority to be open to the Word of God in a process of continual openness to reform in the light of Scripture. This implies, at least, that there must always be an openness to the process of reflecting on the confession of the church, even after a decision-making process by the synods or congregations has been completed.

Article 44 of the CO-DRC thus requires a specific process for amending the church's doctrinal standards and, at the meeting of the DRC General Synod in 2011, the decision was taken to follow this route. Moreover, the process to make the BC part of the confessional base of the DRC in a church-orderly way requires some carefully crafted regulations regarding the process. Some important questions come to the fore in this context, such as: According to what process should concurrence and approbation be sought? In this regard Synod accepted a proposal to add the following footnote to article 44.1: "For the way in which church councils should handle the decision regarding the amendment of the confessional base of the DR Church in order to attain agreement and approbation from congregations, see Church Order Regulation 6:6".

In addition, the new heading of Regulation 6 in the CO-DRC is changed to read 'Regulation for the Multiplication, Combination, Unification and Amalgamation of Congregations, and for the Formation of a New Denomination'. Under Regulation 6.6 on 'The Formation of a New Denomination' the process of seeking agreement and approbation is described in detail (DRC 2011, ATR Report 2.5.2.). Such a well-regulated process is indeed needed.

One should be careful not to oppose the need for carefully crafted church order articles and regulations (that are also sensitive to juridical aspects) with the need for responsible theological speech. Theological speech (also on Reformed ecclesiology and the Reformed Confession) that does not impact church polity remains abstract, while Reformed church polity discourse that is not informed by Reformed theological insights remains reductive. It is therefore important not to juxtapose uncritical church polity discourse and theological discourse, but to see church polity discourse in itself as deeply theological, albeit with its own particularity. In the process we should further be aware of the way power and institutional control function in our discourse.

One way to ensure the theological integrity of church polity discourse is to continually seek the appropriate relationship between Scripture, confession and church polity documents, such as church orders. In our compilation, revision and appropriation of church orders the question of an adequate theological hermeneutics remains of paramount importance (see Van de Beek 1992). Reformed church orders should be the distillation or concentration of the best insights from a Reformed theological, and in particular ecclesiological, perspective. Church orders are our ecclesiology taking on concrete form. With this in mind, I would like to ask whether article 1 of the current CO-DRC (which deals with confession) should not be revisited in the light of the fact that church orders develop out of the confession of the church; they mirror the confession and they are also instruments for the church to be a confessing church (cf. Koffeman 2009, 23).

### *4. Revisiting Article 1 of the CO-DRC?*

Article 1 of the CO-DRC reads as follows: "The Dutch Reformed Church is based on the Bible as the holy and infallible Word of God. The doctrine which the Church confesses in agreement with the Word of God, is expressed in the Forms of Unity as formulated at the Synod of Dordt in 1618–19, namely the thirty-seven articles of the Belgic *Confession*, the *Heidelberg Catechism* and the five *Canons of Dordt*".

This article is short and to the point, and has stood in this form since the constitution of the General Synod of the DRC in 1962 (see Kleynhans 1985, 96). It is important that church order articles be precise and do not try to say too much. But is it not here the case that too little is said?

If one compares article 1 of the current CO-DRC with, for instance, the corresponding articles in the Church Order of the Protestant Church in the Netherlands (Protestantse Kerk in Nederland) or the CO-URCSA, one is immediately struck by the fact that there is no explicit reference to the Ecumenical Symbols (the *Apostles' Creed*, the *Nicene Creed*, the *Athanasian Creed*; cf. CO-PCN, art. I-4)). I would like to argue that a revision is needed in this regard that makes it much more evident that the confession of the church stands in continuity with the 'catholic' church ('die algemene Christelike kerk') of the ages. This seems of special importance, given, among other things, the way in which a certain mindset of ecumenical isolationism has haunted the DRC in the past.

The current article 1 of the CO-DRC does not sufficiently safeguard, in my view, against the danger of atomizing and absolutizing the sixteenth- and seventeenth-century Reformed confessions. It order to challenge such a danger, it is important to affirm the link between the Three Formulae of Unity and the Ecumenical Symbols, as well as to affirm that within the Reformed tradition confessions are never fixed or that new confessions cannot arise. In this regard article 2.3 in the CO-URCSA highlights well the idea that the Reformed tradition is a living tradition and that Reformed churches are not mere communities that have confessions, but that they are *confessing* communities: "The Uniting Reformed Church in Southern Africa accepts that it has not completed its task of confessing the faith. Changed circumstances and a better understanding of God's Word in the future may lead to the acceptance of further articles of faith, or the revision of existing articles of faith".

Therefore it is worthwhile, in my view, for the DRC to consider stating more explicitly the reference to the Ecumenical Symbols in article 1, as well as to emphasise the fact that the church is always open to the possibility of new confessions or revisions to existing confessions.

Two other aspects should also be considered in a possible revision of article 1 of the CO-DRC. First, as this article now stands it lacks explicit reference to the belief in the Triune God. A second aspect that can be noted relates to the lack of any reference to the missional character of the church. It is not my argument that every possible omission should be included in article 1. I do want to argue, however, that the process towards accepting the BC would be well served by a parallel, theologically-informed conversation and process regarding the meaning and nature of Reformed Confessions and what it means for Reformed communities to be confessing churches.

### 5. *Conclusion*

At its meeting in October 2011 the General Synod of the DRC decided to make the BC in a church-orderly manner part of the church's confessional base. Synod commissioned the Moderamen to start the necessary church order processes required in this regard. For this process it is important that responsible church polity discourse should inform and regulate the process. At the same time a parallel theological process of reflection is needed on the nature and meaning of Reformed confession and how these reflections should inform our understanding and concretization of what it means to be a confessing church. In the process we may discover that the BC (with its specific pre-history, origin, theological content and history of reception) is not merely a controversial document that ignites conflict, but that it might prove to be a rich and decisive source as we learn what it means to be a confessing church amidst the challenges and opportunities facing Reformed churches in our southern African context and our global world today.

*Abbreviations and bibliography*

ASK: Algemene Sinodale Kommissie (General Synodical Commission).
ATR: Algemene Taakspan Regte (General Task Group for Legal Affairs).
BC: Belhar Confession
CO-URCSA: Uniting Reformed Church in Southern Africa General Synod, Church Order 1994.
CO-DRC 2002: Church Order of the Dutch Reformed Church. 2002. Die Kerkorde van die Nederduitse Gereformeerde Kerk. Wellington: LuxVerbiBM.
CO-DRC 2004: Church Order of the Dutch Reformed Church. 2004. Die Kerkorde van die Nederduitse Gereformeerde Kerk. Wellington: LuxVerbiBM.
CO-DRC 2007: Church Order of the Dutch Reformed Church. 2007. Die Kerkorde van die Nederduitse Gereformeerde Kerk. Wellington: LuxVerbiBM.
CO-PCN: Church Order of the Protestant Church in the Netherlands. 2004. Kerkorde en ordinanties van de Protestantse Kerk in Nederland inclusief de overgangsbepalingen. Zoetermeer: Boekencentrum. 2nd edition.
DRC: Dutch Reformed Church.
DRC 1982: Dutch Reformed Church, Acts of the General Synod. 1982.
DRC 1986: Dutch Reformed Church, Agenda of the General Synod. 1986.
DRC 1990: Dutch Reformed Church, Agenda of the General Synod. 1990.
DRC 1998: Dutch Reformed Church, Acts of the General Synod. 1998.
DRC 2011: Dutch Reformed Church, Agenda of the General Synod. 2011.
DRCA: Dutch Reformed Church in Africa.
DRMC: Dutch Reformed Mision Church.
URCSA: Uniting Reformed Church in Southern Africa.

Adonis, J. C. (Hannes). 2006. The History of Belhar. In: NGTT 47(2006)/2, 234–239.
Boesak, Allan. 2008. To stand where God stands: Reflections on the Confession of Belhar after 25 years. In: Studia Historiae Ecclesiasticae xxXiv(2008)/1, 143–172.
Botha, Johan, and Piet Naudé. 1998. Op pad met Belhar: Goeie nuus vir gister, vandag en môre! Pretoria: J.L. van Schaik.
Botha, Johan, and Piet Naudé. 2011. Good news to confess: The Belhar Confession and the road to acceptance. Wellington: Bible Media.

Botman, H. Russel. 2001. Belhar and the white DRC: Changes in the DRC: 1974–1990. In: Scriptura 76(2001)/1, 33–42.

Botman, H. Russel. 2006. Barmen to Belhar: A Contemporary Confession Journey. In: NGTT 47(2006)/2, 240–249.

Cloete, G. Daan, and Dirk J. Smit. 1984. A moment of truth: The Confession of the Dutch Reformed Mission Church 1982. Grand Rapids: Eerdmans.

Duvenhage, Hennie. 2011. Dié woorde kon alles verander het. Rapport 22/ 10/2011.

Ernst, Johann. 2011. Tweederdebesluit hou kerk nie gevange. In: Die Kerkbode, June 3, 2011, 19.

Horn, Nico. 2011. The Belhar Confession—29 years on. In: Hansen et al. 2011, 264–276.

Hansen, Len D., Nico Koopman, and Robert Vosloo (eds). 2011. Living Theology: Essays presented to Dirk J. Smit on his sixtieth birthday. Wellington: Bible Media.

Kleynhans, Ewert P. J. 1985. Gereformeerde Kerkreg. Deel 3: Kerkverband en Kerkvergaderinge. Pretoria: NG Kerkboekhandel Transvaal.

Koffeman, Leo J. 2009. Het goed recht van de kerk: Een theologische inleiding op het kerkrecht. Kampen: Kok.

Koopman, Nico. 2007. Reconciliation and the Confession of Belhar 1986: Some challenges for the Uniting Reformed Church in Southern Africa. In: NGTT 48(2007), 96–106.

Koopman, Nico. 2011. Belhar: A Transforming and Dignifying Tradition. In: Journal of Theology for Southern Africa 139(2011), 32–41.

Naudé, Piet J. 2010. Neither Calendar nor Clock: Perspectives on the Belhar Confession. Grand Rapids: Eerdmans.

Smit, Dirk J. 2011. Belhar Confession—Celebrating a Quarter of a Century 'Jesus is Lord!' (1 Peter 3:15–16) (unpublished sermon).

Smit, Dirk J. 2012. Oor die teologiese inhoud van die Belydenis van Belhar. In: Acta Theologica 32(2012)/2, 184–202.

Strauss, Piet J. 2005. Belydenis, kerkverband en Belhar. In: NGTT 46(2005)/3 & 4, 560–575.

Theron, Piet. (ed.). 2012. Belhar geweeg, Pretoria: Kraal-Uitgewers.

Van de Beek, A. (Bram). 1992. Hermeneutiek van het kerkrecht. In: Van't Spijker and Van Drimmelen 1992, 59–72.

Van Niekerk, Attie C.J. 1996. Moet ons die Belydenis van Belhar (1986) as 'n nuwe belydenisskrif aanvaar? In: Skrif en Kerk 12(1996)/2, 445–455.

Van't Spijker, Willem, and Leen C. van Drimmelen (eds). 1992. Inleiding tot de studie van het kerkrecht. Kampen: Kok. 2nd edition.

# THE NATURE OF THE CLASSICAL ASSEMBLY IN CHANGING DUTCH CONTEXTS

## Continuity and Discontinuity in Reformed Church Polity

Leon van den Broeke

*The nature of the classical assembly in changing Dutch contexts*
An interesting ecclesiological question arose in the Reformation as early as the 1520s. As the Roman Catholic monarchical episcopate was rejected, the question *Who should assume episcopal authority and duties?* had to be answered. It appeared concurrent with the question of the nature of the office in general. This essay discusses the question of the nature of collegial cooperation and supervision (*episkopè*) among the Reformed offices.

It was one thing to deconstruct the sixteenth-century Roman Catholic type of ecclesiology and canon law, and quite another thing to construct a new ecclesiology and church polity. Moreover, it was not clear from the start who had to take over episcopal duties from the bishop. The Lutherans instituted on regional level the superintendent as a new office of regional supervision. But the Reformed ecclesiology also rejected this office out of fear of hierarchy. But this fear did not necessarily mean that the reformers rejected every type of *episkopè*. The fear of personal *episkopè* was stressed-over. Any form of lording over someone or some *body* in a Reformed church had to be rejected. Collegial *episkopè* became a central focus in Reformed ecclesiology. Corporate, shared responsibility became typical both at local and supra-local levels. One type of this responsibility is the classical assembly. Its nature is the topic of this article. I focus on the discontinuity and continuity of the nature of the classical assembly in changing *Dutch* contexts. Extension of the research outside the Netherlands is interesting, especially if one has read the challenging remarks of Allan J. Janssen (Janssen 2010) on 'the apostolicity of the classical assembly'; of Joseph Small (Small 2010) on 'the travail of the presbytery'; and of Robert Vosloo (Vosloo 2010) on 'the practice of hospitable dialogue'; but that requires separate treatment. This will hopefully appear some day as part two of a diptych.

*Learning community*

Since we miss a sixteenth-century ecclesiastical manuscript that clearly states the nature of the assemblies in general and the classical assembly in particular, I start with the assemblies of (mostly) ministers, although I am aware that they were not perfect and ideal, nor can we use them as blueprints for the twenty first century. They are important to bring in, however, because they reveal something that was lost in the classical assemblies through the centuries. Some of these sixteenth-century assemblies were more local than others. It depended on the political, societal and ecclesial context of the cities. Such assemblies were the *Prohezey* of Zürich, the *Convocaß* or *Kirchenconvent* in Strasburg, the Classes in Vaud/Waadtland, the Classis Neuchâtel, the *Coetus* in Emden, the *Coetus* in London, the *Vénérable Compagnie des Pasteurs* in Geneva (see De Boer 2012), the *Colloque* in France and the Synod Under the Cross in the Southern Netherlands.

With the exception of the London *Coetus*, the French *Colloque* (also elders and deacons), the *Vénérable Compagnie des Pasteurs* (also professors of theology and humanities) and the Zürich *Prohezey* (also students of the Latin school, visiting scholars and laypeople), only ministers took part in these assemblies.

These assemblies met weekly, fortnightly or monthly for the examination of candidates for the ministry, investigation of the appointments of ministers, mutual supervision of ministers, church visitation, matters of discipline and study of the Bible. This last aspect was important in the education of former Roman Catholic priests and lay ministers, and to safeguard sound Reformed doctrine. A remnant of this is found in the sermon still given in the Dutch classes. The *Coetus* of Emden also functioned as court of appeal with regard to decisions of consistories in the region. As for the study of the Bible and Reformed doctrine, these early sixteenth-century gatherings of ministers and others can be regarded as learning communities. They were more than that alone—they did exercise collegial *episcope*—but the nature of these assemblies was that they were also learning communities.

*Community of neighboring congregations*

These communities of (mostly) ministers developed alongside the young and vulnerable church through the decades of the sixteenth century. In the Netherlands this led to the introduction of the classical assembly by the Synod of Emden in 1571. The classical assembly as it was introduced by this synod was not new. A similar example is the Convent of Wesel in 1568. Despite the academic discussion concerning its date (see Boersma 1994, 197–206), the convent mentioned the classis as a geographic entity in the region in order to consult others outside the congregation in case of supra-local affairs.

Vaud and Neuchatel already had classical assemblies, but with a different nature than the Emden classical assembly. As explained above they were gatherings of ministers. The latter became important for the young, vulnerable and scattered church in the Netherlands. The classical assembly became a wonderful example of the corporate shared responsibilities on the regional level. It was one of the four assemblies, alongside the local consistory, the particular provincial, and the national or general synod.

The acts of the Synod of Emden of 1571 do not contain anything about the nature of the classis, except for section 7. Like the above-mentioned assemblies of ministers, classical assemblies were just there. Sixteenth-century (draft) church orders as well as other ecclesial documents reveal that they did exist, without amplification. Since church orders are expressions of ecclesiology, we must take note of the fact that the classical assembly is also an ecclesiological entity. The Synod of Emden did shed a little light on this matter: the classical assembly was formed by 'some congregations in the neighborhood' (section 7). From section 13 we learn that the classical assembly was involved in matters of ministers who were appointed by a consistory of a church in the classis; it examined ministers (section 16). It was also occupied with matters of admonition and discipline (sections 18, 33, 34), home mission and church organization (section 42), and book visitation (safeguarding the sound Reformed doctrine, section 51). The attachment to the acts contains an agenda. A classical sermon was given by one of the ministers or candidates for the ministry. The president was elected and he said grace. He asked the (delegates of) consistories whether they gathered (not every consistory gathered regularly in those days). Moreover, in some congregations there was not even a consistory, so no elders and deacons were ordained. Further, the president asked whether admonition and discipline were executed, whether there were heresies or doubts about the Reformed doctrine, and whether they took care of the poor and of education. Then the classical assembly studied the Reformed doctrine with regard to the differences with the papal doctrine. The delegates to the particular synod were elected and the brothers listened to and discussed the acts of the previous meeting. They fixed the time, date and place of the next classical assembly. Then another prayer was said and the brothers left, but not before they shared the classical meal. From these tasks and agenda we can learn the corporate, shared responsibility for the congregations and consistories in the region and for the particular synod. Besides, the community of neighboring congregations was also a learning community: the members of the classical assembly listened to and discussed the sermons that were given by ministers and candidates for the ministry.

The brothers who convened at the Synod of Emden did not want the assemblies to only do their ecclesial job. They also had a vision as they established classes, including those areas of the Netherlands still under Spanish authority. It is safe to say that the classical assembly goes back to the diocese in the Roman Catholic Church—to the regional administrative jurisdictions formed around the draining of land and the provision of dikes *(waterschappen)* and the bailiwicks. It is stated in section 42 that the classical assemblies should try to institute local churches or rudiments of churches so that they do not forget and neglect these empty spaces (*ne quid negligantur*). Every square inch had to be included in the Reformed church. This (di)vision of the Emden brothers had a pastoral-organizational character. Therefore the classical assemblies also became agents of home mission as they tried to institute new congregations (see Small 2010, 55).

Despite these classical arrangements the acts concentrate on the local church. This is understandable against the background of the uncertain political context of those days. Moreover, these acts only contain a framework for a young denomination. Its successors—Dordrecht 1574, Dordrecht 1578, Middelburg 1581,'s Gravenhage 1586, and Dordrecht 1618/1619—elaborated on it. The Synod of Dordrecht of 1574 affirmed in section 9 that the classical assembly was an assembly of neighboring congregations. The Synod of Dordrecht of 1578 stated in section 16 that the four assemblies—consistory, the classical assembly, the particular synod and the general or national synod—were instituted to establish and to maintain good and legal order in the Reformed Church. The introductory words in the section wherein the assemblies were introduced were left out in the Acts of the Synod of Middelburg of 1581, section 20. Most likely that was the case because these Middleburg acts can be considered the first official Dutch Reformed church order, naturally starting with section 1 stating the importance of good order in the church of Christ. But it was affirmed again that the classical assemblies were assemblies of some neighboring congregations, in section 30. This was repeated in sections 26 and 38 of the Acts of the Synod of 's Gravenhage of 1586. Most likely this had to do with the fear of dominance of the ministers and the view that the classical assembly was more than just a gathering of the (delegated) offices or office-bearers. It was a community of neighboring congregations.

The sixteenth-century successors to the Synod of Emden of 1571 elaborated the 'church order'. The result was the *Dordt Church Order* (DCO) of 1619 that not only focused on the local church but also on the supra-local church, by means of the classical assembly and of the provincial and the national or general synods. In line with earlier synodical decisions, this church order also stated that classical assemblies were assemblies of neighboring congregations (section 41), and enumerated the four assemblies. However, this church order also did not amplify what the nature of these assemblies was (cf. section 29). Of course, they could only deal with ecclesial, not political matters. Another principle became important.

The general synod could not make decisions with regard to issues properly on the agenda of the particular synod. The same applied to the particular synod with regard to the classical assembly and the classical assembly could not to do likewise with regard to the consistory. The great assemblies were also courts of appeal. Although this gives some insight, sixteenth- and seventeenth-century church orders do not reveal much more pertaining to the nature of the classical assembly.

However, the *Belgic Confession* (*Confessio Belgica,* CB) might be helpful. The Reformed church orders did not contain a preamble with an ecclesiological statement. Sometimes the very first article of a church order gives a hint. This was for example the case in the acts of Emden. Section 1 stated that no congregation, no minister, no elder, no deacon shall lord it over another. This gave the 'church order' an important ecclesiological foundation. Reformed church orders can include a preamble, but this is not necessary because the confessional foundation is to be found in the confession. The CB reveals much about the church in sections 27–29 and about the governance of the church in sections 30–32, though yet nothing can be found about the assemblies. From the confession we can learn that the Reformed supra-local church is a matter more of church order than of confession. Herein the CB differs from the *Confessio Gallicana* as the latter confession reveals more about the supra-local supervision by means of the *superintendans*, section 32. It is understandable, however, that the *Confessio Belgica* does not reveal much about the supra-local church. It was developed for a persecuted church that did not have a supra-local ecclesial structure similar to the one that existed in France around 1559. This explains the emphasis on the local church.

However, the situation in the Northern Netherlands also required supra-local ecclesial structures, as the above-mentioned acts of the Synod of Emden of 1571 and its successors show. The classical assembly as it is envisaged in the DCO was the more elaborated type of the Emden classical assembly and its successors. The DCO did include a definition of the classical assembly on the nature of the classical assembly. Section 29 revealed that there were four assemblies. Section 30 indicated the limitations of their authority: it was based on the subsidiarity principle whereby only ecclesial matters could be treated and, for example, a classical assembly could not deal with matters belonging to a consistory. Section 31 stated that the broader assemblies also functioned as ecclesial courts when someone claimed that the decision of a minor assembly was in discordance with the Word of God. Section 32 demonstrated that every meeting of the assemblies had to begin with invoking the Name of God and end with saying grace. Also important is the fact that ministers and elders were not *de jure* members of the classical assembly. They had to be delegated by their consistories. To validate this, they were to hand over letters of credential from their consistory prior to being admitted to the meeting room of the assembly.

There is more. The golden rule of Emden — no lording over each other, section 1 — was not adopted in the Acts of the Synod of Dordrecht of 1574. We can only guess the reason why that was the case. This synod was more a particular synod and a liturgical synod. In any case the acts of the next synod, Dordrecht 1578, did contain this golden rule, however in the very last section, 101. Nonetheless, this text differed. It was twice as long, because of the addition that "rather, everyone shall mind not to cause any suspicion of lording it over". At the same time, the congregations, the ministers and others not only had the possibility of disciplining each other but were even obliged to do so out of love for each other. In addition, the text did not only prohibit the lording it over each other but also forbade the preeminence of one congregation or office. This addition was omitted by the Synod of Middelburg of 1581, section 68. This was also the case in the Synod of 's Gravenhage of 1586, section 77, and the Synod of Dordrecht of 1619, section 84. Moreover, the golden rule laid down by the Acts of the Synod of Emden of 1571 can be regarded as the preamble that was left out in 1574, included in 1578 as the last section, and also included in 1581, 1586 and 1619 but no longer as the last rule of the church orders. This meant that between 1571 and 1581 the synods struggled with the content and the place of the golden rule of Emden, even though the essence remained intact. The essence was: no congregations or offices lording it over each other. Nevertheless, that did not prohibit ecclesial supervision.

As a result of missionary work of the Dutch Reformed Church, Reformed congregations and denominations around the world were instituted. Part of the ecclesiology of these churches was the existence of the classical assembly. From 1636 the Classical Assembly of Amsterdam executed ecclesial authority regarding the colonial congregations in the world. This assembly delegated the work to the deputies for Indies Affairs. They corresponded with the congregations, consistories, ministers, employees or directors of the United East Indies Company and the West Indies Company around the world. This implies that this classical assembly also became an agent of mission.

Although according to the Emden and Dordtian rules the classical assembly had the task of supervision, the execution of this task was not without the biblical keyword *koinonia*. And it did have a pastoral-organizational nature. The classical assembly was also a learning community as it educated itself by the study of Scriptures, listening to and discussing classical sermons and tending to sound Reformed doctrine. Besides, the Classical Assembly of Amsterdam (and a few others) became agents of mission. This all took place under the ecclesiological umbrella of collegial leadership. Mutual responsibility for each other was felt as a necessity within the classis. These most important aspects of the classical assembly should not be lost in the twenty-first century.

*Managerial body*

A.Th. van Deursen states that the Dutch Reformed Church in the seventeenth century was a construction of classes (see Van Deursen 1998, 5). This denomination was decentralized due to the political situation. A national synod was not allowed by the government between 1618/1619 and 1816. However, things changed; particularly so in the eighteenth century when the classical assemblies became governing bodies rather than being only major assemblies. They no longer practiced book visitation or the classical sermon. Indeed, they were well-organized. Every self-respecting classical assembly that could afford it published its laws or a handbook, and if it could not do so it wrote down its rules (see Nauta 1957). The oldest published manuscript I could find dates from 1683 (Classicale wetten 1683). Whatever its form, it demonstrates how efficiently these classical assemblies operated. They were focused on details — the position and social differences among ministers and elders — but hardly on doctrine or spiritual exchange. It appears trifling, but the social position and order of ranking was important to office-bearers in those days (see Bos 1999, 99). It was the way to stand out. This implies that the role of the classical assembly as a learning community diminished or at least that a transition took place from a learning community and a community of neighboring congregations to a governing body. Why this happened remains unclear.

From this perspective, something completely new happened when king Willem I imposed his own church order (*Algemeen Reglement van 1816*). It is important to note that the Netherlands Reformed Church for the first time became a national church on Dutch soil. This concurred with the institution of the new Kingdom of the Netherlands in 1813. This development implied another ecclesiology. First, until that moment there had been little or even no focus on the supra-national level. Second, the ecclesiology of this denomination was top-down. This appears from section 3. It stated that the governance of the Netherlands Reformed Church was executed at synodical, classical and local levels. The ecclesiology of this denomination was quite hierarchical. This is also underlined when one considers section 49. Classes were considered to be 'subdivisions of the provincial church'. It also appears from the fact that this *Algemeen Reglement van 1816* does not speak of 'major assemblies' in accordance with the DCO, but of 'higher assemblies', sections 5–8. This expressed the hierarchy and top-down structure.

The authority and the position of the classical assembly were minimized. It was only allowed to convene annually, section 65. They could make nominations for the governing bodies in the church and check the finances, section 67.

Something that did not change was the classis meal. But many ministers did not make the effort to join the meetings or the table to share meals together. Only a small classis board was in charge of classical affairs. The classical assembly was not allowed to speak about doctrinal matters. The same applied to the provincial church board and the general synod board. So, the classical assemblies had no power and they were spiritually empty. It also meant that they could not execute their former *episkopè* as in visitation, approbation and supervision (*opzicht*).

Apart from two minor duties, they had nothing to do. The classical board was in charge at the classical level. There were also distinctions made between ministers and elders and former elders. Ministers were *de jure* members of the classical assembly. The position of former elder was new. Yet, the *Algemeen Reglement van 1816* had an advantage. For the first time an elder or former elder was a member of the classical board. This meant an upgrade of the position and authority of the elder.

It appears that the classical board worked with efficiency and great patience with regard to ministers, members of congregations and consistories. This ecclesial and specifically classical machinery was well-oiled. It implies that the nature of the classical board was not as much a theological as a managerial entity. It was a governing body that was in charge of and finished ecclesial business. It meant that both the classical board and the classical assembly were definitely no longer learning communities. Many ministers did not frequent the meetings. All this set an unfortunate trajectory.

### *'Ecclesial authority, granted to them by Christ'*

Two main secessions in the Netherlands Reformed Church took place: the Secession of 1834 and the *Doleantie* of 1886. A large part of the more orthodox believers who left the Netherlands Reformed Church together formed the Reformed Churches in the Netherlands in 1892. Especially in the *Doleantie* the emphasis was laid upon the local church. Although the Netherlands had been a kingdom for seventy years, they considered the ecclesiological structure of the church to be a confederation of local churches. Their classical assemblies and, their particular and general synods existed only when they met. Between meetings the major assemblies functioned through their deputies. The discussion about the authority of the four assemblies, especially concerning the duality between the consistory on the one hand and the larger assemblies on the other, dominated the ecclesial life and work of this denomination.

The church order of the Reformed Churches of the Netherlands was a slightly revised DCO. It is noteworthy that these classical assemblies functioned in closer accordance with this church order than they did in the seventeenth century, although and/or because the political situation differed. The Netherlands was no longer a federation of several independent provinces but one country. Besides, this development fitted into the process of nineteenth-century Neo-Calvinism. In addition, as the DCO became statutory again: typical tasks for the classical assemblies like approbation, church visitation and examination of candidates for the ministry and ministers were given back. The classical assemblies functioned well. This does not necessarily mean that they were ideal or that a classis meeting was just one big spiritual regional event: the Dordtian rules pertaining to the classical sermon and book visitation were not restored.

A revised DCO, the *Reformed Church Order of 1959*, stated —because of the lessons learned from schisms of 1926 (the Geelkerken case) and 1944 (the Schilder case)—that the major assemblies have according to their own nature 'ecclesial authority, granted to them by Christ', section 28. This relates to the ongoing discussion on the authority of the minor and major assemblies, the ecclesial battle over emphasizing either the local congregation and consistory or the supra-local church and the authority of major assemblies, especially with regard to disciplining office-bearers (respectively J.G. Geelkerken and K. Schilder). For the first time it was explicitly stated in a Reformed church order that the nature of the major assemblies and therefore the classical assembly was Christological. Moreover, the previous section, 27, Chapter 2, entitled 'The assemblies of the church', begins with this line: 'the governance of the church and the supervision and the discipline in the church is attributed to its assemblies'. That was already implicitly there in the DCO, article 29, but after the church order was revised it became clearer what the main task of the assemblies in general, and hence of the classical assembly in particular, had to be: governance of the church, supervision and discipline. The Reformed Churches in the Netherlands found this addition necessary because of the secessions that had resulted from the above-mentioned Geelkerken and Schilder cases. These secessions had partially to do with the nature of the major assemblies and especially with the balance between the consistory on the one hand and the major assemblies on the other. Nauta calls this Christological foundation of all the assemblies not a deviation from article 36 of the DCO, but an enrichment (see Nauta 1971, 121).

As congregations were instituted by the classical assemblies in the Reformed Churches in the Netherlands before as well as after 1959, these assemblies functioned again as agents of home mission (see Van den Broeke 2005, 263–269, 409f.).

### *Assembly of offices*

The nature of the classical assembly in the Netherlands Reformed Church has changed after 1951. Its authority came to be considered more from the perspective of the authority of the *office* of delegated office-bearers than from the point of view of their *delegation*. So the focus became not on John or Jane who bore an office, but on the offices. Indeed, after 1951 the classical assembly in the Netherlands Reformed Church became an assembly of the offices. It all had to do with the restoration or revitalization of the office in line with a new development. During the Second World War the Netherlands Reformed Church had reached something that was once considered impossible: an agreement on having a new church order and a restoration of the major assemblies. They received once again the status of assemblies of offices. In this sense, after 135 years they were allowed to deal not only with ecclesial matters but also with spiritual matters. The discussions and preparations had been ecclesiological in nature, and ecclesially-speaking it was quite an event that this new order became statutory in 1951. An innovation was that the section on apostolicity was placed in the church order before the section on its confessional basis.

The classical assembly was a gathering of the offices of the church, said section V of the *Netherlands Reformed Church Order of 1951*. The classical assembly in the Netherlands Reformed Church was definitely not an assembly of delegated office-bearers as it had been in the sixteenth through the early nineteenth centuries and in the Reformed Churches in the Netherlands, but it was an assembly of offices. Although the church order in section I started with the statement that the Netherlands Reformed Church exists through all the congregations, Ordinance 1 (about the assemblies in general) displayed a bottom-up structure as it enumerated first the consistory, second the classical assembly, third the particular assembly and fourth the general synod. As the church order dealt with the offices in section V, it was followed by statements about the assemblies in general in section VI. This again demonstrates the importance of offices in Reformed Church polity. From this point of view it is striking that Ordinance 1 started with the assemblies and that only in Ordinance 3 were rules about the election of office-bearers established.

In any case, the church order expressed in section V the collegial leadership in (major) assemblies as, in line with the Synod of Emden of 1571 and its successors, it rejected the hierarchy of one congregation, one office and one office-bearer over another.

In the *Netherlands Reformed Church Order of 1951*, the classical assembly was not responsible for church visitation, examination, supervision (admonition and discipline), Ordinance 11. However, one cannot assert that the classical assembly was not involved in any form of supervision, Ordinances 1–5. The classical assemblies in the region of the particular assembly elected the church visitors, and the executive committee (*breed moderamen*) of the classical assembly assisted the provincial church visitors. Moreover, the classical assembly was in charge of ecclesial life in the classis, the regional community of congregations.

The rule that deacons and elders-church wardens became members of the major assemblies was new. In short, elders-church wardens were in charge of the financial and material affairs of the congregation. The classical assembly was not only established to make decisions on ecclesiastical affairs, but also to facilitate the so-called 'ecclesial dialogue' between the representatives of the several wings in the church: the orthodox, the confessionals, the liberal and the middle-orthodox. Despite many efforts this dialogue did not get off the ground.

Other innovations were the delegation of the minister and the elder, and the deacon and the elder-church warden. The delegation of the deacon was closely related to developments in the Reformed Churches in the Netherlands. The classical assembly became indeed an assembly of offices as deacons also took part in the supervisory task of the classical assembly. The fact that ministers also had to be delegated by their consistory to the classical assembly, just like the deacons, elders-church wardens and elders was new as well. Ministers were no longer by law members of the classical assembly as was the case in the 135 years that the *Algemeen Reglement van 1816* had been in effect. Nonetheless, there was a small distinction: while all the ministers were delegated, the other office-bearers were delegated according to a schedule. The restoration or revitalization of the classical assembly also included an emphasis on this assembly as a gathering of the offices.

### *'Obedience to Christ'*

The Protestant Church in the Netherlands that was instituted in 2004 was the outcome of the merger of the Netherlands Reformed Church, the Reformed Church in the Netherlands and the Evangelical-Lutheran Church in the Kingdom of the Netherlands. Its church order leaves out one major assembly: the provincial synod. This means that the classical assembly has become the hinge between the consistories and the general synod. Just like in the *Netherlands Reformed Church Order of 1951*, the Protestant classical assembly has an episcopal function and has to facilitate the ecclesial dialogue.

Since the church order is a replication of the *Netherlands Reformed Church Order of 1951*, its classical assembly is more or less a copy too. This also applies to the distinction between major assembly and judicatory. As in the Netherlands Reformed Church, the major assemblies in the Protestant Church in the Netherlands are not judicatories, thus not courts of the church. The *trias politica*—the tripartite system or separation of powers (legislative, executive, and judicial) according to the theory of Charles Montesquieu—was implemented. The

Reformed Churches in the Netherlands had initiated the separation of powers in 1999 (see ACTA 1999, § 98, 100), introducing a separate court of appeal.

Although the above-mentioned section V of the *Netherlands Reformed Church Order of 1951* was taken as a point of departure, it is not identical in the *Protestant Church Order of 2004* because in section VI of the latter a few more, important, lines are added. This section also contains the golden rule of Emden: no one office, office-bearer or congregation lording it over another; however, the order in this section is different. This church order does not start with the congregation, but with the office. This is important to note. Once more, it demonstrates that church polity is not so much about the church, but about office. But even more important is the second part of this section which states that everything will be focused on obedience to Christ, the Head of the Church. Therefore, the responsibility of leading the church is attributed to assemblies. This implies that every task executed by the classical assembly shall be put in the perspective of obedience to Christ, the Head of the Church. It underlines that the work of this major assembly is *Christocratic*. This illustrates a change, not in the sense that assemblies in the Reformed past did not obey Christ, but in that it was written down in an era wherein there is a tendency to shift from what could be called a 'sacramental ecclesiology' toward a 'functional ecclesiology' with the emphasis on efficiency and utility. Likewise, the *Protestant Church Order of 2004*, following the *Netherlands Reformed Church Order of 1951*, states explicitly that the assemblies *guide* or *lead*, so they do not *govern*, although that is ideal.

### *Conclusion*

What was preserved in these developments? There is much continuity in the development of the classical assembly. It survived the past and it still exists, and not only in the (Protestant Church in the) Netherlands. It even returned and regained its power in the Netherlands Reformed Church in 1951 after 135 years. It had been and still is the regional assembly of offices or delegated office-bearers. It has two main tasks: supervision (*episkopè*) and shaping community (*koinonia*). It is not or should not be a managerial body that is merely in charge of, or has to run, an ecclesial business. It is an assembly that receives its power from Christ. This is not clear to all participants in the classical assemblies nowadays. One of the fundamental problems, if not *the* fundamental problem, is the lack of clarity about the nature of the classical assembly. It is not clear in church orders; or office-bearers are not familiar with the nature of this assembly. I notice this every time I lecture in classical assemblies.

What was gained and lost in these developments? There is much discontinuity as the classical assembly developed. *The* classical assembly just does not exist. One can speak for example about the Dordtian classical assembly. But it differs from the classical assembly according to the *Algemeen Reglement of 1816* or the *Netherlands Reformed Church Order of 1951*. The classical assembly in the Protestant Church in the Netherlands looks more like the one of the Netherlands Reformed Church after 1951. And the classical assembly in the Reformed Churches in the Netherlands from the nineteenth century was closer to the Dordtian classical assembly, like the classical assembly in the more orthodox denominations nowadays. Although the classical assembly has survived the ages, its nature has changed since Emden due to ecclesial, ecclesiological, political, and societal developments. The sense of being a learning community was lost. It became a governing body of the community of congregations (until 1816); no longer did it have assigned tasks relating to classical sermons, book visitation, and visitation and examination of candidates for the ministry. After 1951 the classical assembly became a gathering of offices, not of delegated office-bearers. We also see a shift in tendency toward functional rather than sacramental ecclesiology. This shift requires a classical assembly that works efficiently and functionally. The profit of a Christ-oriented assembly — as actually written in the church order — might be a decoy and could become lost. Also, the classical assembly as an agent of mission evaporated. A profit, however, was the implementation of the separation of powers.

What could be altered in the contemporary situation in order to bring ecclesiological strength to Reformed church polity in the Netherlands? Discontinuity could be a blessing-in-disguise as new or other ecclesiological emphases with regard to the classical assembly are laid. We saw above how the nature of the classical assembly was elaborated through the centuries alongside elaboration on the nature of the major assemblies in the church orders. The classical assembly itself should be aware of its Christological foundation and understand that it receives its power from Him. There have been episodes in the past where this has been forgotten by the classical assembly. It is also a decoy for classical assemblies today.

The present and future classical assembly should also gain an eye for being or becoming an agent of mission and for being or becoming a community of neighboring congregations. In addition, it should foster continuity with regard to the 'learning communities' of the sixteenth century in the sense that it should reincorporate into the way it shapes its roles of supervision and communion the challenge of how to become a workshop where the Bible is studied. It is from this angle that supervision, admonition, and discipline and communion should be executed. Such an attitude, based upon its Christological nature, would give space to continuity, and if necessary even discontinuity, with a view to the future of Christ's church.

*Abbreviations and bibliography*

CB: Confessio Belgica (Belgic Confession) (1561).
DCO: Dordt Church Order (1619).
ACTA 1999: Acts of the General Synod of Enkhuizen 1999 of the Reformed Churches in the Netherlands. Kampen: Kok

Boersma, Owe. [1994]. Vluchtig Voorbeeld: De Nederlandse, Franse en Italiaanse Vluchtelingenkerken in Londen, 1568–1585. PhD diss., Theologische Universiteit Kampen. s.l.: s.n.

Bos, David. 1999. In dienst van het Koninkrijk: Beroepsontwikkeling van Hervormde predikanten in negentiende-eeuws Nederland. Amsterdam: Bert Bakker.

Classicale Wetten Gereformeert en Vastgesteld op de Vergaderinge Gehouden tot Swarte-Sluis den 11 April 1683; Conditien en Voorwaerden van de Classicale Weduwe Cassa Opgeregt bij de E. Classis van Vollenhove en Steenwijk, Ingevolge de Resolutien van de Classis Gehouden tot Swarte Sluijs Den 11 April 1683 ... en tot Vollenhove Gehouden den 30 Meij 1683 Zwartsluis en Vollenhove.

De Boer, Erik A. 2012. The Genevan School of the Prophets: The Congrégation of the Company of Pastors and their Influence in the 16th Century. Geneva: Librairie Droz.

Grosheide, Frederik W. et al. (eds). 1957. Christelijke Encyclopedie. Kampen: Kok.

Janssen, Allan J. 2010. The Apostolicity of the Classis. In: Janssen and Van den Broeke 2010, 63–74.

Janssen, Allan J., and Leon Van den Broeke (eds). 2010. A Collegial Bishop? Classis and Presbytery at Issue. The Historical Series of the Reformed Church in America 66. Grand Rapids Mi. — Cambridge: Eerdmans.

Nauta, Doede. 1957. Classicale Handboekjes. In: Grosheide et al. 1957. Vol. 2, 220.

Nauta, Doede. 1971. Verklaring van de kerkorde van de Gereformeerde Kerken in Nederland. Kampen: Kok.

Small, Joseph. 2010. The Travail of the Presbytery. In: Janssen and Van den Broeke 2010, 47–61

Van den Broeke, C. (Leon). 2005. Een geschiedenis van de classis: Classicale typen tussen idee en werkelijkheid 1571–2004. Kok: Kampen.

Van Deursen, Arie Th. 1998. Bavianen en slijkgeuzen: Kerk en kerkvolk ten tijde van Maurits en Oldenbarnevelt. Franeker: Van Wijnen.

Vosloo, Robert. 2010. The Presbytery and Church Reunification in the Dutch Reformed Family of Churches in South Africa: The Story of the United Presbytery of Stellenbosch. In: Janssen and Van den Broeke 2010, 93–109.

# THE CATHOLICITY OF THE CHURCH AND THE IMMIGRANT EXPERIENCE

## A North American Case Study

Allan J. Janssen

*I*

The catholicity of the church is a function of God's intentions for God's created order. God acts in Christ and through the Spirit to "reconcile to himself all things, whether on earth or in heaven, making peace by the blood of his cross" (Col. 1:20). Through Christ, God has broken down the dividing wall between Jew and Gentile (Eph. 2), and thus, principally, between all manner of persons. God uses the *church* as an instrument both to proclaim this reality as having already been accomplished and to embody this reality in a provisional form for the sake of God's world (cf. Janssen 2006, 81–124). Church order, in turn, as the church's obedience in shaping how God desires this exemplary people to be in the world, gives a constitutional configuration to the reality of catholicity. That it can do so only provisionally will be made clear in the following. However, the catholic imperative will disclose not only challenges to Reformed church order as it comes under purview, but a fundamental lack as well. Moreover, catholicity sharpens the question as to what should be understood as essential to a Reformed church order.

This paper will begin with a review of a few notes of the nature of the catholicity of the church. The heart of the essay will report the challenge that a significant immigrant presence, from a non-Western culture, places on a Reformed church with a church order based on the Dordt church order, the Reformed Church in America. I will explore how that church is attempting to respond to the challenge and the issues raised thereby. It turns out that the experience and the attempt to respond make evident that at issue is not only a challenge *to* the catholicity of the church, but that it is a challenge that emerges *from* catholicity.

First, then, notes on the catholicity of the church. I will take as my thesis this observation from Hans Küng's well-known study on the church: "The catholicity of the Church … consists of a notion of entirety, based on identity and resulting in universality" (Küng 1967, 303) Note the three terms in that sentence: entirety, identity and universality. The order is important. Catholicity, one of the creedal 'notes' of the church, has been used polemically. From the notion that catholicity has to do with geography, or the spatial extension of the church, it has been maintained that some churches (particularly the Roman Catholic) is fully catholic as opposed to Protestant churches, limited as most are to national boundaries. As Küng and others argue, the spatial extension is constituent of catholicity, but it is derivative of something more fundamental.

Thinking toward catholicity begins not with the church, which while itself part of the story of God's action with the world, exists only in service to what God has done through Israel and in Christ. Even that is to put the matter too lightly. The church's very identity is rooted not in itself but in Christ: "... catholicity can never be abstracted from Christ Himself" (Berkouwer 1976, 114). One begins then by exploring what God has done in Christ. A number of observers have commented on the notion of 'fullness' or the *pleroma*—Pauline terms (e.g., Berkhof 1962, 52–53; Moltmann 1977, 347; Berkouwer 1976, 112; Küng 1967, 312). This fullness, however, is not the fullness of the church as such, but Christ's fullness, or God's fullness in Christ (see Berkouwer 1976, 112). It is a fullness that presses toward the goal set out in the Christ-hymn of Colossians 1: that Christ reconciles all things in heaven and on earth to himself.Reconciliation with God, then, necessarily includes the reconciliation of those who are estranged. For that reason one such as Herman Bavinck can, at the end of the nineteenth century, talk about 'the absolute universalism' of Christendom in which there are "... no boundaries of sex or age, of status or rank, of nationality or language". And that "[t]he gospel is a glad message not only for the individual human, but for humanity, for the family and society and the state, for art and science, for the entire cosmos, for all sighing creatures" (Bavinck 1888, 11). God has acted in Christ to unite that which is estranged. This happened through the cross, where Jew and Gentile are reunited. This effects a kingdom where all can come and all are welcomed. The house will not only be 'full' in the sense that there is no room, but 'full' the way a family table is full when all are present. In this case, however, it is the welcome of every sort and condition. No one is left out because he or she is of the wrong sort, however that 'sort' may be determined.This fullness is possible, and hence catholicity finds expression, H. Berkhof argues, as a result of what Christ has accomplished: "It is about the essence of the Head of the Church, about the glorified Lord who, in cross and resurrection, has overcome the powers and who is now set at the right hand of God, i.e., participates in the divine rule of the world. Christ is universal, He, the Messiah of Israel is at the same time intended as the Lord of the whole world" (Berkhof 1962, 80).

Hence, no power can establish boundaries that separate people in an essential way. Of course, boundaries exist: national frontiers, language barriers, cultural and historical differences, racial coloring. None, however, can endure so that humanity, and indeed all creation, remains separated. God's kingdom encompasses all, and this is accomplished in Christ's victory over the powers. Hence, "[i]n the new people of God the divisions that destroy mankind will already be deprived of their force here and now. The barriers which people set up against each other, in order to maintain their own position and to put down others, will be broken down through mission and fellowship" (Moltmann 1977, 351; cf. Van Ruler 1969, 139). Only so can the church be what Küng calls 'entire'. This is not first of all spatial, or horizontal, but vertical. It's entirety is an expression of its identity as a people shaped by what God has done in Christ. Here, then, in a particular place, and in all particular places, God gathers a representative people of the whole.

The catholic nature of the church, then, is a *gift*. It is participation in the new reality that overcomes the powers of darkness. It is not something that the church must, or even can, achieve. Nonetheless, because it is a given, it also becomes a possible *task*. The church while living in a non-catholic reality, that is, as it continues to exist, and even persist, in living a practical, if not principled, *apartheid*, is freed, and indeed called, to live into the reality of a reconciled world.

Nonetheless, it is clear that it is not the case that 'every knee' bows to the Victor over the powers of death, sin and evil. For that reason we must admit that the fullness of Christ is not fully present. In fact, catholicity is an eschatological reality. This is the case already when we consider that the *pleroma* before us is in Christ. While the church is the body of Christ it still has to grow toward Christ, or so Küng argues. The "Church has to *become* universal" (Küng 1967, 312; cf. Berkhof 1962, 84). Christ *is* Lord, but his lordship is still hidden. Still, "somewhere in the cosmos is a space in which it is already revealed. Somewhere in the cosmos representative for all, the Head of all is acknowledged and obeyed" (Berkhof 1962, 59).

Hence, even the most expansive church, measured geographically, falls far short of the goal. No church can be claim to be 'catholic' *vis a vis* other communions. The church is becoming. This means, moreover, that catholicity as an attribute is dynamic; it is not an ontological characteristic (see Berkouwer 1976, 112). The church, inclusive of all its separated communions, is called to live toward the future it already has within itself, as the body of Christ and the fellowship of the Holy Spirit.

It does so as it finds itself thrust into the position of crossing boundaries. As such it follows the pattern set out in Acts. The story of Peter in Acts 10 is well known; a dream and a visit push him beyond the boundaries of Israel to the

Gentiles. Less remarked upon is the story in Acts 8 where the community is forced beyond Jerusalem. While the narrative has yet to engage the question of the Gentiles, the community finds itself propelled beyond its place of comfort, its 'home'. So the church has been compelled by the Spirit to mission, to cross boundaries. The story of mission has been told well and often and there is no need to repeat it here. For our task it is sufficient to note that the church is drawn into the eschatological action of God, 'catholic' is "an attribute describing [the church's] mission and its hope" (Moltmann 1977, 349). So Berkouwer: "The Church's charge is to proclaim God's salvation, so that the boundaries are broken through ... the Church may not function as a fearful border guard, but as one who brings good tidings" (Berkouwer 1976, 162). These boundaries include seas and frontiers, cultures and language groups. But they need not be far distant. The church transgresses boundaries to welcome all to the festal joy of the Messianic feast (see Hart 2009). The boundaries may be class and economic groups, racial groups and age groups, sexual orientation and interest.

Here then, Küng's assertion with which we began has become transparent. The catholicity of the church is rooted in its identity in Christ. Because Christ has defeated all that divides humanity, the church not only lives as boundaries have been crossed, but gladly continues to do so against the eschatological horizon. It does so humbly, and in confession of its sin, as the church continually shrinks back into a comfort of persons who live with and among those most like themselves. For that reason Küng's words stand as a comfort and a challenge to the church: "True catholicity is a grace given to the Church and constantly renewed by its Lord. This catholicity cannot be seen, it can only be believed, or seen with the eyes of faith. But catholicity, as glimpsed in faith, is something that we should present to the world through our lives, as something credible" (Küng 1967, 313).

That said, more must be said, and this about the Spirit. I claimed at the outset that God acts in Christ *through the Spirit* to unite all things. God acts eschatologically not simply in Christ, but through the Spirit. The crossing of boundaries happens through the action of the Spirit (Acts). And, I might add, happens at the center of the church, at the Lord's Table. This is catholicity not only of extension, but of intension. It is what Van Ruler is about when he talks about the catholicity not only of persons, but of 'things', meaning God's created order, particularly as taken up in the sacramental life of the church (see Van Ruler 1969, 138). Catholicity then, is realized at the table. This will have implications when we consider that church order, particularly Reformed church order itself, is, as the Reformed confess, a work of the Spirit.

*II*

The Classis of Greater Palisades is situated in the oldest part of the Reformed Church in America. Located in northern New Jersey, its first churches were established soon after the original Manhattan and Brooklyn churches were planted in the New World. Its earliest Dutch constituency has long been Americanized, and in the 1950's and 60's, the years of the highest church membership in the US, the churches that make up the current classis represented the establishment Protestantism regnant in our country. More recent years have seen the decline of most congregations. They have remained, however, largely white, middle and upper middle class churches.

In 2000, the classis received ten Korean ministers as members of the classis. Several of those ministers had already gathered congregations; others were prepared to do so. The church order defines congregations as Christians gathered in one place to conduct worship; they become an organized church when, after they elect elders deacons, the classis establishes them. The classis began to work with gathering Korean congregations as they prepared to become organized churches. The classis took two actions to assist the new Korean presence. First, it purchased a machine by which a person could translate the proceedings of the classis for the Koreans present. Second, it hired a 'Korean coordinator' to assist Korean congregations and ministers as they became acclimated to a new culture.

The Korean congregations have gradually grown in number and about half have found permanent homes; others reside in host churches. First generation Korean pastors remain in leadership in the Korean community, but second generation pastors have begun to occupy a number of pulpits. In the summer of 2010, several Korean pastors began an initiative to establish a separate, Korean-language classis.

Several reasons were given for this initiative. First, language itself is an issue. Korean pastors could not fully participate in the work of the classis. If they attended committee meetings, they could not follow the discussion. Often they were not able to contribute; their lack of skill in English dissuaded them. While the language gap was difficult in itself, it became all the more evident when the matter at hand concerned a Korean congregation or pastor.

Second, there were clear cultural differences. One such difference surfaced early. A Korean church installed a number of women to the office of *kwanza*. It took a great deal of discussion to communicate that the RCA did not have such an 'office', and that there could be a place to honor women without inducting them into a non-existent office. At the same time, Korean churches had (early) difficulty with women in the offices of deacon, elder and minister. Another, more persistent, difference is the understanding of the nature of authority. Korean culture allows a more personal practice of authority. The older, senior, person speaks with authority. Moreover, the pastor exercises great authority in a congregation. The practice and authority of assemblies is more difficult; Koreans find the back and forth of the Caucasian discussions strange (see Janssen 2002, 241–253).

Third, Korean pastors and churches argue that the first two reasons obtaining, they are better able to supervise ministers and congregations in a Korean context. They share not only language and culture, but a shared immigrant experience, one strange to the host Caucasian ecclesiastical culture.

Fourth, Korean pastors could point to recent events in the Reformed church that supported their request. In 2008 the Synod of the West (RCA) established for the first time a 'non-geographic' classis, the City Church Classis. The General Synod received delegates from that classis. It was argued that 'boundaries' as set out in the church order were not reserved for geographic boundaries. While the question of boundaries continues to puzzle the church, the new classis came into existence, thus providing the possibility of a classis put together on a basis other than geographic proximity (see Van den Broeke 2013).

A fifth reason could be noted, although it was not stated; indeed it may not have been perceived as a reason by either the Koreans nor the remainder of the classis. There are theological differences between the immigrant congregations and the resident classis. Korean pastors and first generation Korean Christians are the inheritors of the evangelical-missionary theology of the nineteenth century. Thoroughly Reformed, most Korean Presbyterians were formed by the *Westminster Confession*. While the Caucasian congregations reflect a variety of Reformed expressions, most could be said to live and worship in a post-Enlightenment engagement of scripture and culture.

In the church order of the RCA, a regional synod alone has the authority to form a classis. There was little enthusiasm to do so in the Regional Synod of the Mid-Atlantics. Nor was there a desire within the classis itself to support the break from the Koreans. Among the reasons stated was that of the subject of this paper: a concern for the unity and catholicity of the church. This was stated more concretely when classis members said: "We need each other. We, Caucasians need our Korean sisters and brothers. And we Koreans need our Caucasian (and Taiwanese and Hispanic) sisters and brothers". A second, compelling reason came from the recent adoption of the *Belhar Confession* (BC) as a new confessional 'standard' in the RCA. This confession states, in its second paragraph, that "this unity must become visible so that the world may believe that separation, enmity and hatred between people and groups is sin which Christ has already conquered, and accordingly that anything which threatens this unity may have no place in the church and must be resisted. (….) [w]e reject any doctrine which professes that this spiritual unity is truly being maintained in the bond of peace while believers of the same confession are in effect alienated from one another for the sake of diversity and in despair of reconciliation" (BC, § 2; cf. Naudé 2010, 45).

Still, the classis had ten congregations whose pastors pressed the case for a separate classis. Following a series of negotiations, the classis began discussions to establish what it calls a 'Korean Leadership Committee' that would give limited autonomy to the Korean membership of the classis. The committee would consist of Korean ministers and elders and would be responsible for making recommendations in a number of areas: 1) appointment of classis supervisors [a supervisor is responsible for a local consistory in the absence of an installed minister]; 2) calls and contracts to ministers; 3) establishment of mission churches; and 4) organization of churches. The classis retains final authority on all matters. The recommendations of the Korean Leadership Committee would go to the standing committee responsible for the relevant task. It was stated that the standing committee would accept the recommendation of the KLC unless it is in conflict with the by-laws and procedures of the classis. This left authority ambiguous.

An area that would soon put the classis to the test had to do with 'mission churches'. The Korean Leadership Committee wished to receive congregations from outside the geographic bounds of the classis. There is a history in the RCA of classes superintending distant churches that have no classis near at hand. The Koreans maintain that a number of 'orphan' congregations exist even where a Reformed classis is present; there may be only one or two Korean congregations present; hardly enough to do proper supervision. The confusion within the RCA over the nature of boundaries appeared to leave the door open for such a move. Indeed, a request from a Korean congregation came very soon. In response, the classis moved to put in place a series of 'protocols' to guide any such discussions. The protocols included provisions that required the requesting congregation to show that it could not receive proper ecclesiastical support from the classis where it finds itself; that there be conversation between the resident classis and the Classis of Greater Palisades; that all church order provisions be met; and the like.

In addition to the establishment of the Korean Leadership Committee, two other relevant actions were taking place. First, the classis elected its first Korean president, a first generation Korean pastor. Second, the classis began to hold its meetings in two languages, Korean and English. All matters are translated. Most are done so orally; a number of matters are translated on a large screen that can be seen by all present.

One further note of relevance. The Korean presence is not the only non-Caucasian presence in the classis. The classis also has two congregations that are largely Taiwanese. It also has Hispanic populations in a number of congregations. And one congregation is largely Asian Indian. The multiplicity of language and culture is not limited to Korean. The Korean presence is simply the largest 'minority' presence in the classis.

### *III*

What does this state of affairs tell us about the catholicity of the church within the framework of the church order? On the one hand, the presence of Korean immigrant churches in the U.S. is an expression of catholicity. Indeed, it reflects catholicity as mission. The gospel has reached beyond a particular culture to another. Moreover, it has brought differing cultures together within one ecclesiastical household. It is worth a historical note that the minister who is credited as the missionary who brought Protestantism to Korea is a child of a church in the very same classis of which we speak. The descendants of those mission ventures do not remain distant, but have become fellow ministers, elders and congregants, not just neighbors but are part and parcel of the same church, and then not simply as participants, but full partners in the governance and ministry of the church.

As is evident, however, this places a strain on the church order. The order itself is the product of a particular culture. It is an order that emerged in the Netherlands of the sixteenth and seventeenth centuries. As a church order it became enculturated in the New World where many of its values have become shared within the broader culture (cf. Small 2014). The Reformed system of assemblies looks very much like the representative government of cities, states and nation; Americans understand the republican form of governance. The assumptions that go into that order are not shared by Korean immigrants. The notion of collective authority appears strange to the newcomers.

A further, structural, strain on the church order is evident. It was noted above that configuration of the Korean Leadership Committee left authority ambiguous. The provisions for the new committee state that the classis will in effect ratify the actions of the committee so long as they are congruent with the policies and by-laws of the classis. At the same time, the classis retains a final authority. What happens when the entire classis denies a recommendation by the leadership committee? Or when a committee within the classis comes into conflict? The hope and the intention is that the matter can be worked out in conversation. But that is hardly a satisfying state of affairs in the context of church order. One of the primary functions of church order is, after all, to clarify how authority functions in church governance.

So the question arises: can a church order built on foundations strange to one party sustain and/or encourage the catholicity of the church?

This state of affairs betrays, I think, a fundamental flaw in Reformed church orders, at least seen from the perspective of catholicity. Reformed churches tend at most to be national in character. At least that is the case with the Reformed Church in America, or nearly so. Its church order has as its most encompassing body the General Synod, a body that includes Reformed church in the United States and in Canada. In fact, as a matter of policy, the RCA does not establish Reformed churches in other nations. Churches begun through its mission become part of a native church. The church does not extend beyond certain boundaries. As we saw in the first part of this paper, the church is catholic to *cross* boundaries. This leaves Reformed churches structurally separated.

I suspect that this is the case in part because Reformed churches have seldom thought systematically about catholicity within the context of church order. This may be a result of how Reformed churches have thought about unity, a Nicene attribute closely related to catholicity. One can see unity in many Reformed church orders centered around *confession*. This is unity founded in and through truth. This, however, is not the only way to consider the matter. One need not think of the relation of unity and truth by beginning with truth — unity through truth — but can turn the concepts around — truth through unity (this was J.H. Gunning's point, cf. Balke 1990, 218). The unfortunate upshot is a Reformed propensity to schism (see Van der Borgt 2010, 1). One can safely argue that by ignoring the catholicity of the church, we have contributed to its disunity.

But there is a further lack within Reformed church order. If catholicity is realized in Christ at the table (and we might add, at the font), then a classis/presbytery is poorly situated to give full expression to this attribute of the church. Here I am close to what Leon van den Broeke argues when he maintains that classes/presbyteries pay good attention to the episcopal task of governance, but less attention to the fellowship dimension of what the bishop represents (see Van den Broeke 2010, 75–92). I am adding, however, that this happens at the Lord's Table.

Classes are not church in the full sense; that is, while in their governmental functions they pay close attention to Word and sacrament, they are not sacramental bodies themselves. When the Supper is celebrated in classes, it is an exceptional act. Reformed church order traditionally clearly reserves the sacraments for the local congregation. It is there that elders are present to guard the table. It has been the practice of many Reformed communions that an assembly that wishes to celebrate the sacrament will do so only under the auspices of a local board of elders. It remains a question, then, of how the greater assemblies in Reformed church order will give expression to the catholicity of the church.

The actions of the Classis of Greater Palisades to provide a mechanism to maintain unity and catholicity within one small geographic area (to the extent that one can talk about catholicity as local) express both the strength and weakness of the order of this particular Reformed church. It is a weakness to the extent that the classis found itself forced to go beyond the church order. There is no place in the order for such arrangements. It isn't that the order is not sufficiently plastic for it to be done. It may well happen that the General Synod will initiate a change to the church order to accommodate such a structure. But its plasticity is also the strength of the church order. There is sufficient space to construct the experiment.For experiment it is. I am cautiously optimistic that the experiment will succeed. There are strong reasons to pray earnestly for its success. Nor is it only because the church hopes to live up to its confession of catholicity. Rather it is the lived experience of the church that is at issue. All the different ecclesiastical groups that gather under the roof of the church in Northern New Jersey need each other. Koreans, Taiwanese, African-Americans, Hispanics, Caucasians, all bring different perspectives of the gospel. All have something to offer that the others need. There is no group that holds a privileged access to the gospel. Moreover, no one culture is favored by God. Our mutual presence to one another is a gift that enriches the ecclesial reality. It is now a challenge for the church so to shape its life that its order follows the work of the Spirit who has led the church to this new and exciting place.

I have endeavored in the essay to understand how a Reformed church order gives expression to the catholicity of the church in a concrete instance where ethnic differences press in on the life of the church. That is to see the order of the church through the lens of one of the classic attributes of the church. Further exploration promises to be fruitful as one explores the other Nicene attributes — unity, holiness and apostolicity. Such exploration might not only be felicitous for a Reformed ecclesiology, but might assist churches as they are led by the Spirit to embrace the new global reality and to embrace a way of being church that is not only 'Reformed', but is genuinely catholic.

### *Abbreviations and bibliography*

BC: Belhar Confession.

RCA: Reformed Church in America.

Balke, Willem. 1990. De kerk bij Hoedemaker, Gunning, Kraemer en Van Ruler. In: Van 't Spijker et al. 1990, 202–230.

Bavinck, Herman. 1888. De katholiciteit van Christendom en kerk. Kampen: Zalsman.

Berkhof, Hendrikus. 1962. De katholiciteit der kerk. Nijkerk: Callenbach.

Berkouwer, Gerrit K. 1976. The Church. Grand Rapids: Eerdmans.

Hart, David B. 2009. Atheist Delusions: The Christian Revolution and Its Fashionable Enemies. New Haven: Yale.

Janssen, Allan J. 2002. Plurality in Reformed Church Order. In: Van der Borght et al. 2002, 241–253.

Janssen, Allan J. 2006. Kingdom, Office and Church. Grand Rapids: Eerdmans.

Janssen, Allan J., and Leon van den Broeke (eds). 2010. A Collegial Bishop? Classis and Presbytery at Issue. Grand Rapids: Eerdmans.

Janssen, Allan J., and Leo J. Koffeman (eds). 2014. Protestant Church Polity in Changing Contexts. Ecclesiological and Historical Contributions. Proceedings of the International Conference, Utrecht, The Netherlands, 7–10 November, 2011. Volume I. Church Polity and Ecumenism: Global Perspectives 2. Zürich: LIT-Verlag (forthcoming).

Küng, Hans. 1967. The Church. New York: Sheed and Ward.

Moltmann, Jürgen. 1977. The Church in the Power of the Spirit: A Contribution to Messianic Ecclesiology. New York: Harper Row.

Naudè, Piet. 2010. Neither Calendar nor Clock: Perspectives on the Belhar Confession. Grand Rapids: Eerdmans.

Small, Joseph D. 2014. The Democratic Captivity of the Church. In: Janssen and Koffeman 2014.

Van den Broeke, Leon. 2010. The Protestant Classis: Between Episcopè and Koinonia. In: Janssen and Van den Broeke 2010, 75–92.

Van den Broeke, Leon. 2013. Non-Geographic Classes? Reformed Geography. In: Journal of Reformed Theology, 7(2013)/1, 51–68. DOI: 10.1163/15697312-12341276.

Van der Borgt, Eddy, et al. (eds). 2002. Faith and Ethnicity. Volume 2. Zoetermeer: Meinema.

Van der Borght, Eddy. 2010. The Unity of the Church: The State of the Art and Beyond. Leiden: Brill.

Van Ruler, Arnold A. n.d. [1969]. Ik geloof. Nijkerk: Callenbach. 7th edition.

Van 't Spijker, Willem, et al. (eds). 1990. De Kerk: Wezen, weg en werk van de kerk naar reformatische opvatting. Kampen: De Groot Goudriaan.

# TOWARDS THE RECONSTRUCTION OF CHURCH POLITY IN ZAMBIA

## A Case Study

Godfrey Msiska

### 1. *Introduction*

Church polity in the context of the Scottish Presbyterian tradition in Zambia urgently needs reconstruction. This contribution is meant to show that the inherited church orders do not work in the early years of the twenty-first century. In fact, the inherited church orders are among the factors that delay the difficult process of reconstruction of church polity. The problem with the inherited church orders is that the historical and structural backgrounds were not set up to work for African churches.

For this case study I have selected two cases to illustrate the most serious problems, because each of the cases raises issues that have parallels in other churches as well as issues of concern to the whole of Africa. The first case study is on church discipline: although it is true that most matters that are actionable for ecclesiastical discipline involve behaviors that are unethical and not justifiable, in this case church discipline is used first of all to prove that the church has power. The second case study deals with the church union that brought together Protestant churches in Zambia: however, in my view the union's church order does not reflect the reality of church unity. Both case studies look at what has emerged to be daily practice in churches in Zambia.

While I am taking an approach that is contextually restricted to one area of the world, I do so in the growing awareness that something of the same dynamic is recognized to be the case for churches in other societies — even in Western societies. In Zambia, this is a crucial issue for those of us who wish to engage the 'European missionary encounter of Protestant church polity with our culture', as people like Koffeman have encouraged us to do. How can the missional character of the church be expressed in its polity (see Koffeman 2009, 191f.)? This describes the challenge faced by churches in Zambia. We do not find in the current shape of the inherited church order a model of doing and being church that is highly contextualized. We must admit that it is in fact not overly accommodated and domesticated to Zambian cultural perspectives, values and forms of life. The pattern I will describe and critique comprises one of the most fundamental church polity challenges.

This contribution concludes with brief glimpses to show how the church orders are conditioned by many factors. Those factors include: the need to redefine church polity and church order, a commitment to genuine contextualization, and the role of church polity in a changing context. The answer to the question, How should church polity be reconstructed? rests upon the even more fundamental question, Why should church polity be reconstructed? What is our rationale for considering this? To what end do we consider it? Answering the 'why' question points us towards changing the way we ask the 'how' question. Before introducing the case studies, I will make a few general remarks with regard to church polity, focusing on the Zambian context.

## 2. *The meaning of church polity and church order*

Church polity is an academic discipline with a multi-faceted subject. It deals with issues of organization in the church in relation to discipline, and with all kinds of procedures including the relation of the church to the state. The term 'church polity' among Protestant churches may be used interchangeably with 'church law' or 'canon law'. The reason for the use of one term or another is matter of preference. Church polity is "the sacred science of government for the visible church" (Vorster 2003, 1f.). It studies the church order that applies and should apply in the church. In the same vein it interprets general stipulations of the church to ensure and promote that things go well in church life (see Coertzen 2004, 188). Given the above, Coertzen defines church polity as "the science whose field of interest is in theories on church polity and church order" (Coertzen 1998, 45). He argues that church polity should not only remain "a mere academic interest but should be able to help people in the church" (Ibid.). What that means is that church polity as science must find expression in the church and must be able to help Christians to be more accountable to God.

A church order is "the whole of general stipulations, established by a competent, ecclesiastical instance and written down to ensure and promote that things go well in church life" (Bronkhorst, quoted by Coertzen 2004, 188). According to Coertzen, what is found in church polity must find its expression in the church order (see Coertzen 1998, 45). A church order is a document that has a binding character in a particular religious community, but also a document which intends to help the church live in an accountable way before God in all the facets of its existence.

### 2.1 *Dilemma in church polity models*

The churches in Zambia have church orders that were imposed on them, and therefore the churches are struggling to cope in their changing context. In particular, the Presbyterian Church of Zambia has been in Zambia since 1926, but it still struggles to understand its own church order. Many churches in Zambia can identify with this problem. Most church orders still reflect the reality of the European missionary models of running the church. The Church in Zambia is at a crossroads in its changing context with regard to church polity in general. There is still uncertainty as to which direction church polity can take in Zambia. Basically, there are three options: (a) continuity with the missionary model of church polity; (b) getting rid of the missionary model and making a new model for the Zambian church; (c) adjusting the missionary model in order to make a new model.

Church orders of most Protestant churches that were established by missionaries in Zambia are identical to those of their home churches in Europe. However, that is not only true for Zambia. Presbyterians, Anglicans, Lutherans and Reformed churches replicate their home churches in every corner of the world. They do so because they cannot imagine—as a son who cannot imagine his father being wrong—that any other way could be right. The church orders of their home churches are syntheses of their church polities, faith and practice. It is simply assumed that the inherited church order is the best, if not the only viable, one. This creates a dilemma which most Zambians face in the process of reconstructing their church polity.

## 3. *First case study: church discipline*

In pre-colonial Zambian society, discipline was exercised by parents in a family arrangement: parents had a right to discipline their children. In a community, observation of community morals was used to maintain peace, law and order. When people defaulted in community morals, they were disciplined by the community's leaders. This was especially true for those who were practicing bad behaviors like stealing.

### 3.1 *Inherited model and conception of church discipline*

Verstraelen-Gilhuis says that when dealing with church discipline cases in church councils, the European missionary used as models the courts of traditional society: only instead of the chief who was the head of a village and therefore the judge, the white missionary was the judge. The missionary combined the traditional model with European formal legal procedures. Both systems were used to reinforce one another (Verstraelen-Gilhuis 1982, 327). In many cases missionaries acted as a judge and their word was final. Many disciplinary cases were related to Christian life rather than to doctrinal issues.

The churches in Zambia have inherited a conception of church discipline that is understood 'as a way of purifying the church', in order to say, 'Note how we use church discipline'. They have come to understand that church discipline helps to uphold God's honor against anyone whose grave error or sin would deny and disgrace Christ, and it assists to serve the costly grace of the gospel by calling such sinners to repent. It also facilitates to restore sinners to truth, sanctity and fellowship as brothers and sisters in Christ. Along with that it rallies the community around itself to deter others from being led astray by false doctrine or the temptation to conform to the world's behavior. Apart from that, it helps to save the church from the infection of false doctrine and its witness from public scandal, to maintain the unity of the body of Christ and to save the church from God's judgement (Uniting Presbyterian Church in Southern Africa, *Confession of Faith*, Ch. 2, art. 24, sect. 1–7).

### 3.2 *Meaning of church discipline*

When one talks of 'ecclesiastical discipline', one thinks too willingly only of the maintenance of certain standards of conduct through the enforcement of those standards by appropriate penalties; or it may mean the training of persons that they may conduct themselves according to the given standards. One of the troubles is that the word 'discipline' has a range of meaning. In its widest range 'discipline' comes from the Latin *discipulus*, meaning 'a learner or novice or disciple', and is a derivation of *discere*, 'to learn', and involves the process of inner education (see Oden 1983, 234). In the Hebrew *Talmud*, it refers to a learner, with emphasis on participating in a reflective process instilling both theory and practice. The Christian concept of discipline has the same meaning as the Latin *disciplina*, which signifies the whole range of nurturing, instructional and training procedures that disciple-making requires (see Packer 1993, 220; Childress and Macquarrie 1986, 159). In addition, it has an element of punishment and correction. It refers to approaches that put emphasis on character formation, the teaching of self-discipline and acceptable behavior.

From the study of ascetical theology, we learn that discipline is "concerned with the development of Christian life, and in particular with training in self-discipline and prayer" (Waddams 1967, 18). It deals with ordinary ways of being Christian and can occur only within the fellowship of the church. It is connected to attitudes and practices. Therefore, it is linked with human behavior. Childress and Macquarrie affirm that discipline should aim at reconciliation and at rehabilitation of those who have injured the community. This is where discipline, as the maintenance of standards, passes into the more important kind of discipline which has to do with the forming of disciples and their training in the Christian life (see Childress and Macquarrie 1986, 159).

### 3.3 *Historical perspective on church discipline*

By the sixteenth century the Reformers wanted to re-create disciplinary practice and to restore the godliness of the first and second centuries. And so the reformers instructed their congregations to hear the Word of God and also to practice what they had heard. For this reason they organized bodies comprised of ministers and laymen. The purpose of these bodies was to chastise church members, to correct them, and to settle disputes between them. The members of these bodies were expected to be role models of piety and godliness (see Graham 1996, 4–10).

### 3.4 *John Calvin's position on church discipline*

Calvin had three goals for church discipline. First, he thought that the church was to be kept pure because it was the body of Christ. For example, if a person who could not partake in Holy Communion was admitted to it, for Calvin this was sacrilege, the same "as giving the body of Christ to dogs" (Baxter 2000, 15). Second, church discipline should be used to prevent the corruption of the good in the church. What he meant was that bad examples are easily followed by weaker Christians because they think good examples are difficult to follow. Third, discipline would encourage the sinner to repent and thus be guided back into Christ's flock.

In my view Calvin's position on church discipline can be easily identified in a number of Protestant churches in Zambia, and it has continued to gain ground in Africa. For instance, in Zambia many Protestant churches still discipline Christians by excluding them from the Lord's Supper because of errors they made. In many ways the Protestant churches in Zambia practice and exercise church discipline as in the sixteenth century. In 2001, the Reformed Church of Zambia excommunicated eight ordained ministers based on their doctrinal positions on liturgy (*Post Newspaper of Zambia*, 7 March 2001). In 1993, a part of the United Church of Zambia (UCZ) youth wing broke away in dispute over doctrinal positions on liturgy (which were described as 'Pentecostal practices' and were regarded as not being Reformed practices), to become the Grace Ministries Mission Church. The launching ceremony drew 3,500 people. The UCZ leadership failed to handle this matter adequately. It was argued by UCZ leadership—by the Moderator of the UCZ—that the new ideas about worship about which the UCZ youth wing was talking were contrary to the teaching of the Bible. He said this in justifying the church's position on excommunicating the UCZ youths (see Gifford 1998, 368). I, however, think that there is need to bring harmony to the tension between those who want traditional forms of worship and those (often younger people) who want a more Pentecostal worship style.

### 3.5 *Replica of Scottish church discipline*

The worst types of offenses disciplined in the Church of Scotland were: religious dissent or unorthodox practice, Sabbath breach, disobedience to the church (*kirk*), absence from Holy Communion or sermons, quarrels, magic, witchcraft, and murder. Also disciplinable were marriage offenses such as entering marriage secretly without permission of the minister or civil magistrate (see Cameron 1972, 44). Clandestine (secret) marriages were forbidden, and divorces were only allowed in the case of adultery. Along with that, sexual offenses/sins like fornication, whoredom and adultery were punishable according to the Levitical law of Scripture.

These offenses were the basis for church discipline in Scotland. Although they were not specified in the first *Book of Discipline* or second *Book of Discipline*, they were accepted as punishable offenses during the sixteenth century. When the Scottish missionaries came to Zambia in the nineteenth century, they brought with them the sixteenth-century kind of church discipline, the punishable offenses of which can be still be identified in Zambia today. Although the Scottish missionaries are no longer in charge of the missionary churches in Zambia, their missionary churches still continue sixteenth-century practices.

Some of these punishable offenses are even found in the Zambia Criminal Penal Code (ZCPC), which owes its origin to England during the nineteenth century. It was a model for the new ZCPC that was used in colonies. These offenses came to be included in the ZCPC through the influence of European missionaries, including the Scottish missionaries. The arrival of these missionaries in Zambia coincided with British colonial rule in Zambia. To a large extent the move to control the moral life of the Zambian people was initiated by both the British colonial government and the European missionaries, who worked together to formulate the punishable offenses. According to Verstraelen-Gilhuis, the European missionaries did not like some African practices because they were unchristian (Verstraelen-Gilhuis 1982, 77). For example Zambian traditional dances, drunkenness, and marriage ceremonies without consent of the church and the civil magistrate were prohibited both by the church and by state law (ZCPC, Chapter 87). During the colonial regime the state-church relationship in Zambia was very close, because the missionaries were providing social services like education and health services, with the state giving education grants.

### 3.6 *Church discipline and the case of Alice Mulenga Linshina*

The type of church that came to Zambia was a divided church often following the traditions of the missionary 'mother churches'. This brought about a clash with the African concept of faith and practice, as it conflicted with African traditional religion. The new religious and political context in Zambia gave rise to African nationalism as well as a religious upheaval leading to the birth of African Independent churches such as the Lumpa Church of Zambia (Lumpa was a home village of Alice Mulenga Linshina). Lumpa Church was started by Alice Mulenga Linshina (1924–1978). She was an illiterate woman who, without any formal theological training, managed to come up with a powerful religious overhaul. She was raised as a Presbyterian under the Church of Scotland mission. She was expelled from the church because of her effort to inculturate the gospel. She was excommunicated by the Presbyterian Church who accused her of heresy (see Ipenburg 1992, 240). Lumpa Church shunned the sacrament of Holy Communion because it was viewed as an ancestral rite on account of the theme of memorial attached to the Eucharistic rite. The reason for the problem was that the earlier missionary never considered inculturation and innovative approaches in mission (see Anderson 2001, 11f.).

Lumpa Church, through the religious innovations and teachings of Alice Lenshina, created an alternative enclave of religious authority and power (see Chidester 1992, 113), which did not fully recognise the authority of both the state and mission church. At first, both political and religious authorities played down the influence of the Lumpa Church, thinking that it would fade away and disappear. The Lumpa Church became popular with the people and started to undermine the authority of the mission churches and the desires of nationalist government of President Kenneth Kaunda. This church was banned after independence in 1964 due to the fact that the church had assumed a political orientation and character by refusing to pay taxes and by fortifying its facility so that the government could not enter. Followers of Alice Linshina gathered in Lumpa villages where they became a political body of their own, a sort of independent theocratic peasant state. When Zambia achieved its independence in 1964, this independent theocratic state was perceived as a threat. Many people were killed in the process of the government's attempt to ban them (see Msiska 2010, 60). Her ministry was not easy. She spent most of her life in detention in various isolated places in Zambia. Three years prior to her death she was released from detention and placed under house arrest (see Kondolo 2011, 19–23).

### 3.7 *Church discipline and the case of Emilio Mulolani*

Another African-initiated church was the Sacred Heart of Jesus. It was started by an ex-seminarian of the Roman Catholic Church in Zambia named Emilio Mulolani. The Roman Catholic Church excommunicated him in 1957 because he led the secession that formed the Catholic Church of the Sacred Heart (see Garvey 1994, 165–167). The focus of the church was on the holiness of the church. This church attracted many Africans due to its level of inculturation in the preaching of the gospel. Most of the European missionaries rejected Mulolani's contribution because he was a layperson and they questioned his theology (see Garvey 1994, 16). They condemned him as a heretic. He left Zambia for Southern Rhodesia (Zimbabwe) and South Africa. There in South Africa and Zimbabwe he "witnessed deep-seated racism and apartheid policies of Whites and he became persuaded that Africans have to find their own way towards theology" (Garvey 1994, 16f.). To his point I would add that the formation of African Independent churches is a result of churches' need to be contextual and relevant.

An alternative to forming new, independent churches in response to problems associated with church discipline—especially in Zambia—is to contextualize the older church polity. What is disappointing is that the large number of Africa Independent churches have not received the attention they deserve from the people. The people are not keen to join these churches because they assume that such efforts to inculturate church practices imply departure from true theology.

### 3.8 *Provisional assessment*

Many cases of church discipline in Zambia are extreme, and acts of suppression by the churches. They are extreme and acts of suppression because every person has the right to air his or her grievances, yet some churches do not give opportunity for Christians to defend themselves. Further, some church members are disciplined without having been taught the purpose of discipline. What is worse, some Christians are disciplined on the basis of rumors. As if that is not enough, discipline to some extent has been misunderstood as punishment only. In one way or the other, according to the Apostle Paul the church is the "pillar and foundation of the truth" (1 Tim. 3:15), but in cases like these the church does not reflect justice and fairness. Such outrageous activities in the church, which is the body of Christ, show that church polity and the practice of ecclesiastical discipline do not reflect reality in Zambia. Many mistakes are made in processes of handling church discipline. In fact, church officers are not always aware they are making mistakes.

The increase in the twentieth century of a biblical perspective on church discipline is only true of formal, global conversations, not of individual, particular congregations in Zambia: there we understand discipline to be a replica of the European missionary churches. In reality in Zambia church discipline tends to be used, wrongly, to show that church officers have authority or power. Duncan notes that in Zambia church discipline is used for oppression of church members instead of being used for restoration, reconciliation and reintegration into Christian fellowship (Duncan 2010, 4, 7).

### 3.9 *Is it the church or civil magistrate that has to handle ecclesiastical discipline?*

Church discipline has gone through a long process of development to reach the way it is now practiced in Zambia. The need for church discipline can be identified from the sixteenth century. There we see three options for church discipline. First, ecclesiastical discipline can be separated from the responsibilities of the civil magistrate, as supported by Luther and Bucer. Second, there were those like Zwingli and Bullinger who saw no problem with the civil magistrate handling ecclesiastical disciplinary matters. Third, there can be a combination of the church and the civil magistrate in handling ecclesiastical discipline—a position favored by Calvin and John Knox. In Protestant churches in Zambia we recognize two of these views: both the independence of ecclesiastical discipline from the civil magistrate and the civil magistrate handling ecclesiastical matters.

John Knox's campaign to put church discipline on the same footing as preaching and sacraments shows how important this matter was for the Church of Scotland, and most of the Presbyterian churches have followed this position.

### 3.10 *Reconstruction of procedures of church discipline*

Matters of ecclesiastical discipline have developed through different contexts and with different applications as influenced by different political and ecclesiastical situations. The question is how church discipline can reflect the exigency of Zambian reality. What will this mean for the church order? Of course, this requires the contextualization of church polity.

Coertzen suggests that the church order should contain the procedures of church discipline which help the sinner to be aware of sin rather than to be threatened as in civil law. In the latter case, church discipline loses its pastoral character (see Coertzen 1998, 83). In my view church discipline is the work of Christ and the function of the church. The rules of church disciplinary procedures should help to protect the rights of members. It is easy to see that rules of church disciplinary procedures are difficult to interpret and implement. This calls for theological and juridical reflection. Implementation of church discipline is not always easy. Therefore, the churches require specialized people or education in this area to implement church discipline.

### 3.11 *Ideal interpretation of church discipline*

At the time of the Reformation church discipline was regarded as a mark of true church. It was intended that people should be living the preached gospel. According to Forrester the structure of church discipline then turned into narrow, rigid, oppressive instruments of scrupulous social control rather than guidelines for freedom in fellowship. This has the potential to blind the church to the need for restructuring church discipline in any church (see Forrester 1997, 88–90). Further, Forrester defines church discipline as learning; a process of discipline of individual and community to learn and grow in faithfulness. Discipline is personal, necessary for the disciple: is about following a person rather than obeying rules or fearing to break rules that may be a focus for penalty. He writes, "discipline should bring people into fellowship and hold them back into fellowship" (Forrester 1997, 89). Discipline should help people maintain and restore relationships, in order to grow and develop.

Barth's position is that the church cannot do anything to make itself holy, because holiness is from Jesus Christ who is the Head of the church. In one way or the other, this has implications with regard to the practice of ecclesiastical discipline. Barth suggests that the church cannot control a person with regard to his or her bad actions or behavior. Barth further argues that the church cannot exclude or separate someone who is unholy (Barth 1967, 67f.). We need to rise to the true meaning of church discipline by understanding the nature of sin in the church.

Koffeman says that the issue of the nature of sin is still an unresolved question in the bilateral dialogue between the Roman Catholic and Reformed traditions: is it possible to speak of sin in the church? He suggests that the church should take seriously the faithfulness of God because it is stronger than the unfaithfulness of Christians (see Koffeman 1998, 79–99). In fact, God's faithfulness is stronger than errors and resistances to the Word of God. The traditional Reformed view on the issue of sin is that sin affects the visible church and that the church may sin. Radical forgiveness of sin as a decisive event between God and human is lacking in the ecclesiological concept of constitutions and church orders (Ibid.).

Here Duncan criticizes the European missionaries, arguing that they were not sensitive in handling cases of discipline. He identifies that in mission education the missionaries imposed a hierarchical and authoritarian approach to discipline. Departing from the norm of good forms of discipline, they promoted oppressive forms of discipline. This was very different from African traditional forms of discipline, where counsel was given in order to produce mature members of society, and where sanction was reserved for completely unruly people (see Duncan 2003, 386). I agree with this, but I try to come to the matter from a different, yet compatible perspective, i.e. that church discipline should not be oppressive and should not be a way of controlling the moral behavior of the Christians.

### 4. *Second case study: church unity*

Ecclesiastical documentation points out that the so called 'church union in Zambia' remained inferior to the way it should have been. The church union is still far from complete in Zambia, since the UCZ does not reflect the ecclesial reality of Zambia. In fact, the union was imposed on Zambians by European missionaries.

#### 4.1 *Meaning of church unity*

Unity may be defined as *the state of being in agreement, or many parts of the whole being neatly together*. Unity of the church goes beyond agreement or simply fitting together. Church unity is the state of being united as a church or forming a whole. Church unity means oneness of the church, which is the ecumenical task to make unity visible and effective. This is organic unity which is realized in the coming together of previously independent churches into one, united church. It is the fellowship between churches indicating that churches are on their way from division to unity. This fellowship is expressed in relationships with one another, forms of common prayer, worship, convergence on dividing theological differences, and common witness and service. Unity is the existing fellowship which is either a more direct expression of oneness or consists of steps towards it. For example, churches of the same confession in a particular country have united. Different denominations have come together to form united churches like, for example, the UCZ.

Unity of the church is a major biblical theme and belongs to the essence of the church as a sign of the kingdom and of God. Unity of the church is well-known as one of the four so-called confessed marks of the church: 'one, holy, catholic and apostolic'. It is not just something incidental to the nature of the church; it belongs essentially to its very being, its integrity and identity. This needs to be highly appreciated and recognized.

#### 4.2 *Do we continue to be divided and for how long?*

The growing problem is that amidst ecclesiastical division and disunity, the church in Zambia has seen great numerical growth as people are given a variety of traditions to choose from. In as much as the church continues to grow as a divided force one asks the question: Do we continue to be divided and for how long? Why is church union still far from complete in Zambia? To what extent can we say that the union of the UCZ reflects the reality of Zambia? Why did many churches pull out of the church union negotiations in Zambia? Why are there are no serious negotiations over church union in Zambia? These are very important questions in this discussion.

4.3 *Background of the United Church of Zambia*

Gifford says that the UCZ is the incredible ecumenical undertaking that is more or less exceptional in Africa. It began in the Copperbelt, where Christians moving to the mines found no church to receive them and a variety of Protestant churches formed the Union Church of Copperbelt. In 1965 the new name was adopted—United Church of Zambia—along with the new constitution (see Gifford 1998, 183). Chuba states that the first step in the direction of greater church union was taken on the basis of a common denominational tradition. This resulted in various missionary societies joining to form an organizational and organic union church (see Chuba 2005, 128–135). The first step was taken in 1945, when three churches (the Church of Central Africa Presbyterian, the Church Union in the Copperbelt and the London Missionary Society) properly accomplished the formation of the Church of Central Africa in Rhodesia. It took another twenty years before a wider proposal for church union was accomplished. Another reason which led to church union was that after the Second World War there was an emphasis on making the churches multiracial rather than *Bantu* (Africans or Black people) or native churches.

Three months after national independence on 16 January 1965 (see Luig 1997, 144), the UCZ was formed. The churches which united on this day are the following:

i. The Church of Central Africa in Rhodesia, which was itself the union of the Church of Scotland and London Missionary Society churches, together with the Union Church of Copperbelt. These worked in the Luapula, Northern and Copperbelt provinces.
ii. The congregations of the Copperbelt Free Church Council (see Pons 1982, 4). These worked in the Copperbelt province.
iii. The Methodist Church (formed by the Methodist Missionary Society of Britain). These worked in the Central and Southern provinces.
v. The Church of Barotseland (formed by the Paris Evangelical Missionary Society of France and Switzerland). These worked in the Western province (see Luig 1997, 223).

### 4.4 *Interpretations of the church union*

The implications of the union were open to interpretation. To begin with, it was interpreted as the end of the colonial era, even in the church. The first President of Zambia, Kenneth Kaunda, always bemoaned the way churches had imported European divisions into Zambia; therefore, Kaunda approved the union. What is more, Kaunda was present during the inauguration of the UCZ to show support for the union (see Luig 1997, 223). Freston explains that the formation of the UCZ corresponded with President Kaunda's call to overcome imported denominations; to the political 'One Zambia, One Nation' the religious 'One Church' should correspond. The desire for ecclesiastical unity was thus mixed with desire to please the new state. The government did not want an excess of self-directed religious groups (see Freston 2004, 154–156).

According to Luig, the formation of the UCZ was predominantly attained by European missionaries. Even though the initiative of the independent and viable 'native church' had been a high ideal among the European missionaries from the beginning, only little steps forward were made until the 1950s (see Luig 1997, 221–226). He also argues that there was little clarity on the missionaries' part about the nature that a self-governing, self-supporting and self-propagating church would take, although the post-war years after the Second World War saw an increased eagerness and a greater point of reference toward ecumenical cooperation. As a result, an idea of overcoming the denominational divisions by the creation of an inter-denominational African church gained impetus (see Luig 1997, 221–226). True enough; the basis of the union was weak, because it was based on evangelistic concern and its focus was to overcome confessional differences among the missionary churches.

My argument cuts deeper: the scope of church unity after independence in Zambia corresponded with the political feelings among Africans who believed in national unity, but it is not clear if the African Christians understood the importance of this union of churches because the negotiations towards church union were done by European missionaries (see Verstraelen-Gilhuis 1982, 332). To put this in context, the African Christians came to be aware of the implications of the union for example when church members from the Methodist Church were seen going to UCZ congregations (see Luig 1997, 223). To a large extent the union was a purely European missionary initiative and its vision was not clear for the future of the church in Zambia because it was based on 'non-conformism', i.e. on a refusal to conform to or follow that particular form of governance, belief and church order (see Sundler and Steed 2000, 792). Probably this explains why other Protestant missionary churches did not join the union. Reasons why the South African General Mission, the Plymouth Brethren (Christian Mission in Many

Lands), the Baptist Church and the African Reformed Church did not join were: differences in church polity, language issues, interpretation of church procedures, and racial issues (Ibid.).

Apart from that, the church order that was formulated for UCZ was one-sided: it concentrated on the organizational side of the church rather than on the confessional side of the church. Its main concern was to make a church order for maintaining order in the church and for governance in the church (see Bolink 1967, 366–399). This church order was first prepared in 1947 by Rev. D.K. Francis and it went through six revisions before it was adopted in 1965 (see Bolink 1967, 270–279). It is clear that this church order was made by the European missionaries because the African Christians were not vocal in the negotiations of the union of UCZ and most of them had no knowledge of church polity. In my view this church order was imposed on the African Christians (see also Verstraelen-Gilhuis 1982, 332).

Rev. D.K. Francis, architect of the UCZ church order, made it in such a way that it was open to possibilities of reunion with other Protestants that did not join the union (see Bolink 1967, 380). Since the formation of the UCZ some strides have been made by different Protestant churches toward church union. But not much work has been done by the UCZ to dialogue either with those of traditions different from its tradition or with those churches that demurred from discussions on church union before 1965. At the same time, the discussion about church union has not been clear in the councils of the UCZ, in spite of the fact that its church order states: "The United Church affirms it to be the will of our Lord Jesus Christ that all who believe in him should live together in unity, and acknowledges itself thereby committed to furthering the union of all Christian Churches in Zambia which confess the true faith and follow sound traditions of government, worship, and discipline of the Church" (see *Rules and Regulations of United Church of Zambia* 1994, 1f.).

There has been little effort toward furthering the union of all Christian churches in Zambia by the UCZ, contrary to the clause in the UCZ church order. This shows that there is need to reconstruct the church polity so that it reflects the Zambian reality.

### 4.5 *Fruitful encounter with inherited missionary past.*

Chilekwa argues that "the UCZ has been a passive recipient of much of its missionary inheritance and has lacked the confidence to revisit its received beliefs and practices" (Chilekwa 1998, 93). This is not only a theological weakness. It also shows many other features of theology in Zambia. Zambia needs highly qualified theologians who can produce new models. In order to achieve that, the theologians need to be equipped with tools and creative personnel necessary to have active and fruitful encounter with the inherited missionary past.

### 5. *Toward the reconstruction of church polity*

To begin with, church polity has a responsibility to address this problem of a lack of church union, since the model to enhance church union in Zambia was imposed by foreign partners or by the larger ecumenical community. What is significant at this stage, however, is neither the initiator of unity nor the number of failures that have been recorded. What is important is the determination to imbue unity with a renewed content and fresh objectives, by reconstructing church polity in a contextual way.

It must be realized that the reconstruction of church polity in Zambia will not be built by foreign resources or foreign experts. It will flourish on the basis of the inexhaustible spiritual resources with which God has enriched Zambia from time immemorial. These are the resources that Zambian Christians must discover together, submitting them to the service of the gospel, providing the dynamic by which the current crisis can be overcome and the Zambian Christian dream of reconstructing church polity fulfilled. According to Isichel, the present-day Christian intellectuals in Africa are self-absorbed with inculturation and the search for identity: "This in part is a reaction against white racism in the past, and it is likely that inculturation from above is less effective than the prophetic churches' inculturation from below" (Isichel 1995, 3). She also clarifies that, because of a quest for autonomy by the prophetic churches that are self-supporting, there have been calls for a moratorium on external aid. To some people the quest for inculturation has become a form of false consciousness because of poverty (see Ibid.). It is understandable that a form of false consciousness conceals existing efforts and initiatives aimed at building a faith that is genuinely Christian and authentically African. False consciousness is an ideology that blinds people to their best interest. It is an imposed form of contextualization of the Christian faith. It does not aim at helping people to be influenced by Christian faith in the context of their culture.

According to Verstraelen-Gilhuis, making a new church order would be profitable because in the past there have been Zambian initiatives more or less to develop better models for the handling of church matters (see Verstraelen-Gilhuis 1982, 336). It is necessary to contextualize church polity because as a theological discipline church polity must be relevant to its particular context. Bevans explains that the contextualization of theology is about understanding Christian faith in terms of a particular context. And he locates contextualization as part of the very nature of theology itself. He suggests that contextualization should be made possible. He adds that the time is past when we could speak of unchanging theology. He further contends that we should speak of theology that makes sense at a certain place and in a certain time. For Bevans contextual theology "is a way of doing theology in which one takes into account: the spirit and message of the gospel; the tradition of Christian people; the culture in which one is theologizing; and social change in culture, whether brought about by western technological processes or grass-roots for equality, justice, and liberation" (Bevans 1991, 232).

For Coertzen a church order should be made for a particular church and for a particular time. When making a church order, experts should search for scriptural principles that can help to make a good church order (see Coertzen 1998, 48–53). He also contends that in formulating a church order different literatures should be consulted—literatures such as works on natural law and positive law as well as the confession of faith and other historical documents like minutes and resolutions. At the same time the church fathers, who contributed to the philosophical and theological development of the church polity, should be consulted. When a church order has been formulated, it should be theologically accountable. And it should acknowledge that Jesus Christ is the Head of the church (see Coertzen 2004, 125–130).

According to Verstraelen, the Second Vatican Council serves as a basis for the re-evaluation of the missionary movement, and for the development of a variety of contextual theologies that add greater value to the demand for a shift within the church away from its colonial, racial and dependent roots towards localization and self-reliance (see Verstraelen 1975, 100–125). Again, the Second Vatican Council had a far-reaching impact on the understanding of a participatory ecclesiology of communion. It has expanded the sense of ministry that emerged as a central feature for a local church, particularly in the processes of transition and of reformulating its presence and role in a society, while addressing issues such as ecumenism, education, social justice, communications, liturgy, inculturation, ministerial training and theology. All of these need study from the perspective of the local context.

### *6. Conclusion*

In a word, the church order needs to be contextualized in order to serve its purpose in the practice of church polity. What is needed for Zambia is a model for the reconstruction of church polity, a kind of reconstruction that focuses on training church members and church officers to know the principles and theories of church polity, in order to develop a certain kind of church order for Zambia. At the same time a new church order will create many possibilities for the Protestant churches in Zambia. First, the face of the Protestant churches will change in Zambia. Second, their identity will be clearly defined in the church order. Third, they will be able to develop positions that are in line with their church order in regard to relations with the state. Fourth, it will be easy to revise the church order when the need arises. If the churches in Zambia can have their own homemade church order that speaks directly into the Zambian situation, this will be an important step in area of church polity.

It is clear that the reconstruction of church polity takes the particular context seriously. For that reason, such a reconstruction opens up the possibility of having a new church order. In fact, it means changing the church order to fit the Zambia situation. The reconstruction of church polity has far-reaching benefits for people, as they become able to experience the Christian faith in the context of their culture. Successful reconstruction of church polity occurs when the church that has been planted ceases to be perceived as foreign import, and people own it as theirs (see Shorter 1988, 11).

Given the above points, reconstruction goes beyond including different contexts. It emphasizes the traditional three 'selfs': self-government, self-propagation and self-support. According to Henry Venn (1796–1873), the church is judged to be indigenous if it has the three selfs (see Anderson 1999, 698). Ott adds self-theologizing as the fourth self. Self-theologizing leads to local theologies that are in the hands of the local community (see Ott 2001, 124). It is like the biblical model of incarnation. Incarnation means that Jesus Christ was born in a particular context, which implies that the gospel is like a seed that is planted within a context. It is to be left to grow.

One would expect a full-fledged ecclesiology to be reflected in church polity, as the church is missional by its very nature and its polity expresses the identity and the nature of the church. This is one of the challenges facing the churches in Zambia. In the end, the direction that church polity can take in Zambia is to adjust the missionary model in order to make a new model. The questions for further research include: How can church polity reflect the reality of Zambia? What will this mean for the church order? And what are the implications of this contextual church polity for ecclesiology?

## *Abbreviations and bibliography*

UZC: United Church of Zambia.

ZCPC: Constitution of Zambia. Criminal Penal Code.

Anderson, Allan. 2001. African Reformation: Africa Initiated Christianity in the 20th Century. Asmara: Africa Word Press.

Anderson, Gerald H. 1999. Biographical Dictionary of Christian Missions, Grand Rapids: Eerdmans.

Barth, Karl. 1967. Church Dogmatics. Vol.4/1. transl. G.W. Bromiley. Edinburgh: Clark.

Baxter, Richard. 2000. The Reformed Pastor. Edited by Jay P. Green. Lafayette: Sovereign Grace Trust Fund.

Bevans, Stephen B. 1991. Methods of Contextual Theology. Faith and Culture Series. New York: Orbis Books.

Bolink, Peter. 1967. Towards Church Union in Zambia: A Study of Missionary Co-operation and Church Union Efforts in Central-Africa. Franeker: Wever.

Brinkman, Martien E., and Henk P.J. Witte (eds). 1998. From Roots to Fruits. European Studies of the World Alliance of Reformed Churches 3. Geneva: WARC.

Cameron, James K. 1972. First Book of Discipline: With Introduction and Commentary. Edinburgh: St. Andrews Press.

Chidester, David. 1992. Religions of South Africa. London: Routledge.

Childress, James F., and John Macquarrie (eds). 1986. A New Dictionary for Christian Ethics. London: SCM.

Chilekwa, Mwape. 1998. The United Church of Zambia 1965–1995: A Critical Exploration of History, Faith and Practice of United Church, with Suggestions for the Future Agenda. Master's Thesis. School of Humanities. Oxford: Westminster College.

Chuba, Bwalya S. 2005. A History of Early Christian Missions and Church Unity in Zambia. Ndola: Mission Press.

Coertzen, Pieter. 1998. Church and Order: A Reformed Perspective. Leuven: Peeters.

Coertzen, Pieter. 2004. Decently and in Order: A Theological Reflection on the Order for, and the Order in, the Church. Leuven: Peeters.

Duncan, Graham A. 2003. Lovedale: Coercive Agency, Power and Resistance in Mission Education. Pietermaritzburg: Cluster Publications.

Duncan, Graham A. 2010. Church Discipline: Semper Reformanda in Reformation perspective. In: HTS Teologiese Studies/Theological Studies, Vol. 66(2010)/1, 6 pages. doi: 10.4102/hts.v66i1.789.

Forrester, Duncan B. 1997. The True Church and Morality: Reflections on Ecclesiology and Ethics. Geneva: WCC.

Freston, Paul. 2004. Evangelicals and Politics in Asia, Africa, Latin America. Cambridge: Cambridge University Press.

Gifford, Paul. 1998. African Christianity: Its Public Role. Bloomington: Indiana University Press.

Garvey, Brian. 1994. Bemba Church: Religious and Social Change in South Central Africa, 1892–1964. Leiden: Brill.

Graham, Michael F. 1996. The Uses of Reform: 'Godly Discipline' and Popular Behaviour in and Beyond, 1560–1610. Vol. 58. Leiden: Brill.

Ipenburg, At N. 1992. 'All God People': Development of Lubwa Mission, Chinsali Zambia, 1905–1967. Frankfurt: Peter Lang.

Isichel, Elisabeth. 1995. A History of Africa Christianity in Africa: From Antiquity to the Present. Grand Rapids: Eerdmans.

Koffeman, Leo J. 1998. The Nature of Sin in the Church. In: Brinkman and Witte 1998, 79–99.

Koffeman, Leo J. 2009. Het goed recht van de kerk: Een theologische inleiding op het kerkrecht. Kampen: Kok.

Kondolo, Kapembwa. 2011. The Spread of the African Independent Churches. Berlin: Lambert Academic Publishing.

Luig, Ulrich. 1997. Conversion as a Social Process: A History of Missionary Christianity among the Valley Tonga, Zambia. London: Transaction Publishers.

Macquarrie, John (ed.). 1967. A Dictionary of Christian Ethics. London: SCM.

Msiska, Godfrey. 2010. Towards Inculturation of Church Polity in Zambia: An Assessment based on a Case Study of Church discipline. Master's Thesis. Kampen: Protestant Theological University.

Oden, Thomas C. 1983. Pastoral theology: Essentials of ministry. London: Harper and Row.

Ott, Bernard. 2001. Beyond Fragmentation: Integration of Mission and Theological Education. Oxford: Oxford University Press.

Packer, James I. 1993. Concise theology: A Guide to Historic Christian Beliefs. Wheaton: Tyndale.

Pons, Edwin S. 1982. The Southern and Central Streams of Presbyterianism in Africa. Johannesburg: Presbyterian Church in Southern Africa.

Post Newspaper of Zambia (7th March 2001). Lusaka.

Rules and Regulations of United Church of Zambia. 1994. Constitution.

Shorter, Aylward. 1988. Towards a Theology of Inculturation. London: Geoffrey Chapman.

Sundler, Brent, and Christopher Steed. 2000. A History of the Church in Africa. Cambridge: Cambridge University Press.

Uniting Presbyterian Church in Southern Africa. Confession of Faith. 2007. Manual of Faith and Order.

Verstraelen, Frans J. 1975. An African Church in Transition; From Missionary Dependence to Mutuality in Mission: A Case Study on the Roman Catholic Church in Zambia. Tilburg: Development Research Institute.

Verstraelen-Gilhuis, Gerdien. 1982. From Dutch Mission Church to Reformed Church of Zambia: The Scope for African Leadership and Initiative in the History of a Zambian Mission Church. Franeker: Wever.

Vorster, Jakobus M. 2003. An Introduction to Reformed Church Polity. Potchefstroom: Potchefstroom Theological Publications.

Waddams, Herbert. 1967. Ascetical Theology. In: Macquarrie 1967, 18–20.

# DIACONATE AND CHURCH ORDER IN AN AGING CONTEXT

## A Case Study in Contextualizing Church Polity in The Netherlands

Hans de Waal

### *Introduction*

Contrary to popular belief, the study of church polity in changing contexts is an exciting venture. The dynamics of culture and society, which are usually ambiguous and only partially visible, provide an ongoing challenge for the church and theology in general and for church polity in particular. Contextual changes in society (cultural and socio-economic changes, developments in the relationship between church and state, democracy and populism, human rights, etc.) have an impact on the public presence of the church and the activities of the church in society, and should therefore be taken into account. Context 'co-defines' church (see Van der Ven 1993; Brouwer 2007; De Roest 2011). Regarding a particular church (see Koffeman 2009, 50), changes in context are affecting self-defining 'identity documents' such as the church order of the Protestant Church in the Netherlands (PCN). In the study of church polity and church order, the analysis of context and contextual changes is therefore just as important as the (critical) evaluation of the church's sources and traditions in this respect. It is interesting and worthwhile to examine the church order of a particular church, in this case the church order of the PCN (CO-PCN), for its (in)ability to respond to contextual changes and to integrate (aspects of) context in its 'system'. One of the major contextual changes regarding the PCN has been, and will continue to be, the process of aging. The process of double population aging, demographic and biological aging, is an example of a contextual change that affects society as well as the church. What are the consequences of aging for church polity and church order, and is the CO-PCN equipped enough to assist the church and the congregations to respond to the challenges of aging?

To make such questions of contextualization more tangible, the case study presented in this article originates from the perspective of the diaconate and diaconal studies. In diaconal studies, theological reflection on the diaconal nature of the church is juxtaposed with a preoccupation with practices of church-related societal engagement, which constantly raises the question of contextualization. In several empirical case studies regarding local reflection on diaconal policy in context, it appeared that the CO-PCN was used not only as regulative but also as an inspirational source. In particular the notion of the 'vocation of the congregation', which plays an important role in the CO-PCN, appeared to be a stimulating factor in local reflection on diaconal policy. This discovery of the relevance of church polity in diaconal practices of contextualization stimulated further reflection on what became the subject of this article. The main questions in this article are: (1) What is the importance of ageing as a major contextual change for the PCN and the diaconate? (2) What does diaconate add to the understanding of church polity in a changing context? (3) How can we interpret the articles on diaconate in the church order, in particular on the 'vocation of the congregation', regarding its potential to respond to contextual changes? The concluding paragraph contains a suggestion for discussion and a question for further research.

## 1. *Aging in the Netherlands*

The demographic process of aging is an important development in many Western countries, including the Netherlands. The total number of senior citizens (65+) is growing. Demographic aging is caused by a complex of factors, such as the baby boom after the Second World War and a decreased fertility rate in the second half of the twentieth century. Demographic aging is a proportionate change, i.e., in comparison with other categories of age, measured over a certain period of time. In the Netherlands, the percentage of senior citizens in the population has grown from 7.7% in 1950 to 15.6% in 2011. The percentage will continue to rise up to 25% in 2040 (see CBS 2012). Aging also refers to biological aging. The average life expectancy has been rising from the nineteenth century onwards, due to improved medical interventions and decreased infant mortality rates, from 70 years (men) and 72 years (women) in 1950 to 79 years (men) and 83 years (women) in 2012. These averages will continue to rise and the process of double aging (demographic and biological aging) will continue to change the character of the population of the Netherlands. There are now relatively more senior citizens than ever before, and they are becoming older than earlier generations have ever become before.

What does this mean for the organization of society? This question has been among the most debated topics in the political and societal arena, including the media, over the last ten years (see Van der Steen 2009; Knook 2008). Most attention has been drawn towards the economic consequences of aging, ranging from the sustainability of the pension system, a tight labor market in the near future and a growing need for and costs of senior health care. The social arrangements of the welfare state such as a state pension (AOW, established in 1957) and other regulations are based on an institutionalized form of intergenerational solidarity. These intergenerational arrangements have increasingly been put under pressure by the current shift in the partitioning of the age categories of the population'. Intergenerational solidarity and intergenerational contracts function best as long as they remain implicit and undisputed', critical gerontologist Thomas Scharf recently stated (see Scharf 2012). This does not imply that there is no need for social policy reform in response to the challenges of aging. The current forms of institutionalized solidarity were established in a demographic configuration where the partitioning of the age categories was different and the average life expectancy was lower. Continuation of the social arrangements in any form is therefore in need of revised political and social argumentation.

This is becoming even more urgent with the growing sentiment of unease and worry among the younger generations regarding their own (financial) future. Recently, a pragmatic political initiative by a group of young adults (20-35 years of age) attracted attention with explicitly blaming the traditional political parties for being aged ('*vergrijsd*', i.e., grey) and therefore not able to represent the interests of the younger generations (G500). The political preoccupation with the problematic economic consequences of aging in general has given aging as *termus technicus* primarily a negative association, which makes morally neutral usage of the term barely possible. To complicate matters more, it should be noted that 'senior citizens' hardly comprise a coherent category. Who are the actual (hidden) subjects of the aging statistics and debates? Due to the huge variety among senior citizens in wealth, well-being, health, lifestyle, preferences, level of societal participation, etc., the traditional socio-cultural *strata* of old age are no longer adequate in addressing senior citizens. For the senior citizens themselves, stereotypization and ageism are not imaginary problems.

Gerontologists therefore have constructed new forms of categorization regarding elderly people, e.g., those within the 'third', 'forth' or 'fifth' age. These categories are not primarily defined on the basis of (calendar) age but are applicable to senior citizens who share certain qualifiers, such as 'retired from paid labor', 'relatively healthy', 'multimorbid', etc. But the individual preferences have a key role in the 'dynamic life course' of the new senior citizens (see De Lange 2008A). In short, it appears to be quite a political, economic and social challenge for society in the Netherlands to adapt to the new configuration of an aged population. In terms of public policy, it is important for all stakeholders (national and local governments, senior citizens, civil society organizations, scientists) to participate in processes of reflection on aging, to recognize the increased senior diversity, and to broaden the perspective on aging beyond the economic 'problem narrative' (see Van der Steen 2009; De Waal 2012).

### 2. *Aging and the Protestant Church in the Netherlands*

As a contextual change with a multifaceted impact on society, aging is an interesting phenomenon for theological reflection. What could be the contribution of church and theology to the public debates on aging? Before this question can be answered, it is important to recognize the impact aging has had on the PCN itself. Certain factors can be distinguished that have intensified, and will continue to intensify, the consequences of aging among the population of church members.

Besides the double aging of the population, the church is dealing with a process of so-called 'triple aging' (see De Lange 2008B). The percentage of senior citizens (65+) among all church members was already 25% in 2011 (see PCN 2011). This is especially due to the growing absence of younger generations among church members and churchgoers (see Becker and De Hart 2006, 95). The phenomenon of 'dejuvenation' of church membership is one of the aspects of the process of secularization in the context of the Netherlands (as far as traditional and institutionalized religion is concerned) and is not likely to change in the coming decades. From a sociological perspective, this process can also be qualified as a form of 'institutional aging' which has parallels in other traditional membership organizations such as political parties and trade unions. The younger generations that are still affiliated with the church tend to have a different type (a 'light version') of commitment in terms of church attendance, voluntary involvement and financial support. It is clear that a reference to the process of population aging is not sufficient to explain the 'seniorized' features of the Protestant Church. Aging nonetheless has become a decisive characteristic of this particular church.

It is interesting to analyze whether or not aging is also recognized as such in current church policy documents. Parallel to most of the societal debates on aging, in which the problematic (predominantly economic) consequences of aging prevail, aging within the church is widely considered to be a negative or even fatal development. Aging is associated with a decrease in voluntary work, with the problematic succession of ministers, elders and deacons, with a decrease in church income, with diminished vitality and with church closure or extinction (see De Waal 2011,28). Most of these issues are directly related to the preferences and new types of church commitment of the younger generations. Regarding these issues, it is important to recognize and appreciate the participation and commitment of senior citizens within the church, which is above the average. But in either way, the contextual development of (triple) aging is deeply affecting this particular church in appearance (membership rate, membership age, means), stature and content (member diversity, activities, identity). In the following sections I will explore how a diaconal perspective on an aging church in an aging society could exemplify a relevant process of church polity reflection in a changing context.

*3. A diaconal perspective on aging and the contextualization of church polity*

Within the congregations and the regional and national organization(s) of the Protestant Church, the reflection on aging and the development of relevant policy and activities on this subject is widely considered to be a part of the diaconate of the church. On a local level, congregations traditionally have certain activities for the senior church members, ranging from individual pastoral care, home visits and group activities to material assistance, church transportation service and recreational trips. On a policy level there has been, on a small scale, critical diaconal reflection on the contextual development of aging (see De Waal 2012). This reflection covers the issues of population aging, church aging and the increased variety among senior citizens. For example, a national diaconal working group formulated the following statement in a recent policy document: "On the one hand, there are senior citizens who deserve care and attention. Senior citizens can be vulnerable. The government stimulates senior citizens to remain self-reliant for as long as possible. But due to the loss of partner and family, senior citizens run a risk of social isolation. On the other hand, there is a growing number of senior citizens who are vital and not in need of birthday flowers or annual Christmas gifts. They prefer to share their experience and wisdom with church and society" (KIA 2009).

The contribution of diaconal studies to the contextualization of church polity starts with the recognition of the empirical practices of context analysis in the diaconate. Theological reflection on this topic needs to be grounded in current policy practices in order to avoid becoming a free-floating theoretical exercise. Second, it is neither a coincidence nor a mere organizational circumstance that concern for analysis of context has been part of the diaconate within the church. Diaconate and diaconal work are often considered to be the outward-looking part of the church. Societal developments that are having an impact on social wellbeing—in this case the wellbeing of senior citizens—attract the attention of deacons (office-bearers) and diaconal workers (professionals in diaconal service). Deacons are performing 'border traffic' between 'inside' and 'outside' the church (see Houtepen 2004, 378). They engage themselves with society and stimulate the congregations to do the same. Third, this diaconal 'border traffic' has a preoccupation with those people who are dwelling in the margins of society: the poor, the ill, the neglected, the people who are having a hard time and who cannot live up to the demands of society (physically, financially, mentally or otherwise). In this respect, the iconic biblical stories of the Good Samaritan (Luke 10: 25–37) and the Works of Mercy (Matt. 25:35–45) are often cited as a major source of diaconal inspiration and motivation.

A diaconal contribution to the analysis of aging has to begin with discerning the groups of people who are involved. On what grounds would senior citizens require diaconal attention and become (or remain) a diaconal 'profit group'? Being a senior in itself does not qualify one as being marginalized, poor and in need of support. The example of diaconal policy reflection cited above clearly recognizes the diversity among senior citizens. Processes of marginalization, stereotypization and anonymization however are among the current struggles certain senior citizens are facing. The depiction of aging as a negative development in society and church should lead to (diaconal) protests, and so it does. It has occurred that church policy makers expressed their worries regarding the future sustainability of congregations by, paradoxically, complaining about the fact that the only generations that are actually coming to church are senior citizens. They were (implicitly and unwillingly, but nonetheless) blaming the victim. Those who are involved in the reflection on diaconal policy and diaconal work with senior citizens are detecting the implicit aggression in this line of argumentation. The 'good right' of senior citizens and senior church members needs to be advocated for.

There is more to say about aging than the one-sided 'story of decline', especially within the church: thankfulness, a sense of wonder, a challenge to utilize senior wisdom and stimulate senior participation, the need to recognize the particularity of this church and these congregations with these people. In terms of policy, this could lead to an affirmative approach towards senior volunteers, who are often willing to participate on their own terms and according to their own preferences and qualities. The concept of intergenerational solidarity could be renewed as a means to share life experiences, faith and spiritual wisdom between the generations (see Eurich et al. 2008). This could eventually contribute to the required reinvention of the concept of intergenerational solidarity in society, mentioned earlier.

### *4. Diaconate and church polity in the Protestant Church in the Netherlands*

In protestant theology and in the PCN, the term 'diaconate' is used to describe both diaconal practices and diaconal theology. In definitions of diaconate one usually finds a reference to the variety of (empirical) diaconal work in combination with a reference to normative images and ideals at which these diaconal practices are aimed. For example, a recent ecumenical definition stated: "Diaconate is the acting of churches and other gospel-inspired groups and movements aimed at the prevention, elimination, reduction or the co-endurance of suffering and socio-cultural needs of individuals and groups of people, and at the creation of just relationships within church and society" (Crijns et al. 2011, 392).

In its self-description diaconate tends to highlight its practical and ideal-typical nature. As a result, the relationship between diaconate and church polity remains implicit. This relationship however is solid and multifaceted. We can distinguish at least three aspects.

First, there is the organizational aspect. The existence of the organized diaconate in the Netherlands is the result of effective church polity. Diaconate stems from the office of deacon, which has been a part of the Calvinist ecclesiological tradition of the threefold equal office of minister, elder and deacon (see Van der Borght 2000, 145). Each congregation has a separate diaconal counsel (*diaconie*) which is among other things concerned with the management of diaconal assets and with the recruitment of deacons and diaconal volunteers. The importance of Calvin for the 'rediscovery' of the diaconal function of the church can hardly be exaggerated. The function of the deacon, who had become a liturgical assistant in the church in the middle ages, was redefined by Calvin in terms of the management of the alms for poor relief and the caretaking of the poor and the ill (see McKee 1984; Noordegraaf 2009). The institutionalization of the office of deacon by Calvin on the basis of an exegesis of Acts of the Apostles 6:1-7 was a 'blessing in disguise' according to Berkhof (see Berkhof 1990, 366). Calvin's exegesis may be questionable or even wrong (there is no mentioning of *diakonoi* in Acts) but his intuition of the 'preferential option for the poor' in the Kingdom of God has met broad approval. Exegetical and etymological research in recent years on the meaning of *diakonia* and the *diakonos* in the New Testament has surprisingly led to a reassessment of the 'official' nature of the *diakonos* in the ancient Greek world, who is now understood to have been a representative and a 'go-between' between parties (see Collins 1990; Koet 2011).

A second aspect of the relationship between diaconate and church polity is the inspiring and stimulating potential of the CO-PCN for diaconal practices. As was mentioned in the introduction, the CO-PCN appears to be a relevant factor in the creation of local diaconal policy. As valid church law, the rules and regulations of the ordinances regarding the office of deacon are of course directly influencing local diaconal practices, but especially the theological ('confessing') paragraphs in the church order on diaconate are of interest here. In the CO-PCN, diaconate is connected to what the church is understood to be in its essence. Diaconate shares in the 'vocation of church and congregation'. This perspective of 'vocation' on diaconate, which we I will discuss in the following paragraphs, highlights the theological potential of church polity for diaconal work. A vast number of local diaconal policy plans are citing, and interpreting, the 'vocational' paragraphs of the CO-PCN as a starting point for reflection on diaconate in context. Two (anonymized) examples:

In the CO-PCN one finds paragraphs that refer to diaconal vocation. This diaconal vocation is meant to be understood on a congregational level. All members are involved. The diaconal vocation is not to be limited to the congregation, but stretches worldwide (Local diaconal policy plan 1, 2011). The *diaconie* is of the opinion that it is important for the congregation to realize its diaconal vocation. The *diaconie* should reflect on the ways in which it can stimulate the congregation to become (more) aware of its diaconal vocation. New diaconal initiatives could be stimulated by the establishment of small working groups (Local diaconal policy plan 2, 2010–2013).

A third aspect of the relationship between diaconate and church polity does not so much originate from the empirical diaconal practices but rather from the theological reflection on the concept of *reciprocity* between diaconate and church polity and between church and society. The two examples of local policy reflection quoted above reveal the (direct and indirect) influence of the church order on what can be considered forms of 'local theology'. It is an interesting question to ask whether or not diaconate is, or could be, utilized in return in processes of church polity contextualization. In accordance with the aforementioned characterization of diaconate as 'border traffic' between the church and society, diaconate can be recognized as having experience and expertise in the analysis of context (see Noordegraaf and Witte-Rang 2011). Furthermore, the diaconal sensitivity for the people in the margins of church and society is relevant for reflection on *every* aspect of a particular church in context.

From the perspective of church polity, a further operationalization of the concept of reciprocity could contribute to correcting the tendency of 'one-way traffic' in church polity regarding missionary and diaconal work, as addressed by Koffeman. He describes how the church order tends to focus on the 'work that has to be done', akin to 'the Word that has to be spread'. But then he asks: "Is there not also a movement the other way around, in which the church follows Christ in his movement towards the world, and by doing so, may gather experiences that urge it...to rethink its confession?" (Koffeman 2009, 196, translation HdW). From a diaconal perspective, the answer is certainly affirmative. At stake here is the recognition of the fact that the church not only shares, but also receives; that the church not only teaches, but also learns from others. What is needed is a practical 'vehicle' to elaborate on this type of reciprocity, embedded in the organizational structure of the church. The intermediary character of diaconate as border traffic and the deacon as 'go-between' seems to fit the job description. Deacons monitor congregational and theological reciprocity: they are the 'pathfinders' who enable the congregation to walk unknown routes, as a recent document on the diaconate by the Uniting Church in Australia stated metaphorically (UCA). During their endeavours, the deacons and other diaconal volunteers return what they are finding in (the margins of) society to the congregation in terms of encounters, experiences, knowledge, or simply intriguing questions that can be related to the self-understanding of a particular church.

### 5. *The CO-PCN on vocation and diaconate*

The prominence of the notion of 'vocation' in the CO-PCN offers a surprising perspective on the church and on diaconate in particular. It is interesting to see that the notion of vocation precedes the entire church order, which is divided in three parts: a first part regarding the *vocation* of church and congregation (art. I–VI), a second part regarding the *life* of congregation and church (art. VII–XVI), and a small third part regarding the *order* of the church itself (art. XVII–XIX). In this arrangement, diaconate not only resides in the second part but also (though very modestly) in the first, since diaconate is understood to be a part of the vocation of the congregation:

Article IV, 1
The congregation, blessed for this purpose by the Spirit, is called to ministry of the Word of God in the preaching of the Gospel and the celebration of baptism and the Lord's Supper in public worship, in the ministry of prayers, in missionary work, in diaconal work, in pastoral care, in spiritual education, and also in all other work that serves to build up the body of Christ.

In article VII, 1 and onwards diaconal work is also referred to as the 'ministry of compassion and justice'. In article X, 2 the perspective of vocation is explicitly applied regarding the diaconate of the congregation:

Article X, 2
The congregation fulfils its diaconal vocation in the church and in the world by sharing, in the ministry of compassion and justice, by the gifts bestowed on it, by helping where there is no helper and bearing witness to the justice of God where injustice occurs.

In ordinance 3-11-1, regarding the tasks of the deacons, attention is given to the vocation of the congregation in relation to its social context, and ordinance 8-3-1 further clarifies the content of the diaconal vocation:

Ordinance 3-11-1
[It is entrusted to the deacons] to stimulate the congregation to fulfil its diaconal vocation...to take or to support initiatives that promote societal well-being, to serve the congregation and the church in their involvement in social issues and in addressing the government and society regarding their responsibility....

Ordinance 8-3-1
The congregation is called to the ministry of compassion and justice in mutual support, in offering assistance, care and protection to those in need, in participation in activities regarding societal well-being, in being alert to problematic situations in society, in the stimulation of environmental care for creation.
Ordinances 8-3-2 and 8-3-3 emphasize that the 'diaconal vocation of the congregation' stretches beyond the borders of the congregation and that it is entrusted to all the members of the congregation. The main task of the deacons is to make the members of the congregation aware of their collective diaconal vocation. In their efforts to fulfil this diaconal vocation, congregations should cooperate with other churches, among which are included migrant churches (ordinances 8-5-1 and 8-6-1). In the last ordinance (14) regarding the ecumenical perspective on the life and work of the church, including the responsibility of the General Synod in this respect, special attention is given to the variety of diaconal work as a 'ministry of compassion and justice':

Ordinance 14-9-1
In undertaking diaconal work in the Netherlands and in the world, the church responds to the vocation in the ministry of compassion and justice by supporting those who suffer from poverty, injustice, deprivation and illness, [and the vocation] to stand side by side to those seeking comfort and justice.

### *6. Exploring the theological potential of vocation regarding diaconate*

Diaconate in its various forms finds a firm basis in the CO-PCN: in regard to both its place within the congregations and in society, and the tasks of the deacons and the responsibility of every church member and even the General Synod. The church order's suggestion to approach diaconate from the angle of the vocation of the congregation stimulates further reflection on the potential of 'vocation' in this respect. In an attempt to explore this potential, I will now tentatively point out two aspects of vocation that might be helpful in understanding diaconate in a particular church in a changing context (see also De Waal 2011).

(1) The interesting dynamic between a vocation and the 'fulfilment' or 'answering' of this vocation is helpful in the theological analysis of diaconate in its essence. The definition of diaconate cited above showed the two facets of

*diakonia* in diaconal practices —i.e., a descriptive part regarding the variety of diaconal work and a normative part regarding the ideals and aims of diaconate. This duality is captured in the dynamic of the 'vocation of the congregation' in the CO–PCN. The cited church order articles on diaconate refer to what is actually taking place as well as to what *ought* to be taking place. This twofold character is not restricted to the realm of the diaconate (cf. the articles on missionary work and pastoral care) since it is a result of the theological nature of this particular church order. It is however not a mere theological disguise for an idealist dialectic between 'idea' and 'reality' but rather an expression of what it means 'to be called'. Exploring the potential of the notion of vocation requires a biblical-theological framework. The notion of 'to be called' in the Old and New Testament contains on the one hand the element of grace and promise, regarding 'what has been done' or 'what has been happening' to the one who is called. This refers to individuals concerned with a certain task, but also to collectivities of people: Israel as the 'people of God' and the New Testament community of faith as the *ekklesia*, the church. Vocation is part of the grace that has been bestowed upon the congregation, as a (theological) *indicativus*. On the other hand, 'to be called' contains the element of appeal: the urge 'to do unto others what has been done to you'. Vocation therefore also shares in the new life that wants to be made manifest in the life and work of the congregation, as an *imperativus*. These two elements are inseparable, as for instance the apostle Paul writes in the Epistle to the Galatians: "For you were called to freedom, brethren; only do not use your freedom as an opportunity for the flesh, but through love be servants of one another. For the whole law is fulfilled in one word, 'You shall love your neighbor as yourself'" (Gal. 5:13–14, RSV).

(2) The words 'you were called' in the verse cited above can be interpreted as a *passivum divinum*. In the vocabulary of the apostle, 'to be called' is a synonym for conversion (cf. 1 Cor.7:20). God is the one who calls. This does not mean, however, that the call is a direct and miraculous phenomenon. On the contrary, a vocation often tends to have a veiled and hidden character. Its features have to be unfolded in order to fully grasp its content. Even the origin of the vocation can be unclear. A vocation might be the conclusion of encounters with other people (Matt. 25:35–45), or unexpected events in the context of the church, or as the result of a long period of contemplation. It is up the one who is called (individually or collectively, as a congregation) to constantly discern the vocation, or to adjust the vocation to new insights and developments.

Traces of this 'second-level' duality in the concept of vocation can be found in the distinction the Reformed tradition made between *vocatio interna* and *vocatio externa*, which was used for the vocation to (ordained) ministry (see Koffeman

2009, 144). Internal vocation relates to the faithful acceptance of being called by God; external vocation relates to the calling of a congregation towards the candidates for the offices in the church. Both vocations are correlating with each other without a necessary order. Regarding the vocation of the congregation to diaconate in both its practical and appealing form, this second conceptualization adds to the understanding of the notion of diaconal vocation itself. In the diaconate, the internal vocation relates to the 'internal' sources of diaconate that can be found within the congregation: faith, inspiration from biblical stories and the tradition of the church, including the church order. The external vocation however 'dwells' in the context of the church. The topical questions of this day and age, e.g., regarding new poverty and unemployment, asylum seekers and *in casu* aging, are not the same as those of the past and those of the tradition of the church (see Den Hertog 2009, 125). But without them, the 'internal' diaconate would become a traditional obligation of the congregation and an irrelevant folklore in the eyes of society. In combination, these aspects of vocation constitute the following model of understanding what diaconal vocation stands for (Figure 1).

| | **indicative vocation**<br>*Grace* | **imperative vocation**<br>*Appeal* |
|---|---|---|
| **internal vocation**<br>*Church and congregation* | Encounter with God<br>'I am set free ...<br>'We are being served ... | Mutual support<br>... to set free'<br>... to serve' |
| **external vocation**<br>*Society and people in context* | Encounter with the other/ the Other<br>'I am being noticed ... | Commitment to society<br>(Critical) participation<br>... to notice' |
| 'We are being changed ... | | ... to change' |

*Figure 1: Four elements that constitute the diaconal vocation of the congregation*

This model of understanding demonstrates the spiritual and even 'intimate' aspect of diaconate. The encounter with God and people lies at the heart of all provisional policies, activities, theological reflection and analysis of context. Diaconate is an integral aspect of the vocation and life of the church; equivalent, not subordinate to other offices and aspects (e.g., missionary work and liturgy). It also demonstrates the importance of the awareness and subsequent analysis of the context in which diaconate and church are embedded. Without discerning its external vocation, diaconate would remain incomplete as regards its domains of attention and participation, and in result, its own identity. The reciprocity in church polity Koffeman aims at (see Koffeman 2009, 196) is already, and will continue to be, a diaconal practice.

### *Conclusion, discussion, further research*

In this article I have tried to illustrate the broad theme of church polity in changing contexts through a case study on diaconate and aging. Theological reflection on the impact of aging on society, church and church polity still is in an initial stage. From the perspective of diaconate and diaconal studies, certain factors have been identified that should accompany future reflection on this topic, such as being alert to processes of marginalization of senior citizens, a recognition of the increased variety among senior citizens and the advocacy of intergenerational solidarity. Due to the dominance of the economic discourse in politics and society, people who are not part of the labor force are increasingly regarded as being superfluous, which may result in experiences of loneliness and discrimination. Diaconate (with all its shortcomings) has a history of being alert to and being involved with people who are dwelling in the margins of society. The margins however are changing and likewise should the diaconal expressions of the church in society change. An important prerequisite for the diaconal adaptation to a changing context is reflection on the ecclesiological tradition and the organizational structure in which diaconate is embedded. The CO-PCN is making a valuable contribution to this reflection by approaching diaconate from the perspective of the vocation of the congregation. This vocation can be further conceptualized as an indicative and an imperative vocation and as an internal and an external vocation. All four elements are indispensable in the adequate manifestation of diaconate in context.

Diaconate finds a firm basis in the church order, I concluded earlier, since it is incorporated in the vocation of the congregation. Diaconate thus precedes the realm of the practices ('life') of the congregations, which is important as regards the continuation of diaconate in a changing context. The preservation of the diaconate in an aging or shrinking congregation should remain a top priority in processes of self-evaluation and policy renewal. The church order could further fortify this prioritization by explicitly expanding the articles on diaconate, especially in the first part of the church order. On behalf of the discussion on this subject, it is my suggestion to supplement article I, 2 of the church order with an aspect that relates to the diaconal vocation of the church *as church*. The current article I, 2 stresses the church's fundamental mandate (task) of 'hearing and proclaiming the Word', to which end the church has been called by the Lord:

Art. I, 2 (current)
Living by God's grace in Jesus Christ, the church carries out the mandate of its Lord to hear and proclaim the Word.

In accordance with the paragraphs above, this fundamental self-understanding could be supplemented with an implicit but clear reference to diaconal practices:

Art. I, 2 (suggestion)
Living by God's grace in Jesus Christ, the church carries out the mandate of its Lord to hear, proclaim, *and to act according to* the Word.

A question for further research on church polity in changing contexts would be: which factors determine the *pace* in which contextual changes are detected, analyzed, evaluated and incorporated in the church order? The correlation between church order and context is evident. Church polity is in itself a contextual phenomenon, even if ecclesiological and theological traditions completely determine the principles of a certain church order. The people who epitomize the church in a certain context, in reality and in practices, are specific by definition. In relation to the process of aging, which probably will be an irreversible development determining the features of the PCN, the question can thus be made specific: how long will it take before the church order will, preferably in an affirmative way, contain a reference to the aged character of this particular church?

## *Abbreviations and bibliography*

CBS 2012: Central Bureau for Statistics in the Netherlands. 2012. Accessed August 20, 2012. http://www.statline.cbs.nl.

CO-PCN: Church order of the Protestant Church in the Netherlands (2004).

G500: Accessed August 20, 2012. http://www.g500.nl.

KIA 2009: Kerk in Actie. 2009. Diaconate and care project 'Grey is more than a colour'. Accessed August, 20, 2012. http://www.kerkinactie.nl/kerkengemeenten/diaconaat/zorg-in-nederland/ouderen--i13117.

PCN 2011: Protestant Church in the Netherlands. 2011. Annual Statistic Report 2011. Utrecht: Protestants Landelijk Dienstencentrum.

RSV: Revised Standard Version.

UCA: Uniting Church in Australia. n.d. Deacon. Accessed December 2, 2012. http://www.ministry.ucaqld.com.au/deacon.aspx.

Becker, Jos, and Joep de Hart. 2006. Godsdienstige veranderingen in Nederland: Verschuivingen in de binding met de kerken en de christelijke traditie. Den Haag: Sociaal en Cultureel Planbureau.

Berkhof, Hendrikus. 1990. Christelijk geloof: Een inleiding tot de geloofsleer. Nijkerk: Callenbach. 6th edition.

Bisseling, Harry, Henk de Roest and Peet Valstar (eds). 2011. Meer dan hout en steen: Handboek bij sluiting en herbestemming van kerkgebouwen. Zoetermeer: Boekencentrum.

Brouwer, Rein. 2007. Perspectieven en spanningsvelden. In: Brouwer et al. 2007, 46–67.

Brouwer, Rein, Kees de Groot, Henk de Roest, Erik Sengers, and Sake Stoppels. 2007. Levend lichaam: Dynamiek van christelijke geloofsgemeenschappen in Nederland. Kok: Kampen.

Collins, John N. 1990. Diakonia: Re-interpreting the ancient sources. Oxford: Oxford University Press.

Crijns, Huub, et al. (eds). 2011. Diaconie in beweging: Handboek diaconiewetenschap. Kampen: Kok.

De Lange, Frits. 2008A. De armoede van het zwitserlevengevoel: Pleidooi voor beter ouder worden. Zoetermeer: Meinema.

De Lange, Frits. 2008B. De 'grijze kerk' als uitdaging. In: Ouderlingenblad no. 987, November 2008, 16–19.

Den Hertog, Gerard C. 2009. Theologische en hermeneutische verkenningen in het diaconaat. In: Den Hertog and Noordegraaf 2009, 107–141.

Den Hertog, Gerard C., and Albert Noordegraaf (eds). 2009. Dienen en delen: Basisboek diaconaat. Zoetermeer: Boekencentrum.

De Roest, Henk. 2011. Kerksluiting in perspectief. In: Bisseling et al. 2011, 27–75.

De Waal, Hans. 2011. Diaconaat en het ouder worden van kerk en samenleving. Groningen: Stichting Rotterdam.

De Waal, Hans. 2012. Colourful shades of grey: Diaconal responses to the challenge of aging in the Protestant Church in the Netherlands. In: Diaconia, Journal for the study of Christian social practice, 3(2012)/2, December 2012, 39–157.

Eurich, Johannes, Peter Dabrock, and Wolfgang Maaser (eds). 2008. Intergenerationalität zwischen Solidarität und Gerechtigkeit. Heidelberg: Winter.

Houtepen, Anton J. 2004. Diakonia opnieuw geïnterpreteerd. In: Crijns et al. 2004, 366–379.

Knook, Dick. 2008. Het Methusalem-mysterie; Vergrijzing: zegen of bedreiging. Amsterdam — Rotterdam: Prometheus — NRC Handelsblad.

Koet, Bart. 2011. Exegetische kanttekeningen over diakonia in het Nieuwe Testament. In: Crijns et al. 2011, 69–96.

Koffeman, Leo J. 2009. Het goed recht van de kerk: Een theologische inleiding op het kerkrecht. Kampen: Kok.

McKee, Elsie A. 1984. John Calvin on the diaconate and liturgical almsgiving. Geneva: Librairie Droz S.A.

Noordegraaf, Herman. 2009. De diaconale C-factor: De betekenis van Calvijn voor het diaconaat. Groningen: Stichting Rotterdam.

Noordegraaf, Herman, and Greetje Witte-Rang. 2011. In de wereld werkzaam zijn: Anders denken over kerkelijk optreden door het MCKS 1981–1998. Vught: Skandalon.

Scharf, Thomas. 2012. Why isn't Active Aging a Right Approach. Lecture at the expert meeting Active Aging: Support or Obstacle for Intergenerational Solidarity. February 9, 2012. Den Haag: Haagse Hogeschool.

Van der Borght, Eddy A.J.G. 2000. Het ambt her-dacht: De gereformeerde ambtstheologie in het licht van het rapport Baptism, Eucharist and Ministry (Lima, 1982) van de theologische commissie Faith and Order van de Wereldraad van Kerken. Zoetermeer: Meinema.

Van der Steen, Martijn. 2009. Een sterk verhaal: Een analyse van het discours over vergrijzing. Den Haag: Lemma.

Van der Ven, Johannes A. 1993. Ecclesiologie in context. Kampen: Kok.

# CHURCH POLITY AND 'CONSTITUTIONALISM'

Helena van Coller

## *1. Introduction*

In liberal society, the government has no competence to determine moral ends. In theory, at least, the goals of the liberal democratic government must depend on the values held by those it governs — values that originate outside of government in churches, families, political parties, trade unions, private schools, and other voluntary associations. In the absence of these groups, government and society would be deprived of the enriching world-views that these groups contribute to...culture and politics (see Ahdar 2001).

The social, political and religious landscape of South Africa at present resembles a transition from a strong Christian-orientated society to a society characterized by strong secular views, where the church is slowly losing its once-powerful position and voice within the public sphere. The South African society exhibits a growing multicultural character, which find expression in a religious pluralism with much more diversity than in the past, and which is enriched by new experiences and different needs concerning religion. The former Chief Justice, Pius Langa, described 'transformative constitutionalism' as "a permanent ideal which embraces openness to the other, a commitment to inclusive, democratic dialogue, and a sharing of the responsibility of transformation between all three branches of government in partnership with a vibrant, *independent civil society*" (Langa 2008, emphasis added).

Within a framework of religious freedom, the government is required to respect the status of religious organizations and churches in South Africa. However, changing social, political and constitutional contexts also place a duty on churches to adapt their structures and church orders in the light of constitutional demands. In *Van Rooyen and Others v S* 2002 (§ 50), Chaskalson CJ states that "transformation involves not only changes in the legal order, but also changes in the composition of the institutions of society [...] ", which include churches and religious organizations.

Drawing from this example, this article will focus on South African developments where it is becoming increasingly important to recognize the need for religious diversity in a pluralistic society. The article will focus on the nature and position of churches as organizations of civil society and the importance of the right of freedom of association for religious organizations in general, and churches in particular, when evaluating and adapting existing policies. It will also assess the role of the civil courts in determining religious disputes and the role of the church order in this process.

## 2. *The nature, position and functioning of churches and religious organizations in civil society*

Despite the premise that religious organizations and churches are *sui generis* organizations based on an internal ecclesiastical law, they still function as private organizations in accordance with the rules and regulations laid down in their respective constitutions or church orders. In general, churches and religious organizations function as voluntary associations in civil society, either as churches and congregations in support and development of religious convictions and practices, or as faith-based community or service organizations. It is generally accepted that not only an organized society, but also an active society, is important for inclusive democracy and development (Legal Resources Centre 2006). Various forms of community organizations exist, and the most important characteristic that they have in common is that they do not form part of the state. The emphasis is therefore not on commercial or profit-making organizations, but on non-governmental or non-profit organizations that make a contribution to the society at large. It is within this category that we find churches and religious organizations.

The question is: what do we mean when we refer to the 'non-profit sector'? Various forms, types and definitions exist: non-governmental organizations (NGO's), voluntary organizations, faith-based organizations, non-profit organizations, and many more. Salamon and Anheier briefly outline four types of definitions that can assist in classifying an organization:

a. The legal definition (in straightforward terms: what does the law say? A non-profit organization is what the law of a specific country says it is);
b. The economic/financial definition (what is the source of income for the organization?);
c. The functional definition (what is the purpose of the organization; what functions does it carry out and what activities is it engaged in?);
d. The structural/operational definition (what is the basic structure of the organization and how does it operate?) (see Salamon and Anheier 1992, 133–135).

The last two categories, the functional and structural definition, are of particular importance when assessing how churches and religious organizations function in civil society. The actual features included in these definitions may vary. Some key features have been identified, and it is argued that a non-profit organization must at least be *organized*; it must be *private* and separated from the state; it must be *non-profit*; it must be *self-governing*, that is, not controlled by outside entities but is in charge of its own internal procedures; and it must be *voluntary*. Since various organizations exist that exhibit these features, a more specific classification might be necessary. A classification system can assist, in order to classify and describe in more detail the types of organizations this definition encompasses.

A few classification systems are available for differentiating the non-profit sector at the international level, including the International Standard Classification (ISIC), the General Industrial Classification of Economic Activities (NACE), and the National Taxonomy of Exempt Entities (NTEE), a very comprehensive classification system used in the USA. In the ISIC system religious organizations are only mentioned in passing and classified under the heading, 'Other community social and personal service activities', and more specifically as 'Other membership organizations (including religious, political)'. In the NACE system, religious organizations are grouped together with social services, unions, tourism and professional organizations as 'Other services to the public'. In the NTEE, probably one of the most comprehensive classification systems—having over twenty-five categories and more than 100 sub-categories—only one reference is made to 'religion-related' entities. The International Classification of Non-profit Organizations (ICNPO) serves as a good example of a system that is not as complex as the NTEE but also not as limited as the ISIC and the NACE. The ICNPO provides for the classification of distinct and separate units and groups rather than organizations in general. Organizations are often made up of different units or establishments that may have their own activities. The ICNPO therefore provides for different units and establishments, and groups them into twelve main activity groups subdivided into twenty-four sub-groups. Group 10 focuses on 'Religion' and includes the following: "organisations promoting religious beliefs and administering religious services and rituals; includes churches, mosques, synagogues, temples, shrines, seminaries, monasteries and similar religious institutions, in addition to related associations and auxiliaries of such organizations" (Salamon and Anheier 1992A, 297).

This system specifically distinguishes churches and religious organizations from all other organizations. Group 10 further differentiates between congregations on the one hand and associations of congregations on the other hand as follows:

- *Congregations*: churches, synagogues, temples, mosques, shrines, monasteries, seminaries and similar organisations promoting religious beliefs and administering religious services and rituals.
- *Associations of congregations*: associations and auxiliaries of religious congregations and organisations supporting and promoting religious beliefs, services and rituals (see Salamon and Anheier 1992A).

'Religious organizations' is a very broad concept and can include congregations on the one hand but also more general religious organizations such as faith-based organizations on the other hand. Jeavons argues that it would be wrong to classify congregations as faith-based organizations, since a pastor, rabbi, imam or minister would rarely see themselves as leaders of faith-based organizations, but rather as leaders of a church, temple, synagogue or mosque (see Jeavons 2003, 27). The primary function of these organizations is to worship. Congregations are of course also involved in various service activities, but often as a manifestation of their religion and belief. Congregations are also described as "the basic units of organized religious life in almost every spiritual tradition visible" (Jeavons 2003, 28). Faith-based organizations are often dependent on outside funding for survival, which places them in a bit of a different category than congregations. That however does not mean that congregations are not involved in this type of service delivery, as Jeavons correctly points out: "congregations are amongst the most independent of all the organizations in the independent sector. They are also very active in serving public needs in many ways, in addition to meeting the spiritual and practical needs of their members" (Jeavons 2003, 36).

Faith-based organizations are often non-profit organizations that are involved in some form of service delivery, including religious education, charity, elder care, health services and missionary work. These are activities that "in medieval times...would have come primarily within the jurisdiction of the church rather than the state" (Jeavons 2003, 32). Many of these organizations have religious objectives either to provide religious education or to be involved in missionary work. Some of them are funded by churches or congregations to run religious schools or old age homes, and some have no religious objectives at all but are inspired by religious values. Most of these organizations, especially in the field of social services, are fully dependent on the state for funding, and according to Jeavons "[t]he availability of new funds, the ways they are provided, and the demands for accountability that must come with them certainly have the potential to cause goal displacement and mission drift, a loss of independence and vitality, and an erosion of the separation of church and state for both congregations and religious service agencies as government seek to use these organizations to pursue public policy agendas" (Jeavons 2003, 35).

The South African Council of Churches (SACC) is of the view that any voluntary association (including religious organizations) will qualify for public funds if they provide a service to the public or at least a section of the public. According to it: "An association that admits any person who subscribes to and supports its aims and objectives can be classified as an open association and should ... be entitled to public funding" (SAHRC 2006).

If an organization's objectives are regarded to be constitutionally permissible goals, it should be eligible to apply for state funding and "then the state is precluded from denying funding to that body solely because it disapproves of its policies, practices, or activities" (SAHRC 2006). An example is the Highlands House, an old age home for members of the Jewish Community. The home is restricted to persons of the Jewish faith. The home is supported by contributions by members of the Jewish community, payments from residents, and a contribution from the state which amounts to 7.5 percent of the home's operating costs. This is not a direct contribution; it comes in the form of subsidies to individual members. The Chairperson of the Council acknowledged that the restrictive admission policy was discriminatory against non-Jewish people. However, the argument was that the discrimination was not unfair "as the admission policy is designed to promote the continuity of the Jewish community and its adherence to the principles and precepts of the Jewish religion" (SAHRC 2006). The South African Human Rights Commission (SAHRC) is of the view that a home for the aged, like Highlands Home, which is set up and maintained by the organization itself for the purposes of providing for religious needs of those in the community, and which does not discriminate on the basis of any irrational criteria, may be constitutionally permissible. The Human Rights Commission further highlighted the importance of these homes and other religiously-based organizations as follows: "There can be no doubt that homes for the aged like Highlands Home play a useful and constructive role for members of the community that it serves. It provides them with the comfort and security of being in an environment that is supportive of them and is deeply committed to upholding and promoting their religion in all its manifestations without compromise" (SAHRC 2006, 33). This provides great solace and reassurance at a time when religion and religious affiliations are particularly important in the lives of people. These homes are often set up and operated largely from funds obtained from the community that they serve. The reality is that opening a home to persons of different religious beliefs may profoundly change the character of the homes, as a variety of compromises, some pertaining to religious beliefs, may have to be made. This may diminish the fund raising potential to such an extent that the existence of the homes may be threatened. Self-supporting institutions also reduce the fiscal burden on the state and enable funding to be diverted to needier communities.

According to the SACC, allocation of state funding should depend on the following criteria:

1. Does the voluntary association seek to achieve an objective that is either directly or indirectly protected by the Constitution.
2. The extent to which the organization seeks to improve the quality of life and free the potential of all people by contributing to the progressive realization of socio-economic rights.
3. The nature, purpose, and objectives of the organization, and the benefit it actually confers on the community it serves and the broader South African society.
4. The extent to which the organization addresses disadvantage arising from past patterns of discrimination, and
5. Competing priorities in respect of budgetary allocations (see SAHRC 2006).

The question arises: does state funding mean state interference in the affairs of these organizations, and a possible infringement of the autonomy of these organizations? It must be noted that churches and religious organizations can co-operate with the state without compromising their religious identity. In a constitutional democracy with guaranteed freedom of religion, there *should* be cooperation between the state and all religious communities. However, it is important that the state: should not give preference to a particular religious belief, should refrain from interfering with the internal organization of the church, and should respect the religious identity of these religious organizations. This approach would be in line with the approach taken in Ireland, where all religious organizations function as voluntary associations, and where the term 'religious/church denomination' refers to "a generic term wide enough to cover the various churches, religious societies or religious congregations under whatever name they wished to describe themselves...[and also]...that each religious denomination should be respected when it says what its ethos is" (Colton 2007, 128).

For purposes of the right to freedom of religion, it is argued that all the above organizations should be treated the same, and are equally entitled to the protection offered by the Constitution — especially protection of the institutional right to freedom of religion and the right to freedom of association. Members of different religions and religious communities have the right to practice their religion jointly, and to form, join and maintain religious institutions. Section 4 of the *South African Charter of Religious Rights and Freedoms* (or: *Bill of Rights*) specifically provides that persons of the same conviction have the right to associate with one another, to form, join and maintain religious and other associations, institutions and denominations, to organize religious meetings and other collective activities, and to establish and maintain places of worship.

For churches and religious organizations to operate effectively as organizations of civil society, it is of the utmost importance that not only should their institutional right to freedom of religion be respected, but also their right to freedom of association, which will be discussed in more detail below.

### 3. *The right to freedom of association*

"Associational rights safeguard primordial religious and cultural attachments from undue state interference" (Woolman 2005). The right to freedom of association is one of the most fundamental rights in a democratic society, and is described as a right that entails "a general capacity for citizens to join, without interference by the state, in associations in order to attain various ends" (Cheadle and Davis 2002, 251). The importance for religious organizations in particular is that "associations, such as religious communities, are integral to self-understanding, and that there can be no self without the host of associations that give the self content" (Woolman 2009A, 286). An important aspect of the right to freedom of association is that it fosters diversity. Lenta uses the aspect of diversity to emphasize the importance of organizations and the right to freedom of association in society. He puts it as follows: "Associations should not always be expected to conform to public principles, including non-discrimination, when those principles clash with the convictions of members, and the state should refrain as far as possible from interfering with the internal affairs of associations. *This is what the protection of diversity requires*" (Lenta 2009, 832; emphasis added).

Section 18 of the *Constitution of the Republic of South Africa* (1996) guarantees everyone the right to freedom of association. One aspect of this right incorporates the right of individuals as members of particular organizations to decide freely with whom they want to associate, whether for social, political or religious reasons, as a manifestation of a particular freedom of culture, belief or religion. This associational right encompasses certain membership and admission requirements. Woolman refers to this as "capture [which] justifies the ability of associations to control their association through selective membership policies, the manner in which they order their internal affairs and the discharge of members or users" (Woolman 2009A, 287).

Section 15 (freedom of religion), section 18 (freedom of association) and section 31 (the right to associate in religious communities) of the *Constitution* play a very important role in respect of religious institutions in relation to the degree of interference by the state in the internal affairs of the association (membership, activities etc). Government interference can occur due to discriminatory practices by the organization, but only in accordance with section 36 of the *Constitution*. It reads: "The rights in the Bill of Rights may be limited only in terms of law of general application to the extent that the limitation is reasonable and justifiable in an open and democratic society based on human dignity, equality and freedom" Examples include: activities or provisions in the organization's constitution that are in conflict with the principles of a society based on human dignity, equality and freedom; where membership is declined on the basis of discriminatory practices; and where the internal affairs of the organization are not conducted in accordance with democratic principles (see Pienaar 1997, 576f.).

The *nature* of the religious institution together with the operation of sections 15, 18, and 31 of the *Constitution* should limit state interference in the internal affairs of religious institutions and allow interference only in very exceptional cases. Religious institutions are afforded this privileged position for so long as and to the extent that their activities are of a *bona fide* religious nature. Where religious institutions therefore are pursuing purely economic or political objectives, "state interference with the membership policies — and perhaps even the internal affairs — of the association may well pass constitutional muster" (Woolman 2005, 434). However, the threshold for interference with certain kinds of association ought to be quite high. As Woolman correctly points out: "[w]ith families, *religious groups* and traditional communities, the first inclination of a liberal state ought to be to allow the members to work out their voice on their own" (Woolman 2009; emphasis added). This flows from the important premise that churches and religious associations are not just ordinary associations; they are *religious* organizations. Therefore it requires observance not only of the right to freedom of association, but also of the right to freedom of religion. No rights are absolute, including the rights enshrined in Sections 15, 18 and 31 of the *Constitution.* The court in *Christian Education SA v Minister of Education* 2000 (§ 26) made it clear that in accordance with section 31(2), the rights in section 31(1) may not be exercised in a manner inconsistent with any provision of the Bill of Rights, and states as follows: "It should be observed, further, that special care has been taken expressly to acknowledge the supremacy of the Constitution and the Bill of Rights". Section 31(2) ensures that the concept of rights of members of communities that associate on the basis of language, culture and religion, cannot be used to shield practices which offend the *Bill of Rights.* These explicit qualifications may be seen as serving a double purpose. The first is to prevent protected associational rights of members of communities from being used to 'privatise' constitutionally offensive group practices and thereby immunize them from external legislative regulation or judicial control. This will be particularly important in relation to practices previously associated with the abuse of the notion of pluralism to achieve exclusivity, privilege and domination. The second relates to oppressive features of internal relationships primarily within the communities concerned, where section 8, which regulates the horizontal application of the *Bill of Rights*, might be especially relevant.

Section 31(1) makes it clear that any exclusionary policies, actions or procedures by voluntary associations, including religious entities, would not be allowed unconditionally and can be limited only in accordance with the requirements of the limitation clause, section 36 of the *Constitution*, and the test for proportionality. There rests a duty on religious institutions to evaluate their exclusionary policies, rules and conduct in accordance with the requirements set out in the Constitution. Religious institutions, whose objectives are to achieve constitutionally-legitimate goals must be allowed to adopt exclusionary rules and policies in order to afford appropriate weight to associational rights aimed at developing and protecting religious liberties.

The court in both *Taylor v Kurtstag* 2005 and *Wittman v Deutscher Schulverein* 1998 recognized the right of religious organizations "to have one's life shaped in a manner that does not readily permit the alteration of either belief or act and that to be a member of a liberal society is to live in a state committed to not so readily dictating the ends of its citizens" (Woolman 2005, 442). That does not give religious organizations a blank check to act however they want. The state can still interfere with the functioning of such an organization. It merely means that the state should recognize and respect the religious nature of the organization and should afford the organization an appropriate amount of deference. The right to freedom of association also incorporates the right of everyone to decide to join any organization of choice. In the context of the horizontal application of the *Bill of Rights*, it means that no one may be discriminated against on one or more of the grounds listed in Section 9 of the *Constitution*, including race, gender, sexual orientation or religion. If a religious organization can prove that discriminatory practices or admission policies are lawfully designed for the protection and promotion of a particular community's cultural or religious precepts and principles, the right to freedom of association of the particular organization to set discriminatory admission requirements should trump other considerations.

If an organization's exclusionary policies or admission requirements violate the right to equality in terms of section 9 of the *Constitution*, a somewhat different test applies (see *Harksen v Lane NO and Others* 1998, and later cases such as *Van Heerden v Minister of Finance* 2004) that refined the test for discrimination). An inquiry will be done into the rational connection between the differentiation and a lawful government purpose. If the differentiation is based on one of the listed grounds in section 9(3), it is to be regarded as discrimination that is unfair. The unfairness of the discrimination must be determined on the basis of whether the discrimination is reasonable and justifiable in an open and democratic society based on human dignity, equality and freedom, in terms of section 36 of the *Constitution*. A decision by the SAHRC in the ATKV/Goudinie matter, can serve as a good example.

The *Afrikaanse Taal- en Kultuurvereniging* (ATKV) came into existence in 1930 as a cultural organization of which membership was open only to whites until the 1980s. The ATKV runs and operates five holiday resorts in South Africa, open to all members of the public, but the activities at the resorts promote the Afrikaans language and Christian values. ATKV members receive a 30 percent discount at the resort, while other members of the public must pay full price. On the question of whether the admission requirements of the ATKV constituted unfair discrimination, Dr. Kok argued on behalf of the ATKV that the admission requirements did constitute discrimination on religious grounds, but that the discrimination was fair in that it served the legitimate and lawful purpose of promoting the religious grounds and commitment of the ATKV to Christian values. He then argued that the admission requirements did not constitute unfair discrimination.

In the ATKV/Goudinie-matter, the SAHRC had to determine whether an organization that was not only a language organization but also a cultural and religious organization can limit its membership to members of one particular faith (in this instance, the Christian faith). Membership was refused to members that would have qualified on language or cultural grounds; it was excluded as a result of their belief (in this instance, Islam). The ATKV requires all its members to commit to upholding the Christian faith and to promote, advance and develop the Afrikaans language and culture. The applicants, being of the Muslim faith, did not wish to subscribe to the founding principles of the ATKV. They alleged that they were being unfairly discriminated against on the basis of religion. The Commission found that while the practices of ATKV were in fact discriminatory, they were not unfair as the organization permitted non-Christian and non-Afrikaners to attend their resorts. The Commission also found that the ATKV was entitled to set particular religious convictions as admission requirements and consequently to exclude certain members on religious grounds (SAHRC 2006). The discussion above has clearly emphasized the importance of the right to freedom of association for religious institutions and has indicated that "[w]ith certain kinds of association the threshold for interference in determining the voice ought to be quite high. With families, *religious groups* and traditional communities, the first inclination of a liberal state ought to be to allow the members to work out their voice on their own" (Woolman 2009; emphasis added).

Van Coller in *United Methodist Church of South Africa v Sokufundumala* (§ D-E) makes the following remark: "I trust that the parties, being church men and women, will try to resolve their differences in the spirit that the Bible teaches us we should adopt, namely the spirit of brotherly love, and I think an attempt should be made, by the parties, to solve this problem and not to come to Court".

Unfortunately, in practice, this is often not the case and churches and religious organizations do get involved in legal battles and have to approach the courts for appropriate relief. The next section will briefly assess the role of the courts in determining religious disputes.

### *4. The civil courts and religious disputes*

An important case for the institutional right to freedom of religion applicable to religious organizations and churches in South Africa is the case of *Taylor v Kurtstag* 2005. It also illustrates the important connection between the right to institutional freedom of religion (section 31) and the right to freedom of association (section 18). A member of the Jewish community was excommunicated by the relevant Jewish community authority, the *Beth Din*, by means of a *Cherem*. He applied for the setting aside of the *Cherem* in that it not only violated his right to freedom of association in accordance with section 18, but also that it violated his institutional right to freedom of religion

Other than the minority decision of Ngocobo in *Prince v President, Cape Law Society* 2002 (§ 42) where he stated that "[i]t is undesirable for courts to enter into the debate whether a particular practice is central to a religion unless there is a genuine dispute as to the centrality of a practice", the court in *Kurtstag* confirmed that the *Cherem* forms part of the Jewish religion and that as part of the particular religion members are bound by it and that "they are not coerced; assumption of the obligation is consensual" (Ibid., § 35). Consequently, the court had to determine whether there was a violation of the individual's rights and whether the *Cherem* must be lifted. Although the *Cherem* may have severe consequences on a particular member's position within the Jewish faith in the particular community, the court confirmed that the question involved religious doctrine and that "the threshold for intervention is and should be high" and that if the court should interfere "it would be impossible for voluntary organizations, particularly religious communities, to require conformity with particular values and to impose sanctions for their contravention. The members of the faith, exercising their own rights in terms of s 31, have the right to protect the integrity of their common bond by disciplining those who do not conform" (Ibid., § 58).

In the light of the fact that courts are in fact willing to scrutinize the particular religious doctrines of a church or religious organizations in order to determine whether they form part of the particular religion in question, a huge responsibility rests on churches and religious organizations to have clarity on their own doctrines and beliefs and related procedures. As the court correctly points out in

*Minister of Home Affairs v Fourie; Gay and Lesbian Equality Project v Minister of Home Affairs* 2006 (§ 92): "Judges would be placed in an intolerable situation if they were called upon to construe religious texts and take side on issues which have caused deep schisms within religious bodies".

Cases such as *De Vos v Die Ringskommissie van die Ring van die NG Kerk, Bloemfontein and Another* 1952, *Odendaal v Kerkraad van die Gemeente Bloemfontein-Wes van die NG Kerk in OVS en Andere* 1960, and *Theron v Ring van Wellington van die NG Sendingkerk in Suid-Afrika* 1976 confirm the position and serves as authority for the fact that civil courts do have the authority to interpret a church order and to act accordingly. However, courts should act with deference in respect of church customs and interpretations. It is therefore necessary to look more closely at the role of the courts in interpreting a church order. According to Van Eikema Hommes, it is a fundamental principle that all law-making bodies of churches should abide by the law as laid down in their respective church orders, rules and regulations (see Van Eikema Hommes 1983, 101).

In *Yiba and Others v African Gospel Church* 1999 the court confirmed the principles applicable to the nature of the relationship between a voluntary association and its members, and the interpretation of its constitution in the context of disciplinary action. The constitution, together with the rules and regulations, form the agreement that sets out the nature and scope of authority of the organization, as well as the functionaries and members of the organization. The organization explicitly undertakes to treat members fairly in accordance with the rules and regulations of the constitution, and these rules cannot be ignored. The question that comes to mind is: what exactly is regulated by the organization's constitution? In the context of churches and religious organizations, the church order or constitution determines that the particular organization is regulated by means of internal church or organizational rules, compiled by the institution itself and not the state. Does that necessarily mean that a Mosque can dismiss its Imam without complying with the rules of labor law? Or that an association or church can suspend a member without complying with basic procedural rules? According to Van der Vyver, "[i]t is not for state institutions to judge the substance, or the truth or falsity, of religious belief per se. However, it is a vital function of government to resolve, through its judicial arm, disputes pertaining to the rights and obligations of its subjects. Courts of law ought not to shy away from that function merely because those rights and obligations cannot in a given case be established without doctrinal issues" (Van der Vyver 1999, 670).

Malherbe is of the view that it is important for churches and religious organizations to note that the *Constitution* is not interpreted in neutral terms, but that certain worldly views can be applicable (see Malherbe 2008, 274). The South

African Constitutional Court in *S v Makwanyane* 1995 followed a 'generous and purposive' approach, but in the light of Malherbe's view, such an approach can still be influenced by the applicable worldly views of the court in question. According to him, various courts have, in fact, indicated a strong humanitarian outlook on certain issues (see Malherbe 2008, 274–276). The Court of Appeal in *Nederduits Gereformeerde Kerk in Afrika (OVS); Nederduitse Gereformeerde Kerk in Afrika (Phororo) v Verenigde Gereformeerde Kerk in Suider-Afrika* (case number 536/96), confirms that an appropriate interpretation of a church order should include an interpretation where words are interpreted in the context of its nature and purpose, and that the relationship between words should be looked at in the context of the church order as a whole. The court was in favor of the approach taken by Lord Wilberforce in *Prenn v Simmonds* 1971, where the court was of the view that the broad contextual background includes the so-called 'matrix of facts', in which the church order is set when interpreting the church order. According to the court, "the time has long passed when agreements, even those under seal, were isolated from the matrix of facts in which they were set and interpreted purely on internal linguistic considerations....We must enquire beyond the language and see what the circumstances were with reference to which the words were used, and the object, appearing from those circumstances, which the person using them had in view".

It is not always easy to determine which matters (suspension, dismissal, co-ownership, decision-making) are regulated by church law and which by the civil law. The church order and church constitution play an important role in assisting the courts to determine the scope of interference and review, when the lawfulness of a decision is challenged. Because disciplinary action in various churches goes hand-in-hand with the particular religious doctrines and convictions of the church, courts should act with deference. Each case should be assessed on its own merits and therefore the particular factual context is of the utmost importance. Also, associations do not have any inherent power to discipline members. The respective constitution, rules and regulations of the association must provide for that. An association must therefore exercise its disciplinary authority in accordance with the said rules and regulations and a court shall not interfere where an association has acted in accordance with its own rules. A court will however interfere where a domestic tribunal has not acted within the scope of its own rules, or has not exercised its discretion properly or has acted *ultra vires* and therefore outside the scope of its authority. Because a dismissal or suspension is one of the most severe forms of punishment, it has to be explicitly provided for by the constitution. An organization, or a church for that matter, cannot suspend a member if it is contrary to its rules, nor can a member be dismissed by an organ other than the one authorized to do so (*Yiba and Others v African Gospel Church* 1999, 960D–961H).

Domestic tribunals must exercise their functions in accordance with the requirements as laid down in the organization's constitution, but also in accordance with the rules of natural justice. What also needs to be taken into account is that it is a domestic tribunal of a voluntary association and not a court of law. Therefore, it is important to note the following words by MT Steyn in *Motaung v Mukubela and Another, NNO; Motaung v Mothiba* 1975 (618H–619A): "In considering whether there has been a material breach of the constitutional provisions of a voluntary association (such as a Church), a Court of law should not view the matter as if under a strong magnifying glass and should not carpingly ferret out and unduly enlarge every minor deviation from the strict letter of the constitutional provision being examined. Much rather should it adopt a practical, common-sense approach to the matter, constantly bearing in mind that the persons called upon to administer such a constitution are usually laymen who are unversed in the ways of the law. Where, however, despite the adoption of this benevolent approach, the Court is satisfied that there has in fact been a serious breach of the constitutional provisions of such an association and that such breach is therefore not a 'mere matter of form without any interference with the substance' of the decision involved, it should not hesitate to give full effect to the legal consequences of such a breach".

In *Odendaal v Loggerenberg en Andere NNO* 1961, the court confirmed its authority to review the decisions of domestic tribunals, and stated that it is common cause that a court of law will interfere with the decision of a domestic tribunal only when there was a violation of the rules or constitution of the association or where elementary principles of fairness were ignored and the accused was in fact prejudiced as a result of the violation. In *United Methodist Church of South Africa v Sokufundumala* 1989, a minister of the Methodist Church's service was terminated unilaterally by the congregation. The court confirmed that the respondent had the right to state his case and that the rules of natural justice had not been complied with. The court also confirmed the earlier view of Steyn in *Turner v Jockey Club of South Africa* 1974, where Botha emphasized that the rules of natural justice do not require a domestic tribunal to follow the strict procedural and technical rules of a court of law, but that "[T]hey do require such a tribunal to adopt a procedure which would afford the person charged a proper hearing by the tribunal, and an opportunity of producing his evidence and of correcting or contradicting any prejudicial statement or allegation made against him. The tribunal is required to listen fairly to both sides and to observe 'the principles of fair play'....In addition to what may be described as the procedural requirements, the fundamental principles of justice require a domestic tribunal to discharge its duties honestly and impartially....They require also that the tribunal's finding of the facts on which its decision is to be based shall be 'fair and bona fide'....It is, in other words, 'under an obligation to act honestly and in good faith".

The court came to the conclusion that the respondent in *United Methodist Church* did not get a fair hearing and an opportunity to state his case, and the decision was accordingly set aside.

### 5. *Conclusion and recommendation*

The right to freedom of religion provides churches and religious organizations with the opportunity, but also the responsibility, not only to give content to this right, but also to formulate and defend their own religious identities within the limitations set by the *Constitution* and the law. Churches and religious organizations must be able to indicate why certain secular legislation or specific procedures do not apply to them. Churches and religious organizations have a duty to adapt and evaluate their existing structures, church orders, rules and regulations in the light of the requirements of the *Constitution* and the *Bill of Rights*. These changes do not have to result in the restriction or limitation of the religious identity of the church or organization, but they should make sure that they have a thorough understanding and formulation of their own religious convictions, identity, rules and procedures.

A report by the SAHRC (SAHRC 2006, 31), sets out various guidelines for voluntary associations when they want to evaluate and adapt their constitutions, especially where they contain exclusionary policies. It can equally assist churches and religious organizations when they want to evaluate and adapt their existing church orders and constitutions. It is recommended that churches and religious organizations adopting any exclusionary policies have regard to the following:

1. Identify the right or interest that it seeks to protect [whether to exclude women or homosexuals or not incorporating certain procedures];
2. Identify the rights that may be infringed or limited by the adoption of the policy [the right to equality and non-discrimination or the right to freedom of association];
3. Determine alternative ways of achieving its objectives;
4. Adopt the alternative that achieves its objectives without unreasonably and unfairly limiting or restricting rights;
5. Maintain reasons as to why a particular method or means was adopted and other alternatives discarded or disregarded.

It is important to note that churches and religious organizations must be able to provide adequate reasons when certain fundamental rights are limited as a result of specific provisions in a church order or policy document, or where certain procedural guarantees are not incorporated. Churches and religious organizations must make sure that if they do have discriminatory provisions or policies, that they are reasonable and justifiable in accordance with the legitimate religious identity of the church or organization, and in accordance with the right to freedom of religion. While this can mean that churches will be allowed to have certain restrictive rules or policies, they are not absolute. All restrictions and limitations will always be tested in accordance with the limitation provision in section 36 of the *Constitution*. The disciplinary procedures of a church or religious organization must provide for the necessary procedural guarantees that comply with the requirements of a fair hearing, taking account of the view by Malan in *Taylor v Kurtstag* 2004 (§ 63).

Clearly, when deciding the fairness of the process, its nature must be taken into account. A religious tribunal is subject to the discipline of the *Constitution*, but its being a religious body giving effect to the associational rights of its members, must be accounted for.

Churches and congregations are among the most important of non-profit, public benefit organizations. The more they operate in the public sphere and are dependent on public funds, the greater the need for accountability and the potential for a loss of independence and vitality. If this is not taken seriously, it can lead to the erosion of the separation of church and state and to interference by the state in the internal organization of religious organizations to pursue their own public policy agendas. The important issues of autonomy of religious organizations and resolving the tension between private and public, profit and non-profit, and secular and religious, still remains relevant.

## *Abbreviations, bibliography, and cases*

ATKV: Afrikaanse Taal- en Kultuurvereniging (African Language and Culture Association).

ICNPO: International Classification of Non-profit Organizations.

ISIC: International Standard Classification.

NACE: General Industrial Classification of Economic Activities.

NTEE: National Taxonomy of Exempt Entities.

SACC: South African Council of Churches.

SAHRC: South African Human Rights Commission.

SAHRC 2006: South African Human Rights Commission 2006. Report: Public Inquiry Exclusionary Policies of Voluntary Associations: Constitutional Considerations. South African Human Rights Commission 32. Accessed October 2011. http://www.sahrc.org.za.

Ahdar, Rex J. 2001. Religious Group Autonomy, Gay Ordination, and Human Rights Law. In: O'Dair and Lewis 2001, 275–297.

Bill of Rights: South African Charter of Religious Rights and Freedoms (as amended 6th August and 1st October 2009), publicly endorsed on 21 October 2010.

Chaskalson, Mattthew, Janet Kentridge, Jonathan Klaaren, Gilbert Marcus, Derek Spitz, and Stu Woolman (eds). 2009. Constitutional Law of South Africa. Cape Town: Juta. 2nd edition.

Cheadle, Halton, and Dennis Davis. 2002. South African Constitutional Law: The Bill of Rights. Durban: Butterworths.

Colton, Paul. 2007. Religious Entities as Legal Persons — Ireland. In: Friedner 2007, 125–138.

Constitution of the Republic of South Africa (1996).

Currie, Iain, and Johan De Waal, 2005. Bill of Rights Handbook. Cape Town: Juta.

Friedner, Lars (ed.). 2007. Churches and Other Religious Organisations as Legal Persons. Leuven: Peeters.

Jeavons, Thomas H. 2003. The Vitality and Independence of Religious Organizations. In: Society 40(2003)/4, 27–36.

Langa, Pius. 2008. The Future of 'Transformative Constitutionalism' in South Africa. In: Legalbrief Today, 12 August 2008.

Legal Resources Centre (LRC). 2006. 'n Gids tot die Wet op Organisasies sonder 'n Winsoogmerk 71 van 1997. In: Information Series 2006, Number 2.

Lenta, Patrick. 2009. Taking Diversity Seriously: Religious Associations and Work-Related Discrimination. In: South African Law Journal 126(2009), 827–860.

Malherbe, Rassie. 2008. Die Impak van die Grondwet op Godsdiens: 'n Voorlopige Waarneming. In: Nederduits Gereformeerde Teologiese Tydskrif 49(2008), 263–278.

O'Dair, Richard, and Andrew Lewis (eds). Law and Religion: Current Legal Issues. Oxford: Oxford University Press.

Pienaar, Gerrit. 1997. Konstitusionele Voorskrifte rakende Regspersone. In: THRHR 60(1997), 576–577.

Salamon, Lester, and Helmut K. Anheier. 1992. In Search of the Non-profit Sector. I: The Question of Definitions. In: Voluntas 3(1992)/2, 125–151.

Salamon, Lester, and Helmut K. Anheier. 1992A. In Search of the Non-profit Sector. II: The Problem of Classification. In: Voluntas 3(1992)/3, 267–309.

Van der Vyver, Johan D. 1999. Constitutional Perspective of Church-State Relations in South Africa. In: Brigham Young University Law Review 1999, 635–672.

Van Eikema Hommes, Hendrik J. 1983. Hoofdlijnen der Rechtssociologie en De Materiële Indeling van Publiek- en Privaatrecht. Encyclopedie der Rechtswetenschap. Zwolle: Tjeenk Willink.

Woolman, Stu. 2005. Association. In: Currie and De Waal 2005, 423.

Woolman, Stu. 2009. Freedom of Association. In: Chaskalson et al. 2009, § 44.20.

Woolman, Stu. 2009A. On the Fragility of Associational Life: A Constitutional Liberal's Response to Patrick Lenta. In: SAJHR 25(2009), 280–305.

*Christian Education SA v Minister of Education* 2000 (4) SA 757 (CC).

*De Vos v Die Ringskommissie van die Ring van die NG Kerk, Bloemfontein and Another* 1952 (2) SA 83 (O).

*Harksen v Lane NO and Others* 1998 (1) SA 300 (CC).

*Minister of Home Affairs v Fourie; Gay and Lesbian Equality Project v Minister of Home Affairs* 2006 (3) BCLR 355 (CC).

*Motaung v Mukubela and Another, NNO; Motaung v Mothiba, NO* 1975 (1) SA 618 (O).

*Nederduitse Gereformeerde Kerk in Afrika (OVS); Nederduits Gereformeerde Kerk in Afrika (Phororo) v Verenigde Gereformeerde Kerk in Suider-Afrika* case number 536/96.

*Odendaal v Kerkraad van die Gemeente Bloemfontein-Wes van die NG Kerk in OVS en Andere* 1960 (1) SA 160 (O).

*Odendaal v Loggerenberg en Andere NNO* 1961 (1) SA 712 (O).

*Prenn v Simmonds* [1971] 3 All ER 237 (HL).

*Prince v President,Cape Law Society* 2002 (2) SA 794 (CC).

*Roberts v United States Jaycees* 468 US 609 (1984).

*S v Makwanyane* 1995 (6) BCLLR 665 (CC).

*Taylor v Kurtstag* 2004 (4) All SA 317 (W).

*Taylor v Kurtstag* 2005 (1) SA 362 (W).

*Theron v Ring van Wellington van die NG Sendingkerk in Suid-Afrika* 1976 (2) SA 1 (SCA).

*Turner v Jockey Club of South Africa* 1974 (3) SA 633 (SCA).

*United Methodist Church of South Africa v Sokufundumala* 1989 (4) SA 1055 (O).

*Van Heerden v Minister of Finance* 2004 (6) SA 121 (CC)

*Van Rooyen and Others v S* 2002 (8) BCLR 810 (CC)

*Wittman v Deutscher Schulverein* 1998 (4) SA 423 (T)

*Yiba and Others v African Gospel Church* 1999 (2) SA 949 (C)

# 'CHRIST, THE HEAD OF THE CHURCH'

## Authority, Leadership and Organizational Structure Within the CCAP – Nkhoma Synod in Malawi

Willie S.D. Zeze

### 1. *Introduction*

This contribution, which is an extract of my dissertation (see Zeze 2006), intends to examine critically the notion in the Church Order (*Zolamulira*: '*Zopangana ndi Zolangiza*) of the Nkhoma Synod in Malawi as stated in its Preamble: "Our Lord Jesus Christ is the Head of the Church (Ephesians 1:22; Colossians 1:18). His authority is executed by office-bearers such as ministers, elders and deacons (Acts 6:1–7; Romans 10:14–17; Philippians 1:1; 1 Timothy 5:17; 2 Timothy 2:2; Titus 1:5 Ephesians 4:11; 16)... These office-bearers exercise the authority in the church through four ecclesiastical assemblies; namely church council, Presbytery, Synod and General Synod" (CO-CCAP, Preamble). Though in the Preamble Christ is rightly acknowledged as Head of the Church and that He governs his Church through office-bearers, who associate with each other in the ecclesiastical assemblies, the Preamble of the CO-CCAP fails to say that Jesus Christ exercises his rule and reign through his Word and the Holy Spirit using the service of office-bearers. I argue in this article that a failure to say Christ's rule and authority are exercised by means of the Word of God and the Holy Spirit is a major theological shortfall that might have serious implications for church leadership and the organizational structure of the Nkhoma Synod. The absence of such a statement has negatively affected both theological and church polity discourses as well as church practice in the Church of Central Africa, Presbyterian — Nkhoma Synod (CCAP). This article critically examines and assesses how the notion in the Preamble of CO-CCAP, that Christ rules His Church through office-bearers, has negatively influenced the church polity discourse and practice in the CCAP — Nkhoma Synod.

I will address the following questions: Which church polity sources did the Nkhoma Synod use when writing its *Zolamulira*? And which contextual factors influenced its *Zolamulira*? In the first part, I discuss the context in which the church government discourse and practice of the Nkhoma Synod in Malawi took form. In discussing this, I am sensitive to the assumption that contexts are able to negatively influence church polity discourse and practice. Then I discuss the church polity sources.

## 2. *The Influence of the Malawian Context*

Malawi (formerly Nyasaland) is a long, narrow strip of land which is administratively divided into three regions comprised of twenty-eight districts: the Northern Region, the Southern Region, and the Central Region. The Nkhoma Synod is situated in the Central Region and its headquarters is at Nkhoma in the district of Lilongwe, Malawi's capital. The CCAP, of which the Nkhoma Synod is part, is divided into three Synods: the Livingstonia Synod in the Northern Region, the Blantyre Synod in South Region and the Nkhoma Synod in the Central Region. Although the political boundaries do not overlap exactly with synod boundaries, it is interesting to note that the boundaries of Malawi's political regions and the boundaries of the CCAP's synods resemble each other. The synods' administrative headquarters and the regions' administrative centers are situated in the same districts.

### 2.1 *The Social-Economic and Political Influence*

From the ancient times, Malawi's economic system relied on hunting, fishing, gathering, farming, barter, agriculture and business. These activities contributed to the development of classes of people in a hierarchy of communities, and to a certain extent people's differing positions in the economic system caused frictions in the church. This is illustrated by Joda-Mbwe's study of the relationship between church ministers and elders in congregations in towns and cities, particularly where he shows that church ministers find it difficult to relate well to upper class people in cities because most of these people are highly educated and hold senior positions in either government or non-governmental organizations (see Joda-Mbwe 2002, 107). He points out that "ministers in Malawi see themselves as holding authority and high status. They feel they can do anything that they want without any objection from the laity" (Joda-Mbwe 2002, 294).

For Msangaambe, a church minister in the Nkhoma Synod holds "a highly respectable position" (Msangaambe 2011, 63). According to him, "in general, people believe that the church minister is extremely wise and cannot be advised regarding church issues" (Msangaambe 2011, 63). It should be taken into account, however, that in many Malawian communities people have been highly respected because of their economic status. Most elders who have become executive members in presbytery and at the synod levels originate from the middle- and high-income areas of the urban Central Region. In addition to this, the hierarchical structures of the local societies, i.e., those of the Chewa and Ngoni people who constitute the majority of membership in the Nkhoma Synod, have influenced the organization of the church. According to Paas, the governing structures of the Malawian churches, including the CCAP, became an imitation of the ruling structures of society and state. He was led to this conclusion because ministers in the local churches are considered to be the exclusive principal leaders and behave like autocratic rulers (see Paas 2007, 8).

From a sociological point of view, it can be observed that historically there was no parity between the whites and the natives. It was said that "our native pastors are not equal with European ministers" (Thompson 1995, 178; cf. McCracken 2000, 290). There was a vertical social relationship between the whites and the indigenous people, which may have contributed to the development of a feeling of inferiority in Malawian communities and society. Pretorius described how local chiefs viewed the whites: first, white people were seen as valuable instruments that provided security and protection to Malawian local communities against their enemies (Pretorius 1971, 366f.; cf. Pauw 1980, 66). Second, their presence was a valuable insurance against plotting by civil counselors, particularly against war-like tribes such as the Ngoni and the Yao. Third, the missionaries were regarded as persons who had power to manipulate supernatural forces; hence it was prudent and advantageous to have them near. We can add another reason why the whites, particularly the missionaries, were not equal with the natives. It was because of their unique role as go-betweens in negotiations with chiefs who quarreled, and between chiefs and the state. In his recent research, Msangaambe concludes that in the Nkhoma Synod the social relationship between church leaders and members is partly influenced by the Nyau cult which in its occult practices demands strict and immediate obedience of subordinates to their leaders (see Msangaambe 2011, 163). We can preliminarily conclude that the church uncritically derived its polity from the polity of the Nyau cult, and drew its leadership from the village headmen and other leaders within Malawian society. Leadership ideas inherited from them influenced to a certain extent, either positively or negatively, the church's polity discourse and the practice of church government.

Malawi's political system at village, town, district and national levels is another factor that has had direct influence on church polity practice and church government discourse in the Nkhoma Synod. Historically, on each level one officer was in authority; he hovered above the office-bearers who were considered his assistants. Pachai observes a similar system during pre-missionary and pre-colonial era: "As for the political history of the Maravi peoples, involving both local and external relations, the senior kings had a number of subordinate or tributary kings who owed allegiance to him locally....Where there was a single political structure when the settlements were close and the *Karonga* [title of the paramount chief of the Chewa -WZ] was at the head, now there were as many political units as there were rulers" (Pachai 1972, 8f.). It is interesting to note that in the systems of the Chewa and the Ngoni all tribal matters and laws were discussed at the so-called 'great council', i.e., a gathering of chiefs, nobles and village-headmen and their *indunas*. They employed a top-down system in which the great councils made the decisions. In addition, the Ngoni political system was characterized by a military organization with a related system of age grades, organized under the paramount chief with his hierarchy of local office-bearers, together with a system of courts, again in a strict hierarchy (cf. Phiri 2000, 61f.).

In 1891 when the country became a British protectorate, a new system of ruling was introduced called 'Indirect Rule' (see Baker 1971, 7). In it the British used African traditional rulers to work on their behalf to subjugate their fellow Africans. These Africans ruled nominally; the actual decisions were made by the British colonial officers. A British Consul or the Governor executed rule of the country through commissioners who were appointed in each district. Seniors assisted each district commissioner. From 1891 to 1961 the administrative system of the country largely consisted of a hierarchy from consul-general to district commissioners to chiefs (see Baker 1971, 7). Jones concludes that "[T]he Nyasaland government in its early days was autocratic. Sir Harry Johnston, the first Governor, derived his authority from the British; provided he kept the support of the government, his decision in Nyasaland was final" (Jones 1966, 190).

According to Ross, between 1961 and 1994 power was conditioned by the authoritarianism of the one-party system (see Ross 1996, 265). This influenced the church. Ross quotes Silas Ncosana, a former Blantyre Synod General Secretary: "The one-party system certainly influenced the way the church exercised its power...so the church became much more clerical than it ought to have been.... Clearly, the church has not been immune to the tendency to think of the exercise of power in authoritarian terms....Similarly, church leadership too often mirrors the corruption and graft prevalent in wider society, rather than offering a challenge to it. Clergy seek power within the church structures in order to gain access to resources, principally money and women" (Ross 1996, 265).

Ross again points out that during Dr. Hasting Kamuzu Banda's regime CCAP clergy exercised power and authority in the same way as political leaders did (see Ross 1996, 66). One of the reasons is that most of the ministers, elders and deacons were once members of the Malawi Congress Party youth league as branch or area chairpersons. In his research regarding office-bearers, i.e., ministers and elders,

Paas rightly observes: "In Presbyterian and other denominations, the government of the church has often become an imitation of the ruling structures in state and society. Depending on the prevailing culture and political climate the minister is the principal leader. He may behave as an autocratic ruler or he may have adopted the style of a modern manager in a more democratic way. Under him, the elders are a body of executives" (Paas 2007, 8).

Paas does not, however, specify to which Malawian Presbyterian church and to which other denominations he is referring, and he gives no further evidence. Yet his observation is slightly supported by Brown: "The evolution of the office of General Secretary bears mention, because he continues to wield considerable power like the Stated Clerk of American Presbyterianism; while not a dictator, he nevertheless commands great respect and the role of the Moderamen, which includes the General Secretary, wields significant power. The authoritative character of CCAP — Nkhoma Synod *abusa* (ministers) is also revealing. In some cases they appear to be similar to traditional village headman" (Brown 2004, 73).

In conclusion, what Brown and Paas observe regarding how Malawian society and its political system negatively influenced the organizational system of the church urges us to ask the following question: How was the integrity of the Nkhoma Synod endangered by the Malawian political system?

The integrity of the Nkhoma Synod in matters of church polity was endangered by the political system of Malawi in the sense that the country's political system became characteristic of its church government. The tendencies toward autocracy, dictatorship and clerocracy that can be noticed in the church's polity discourse and practice certainly mirror the political system of Malawian society, although other contexts also played important roles.

So far, what has been observed above leads us to a second question: Should developments in church polity be dictated by political context? This question is answered in article 30 of the *Belgic Confession of Faith* which states, 'We believe that this true Church must be governed by that spiritual policy [polity] which our Lord hath taught us in his Word'. And also in article 32 of the same confession we read that 'those who govern the churches should establish and set up a certain order for maintaining the body of the church' and 'they ought always to guard against deviating from what Christ, the only Master, has ordained' It is clear from these two articles that church polity must not be dictated by political context, because if it does its identity and essence may be compromised.

### 2.2 *The Christian Ecclesial Influence*

The Episcopal, Presbyterian, Reformed/Presbyterial, and congregational systems of church government were established in Malawi in the nineteenth and twentieth centuries. Anglican missionaries and Roman Catholic missionaries established their respective Episcopal systems. Scottish missionaries of the Church of Scotland and the Free Church of Scotland established the Presbyterian system. South African missionaries of the Afrikaans Dutch Reformed Church established the Reformed/Presbyterial system. Lutheran missionaries, especially from America, established the Lutheran system. Missionaries of Baptist, Pentecostal, evangelical, Seventh Day Adventist, etc. churches, either through faith missions or through their own denominations, established the congregational system.

When Christian missionaries from different parts of the world came to Malawi, they found it difficult to agree which system of church government would be suitable for the African churches. In 1932 Hetherwick said: "The question of what form such organized life should take is one that no one can or dare attempt to answer at this early stage in the history of the Church of Central Africa. Naturally, each mission will set itself to organize its converts on the lines of the system of government which rules in the mother church of the mission. A Presbyterian Mission will order its daughter on the Presbyterian system, an Episcopalian Mission on Episcopalian lines and so on in the many forms of Christian activity in the homeland" (Hetherwick 1932, 140).

This section will examine and assess whether and how the episcopal, the congregational, the Presbyterian and the Reformed systems of church government negatively influenced the Nkhoma Synod's church polity discourse as well as its church government practice.

#### 2.2.1 *Episcopalism*

In Malawi the Roman Catholic Church polity was the second Episcopal polity to be established, after the Anglican. It was founded in 1902 through the enterprise of the priests of the White Fathers and the Montfort Fathers (see Linden and Weller 1984, 100). Roman Catholicism spread through central mission stations, vicariates and ultimately parishes. Each parish is under the leadership of an *Abambo Mfumu* (lit.: 'Mr. King'), who is priest-in-charge or 'father superior' A group of parishes forms a diocese with a bishop as its head. In Nyasaland, all mission stations collectively attained the status of The Nyasa Apostolic Prefecture on 21 July 1889. Joseph DuPont became its head (see Veveau 1989, 157–168). Today the Roman Catholic Church in Malawi has a fully-empowered hierarchy, consisting of the Blantyre Archdiocese and six dioceses (Chikwawa, Dedza, Lilongwe, Mangochi, Mzuzu, and Zomba) (see Ott 2000, 225–226; Paas 2006, 198–200).

Reijnaerts and others observe that the offices in the Roman Catholic Church are highly regarded (see Reijnaerts et al. 1997, 353). At every level they demand honor and respect from lower office-bearers. The hierarchical structure is centered on the priest at parish level, on the bishop at diocese level and on the pope at world level. Ott reports that in more recent times people who want to reorganize the Roman Catholic Church into small Christian communities would like to give up the church as a hierarchy and replace it with the 'Church as people of God' in a system of 'collegiality' (see Ott 2000, 228).

The CCAP has a historical link with the Anglican Church, which also maintains an episcopal structure. From 1978 to 2008 Anglican students for the priesthood were trained at Zomba Theological College (ZTC). Anglican clergy were among the full-time lecturers there, e.g., Rodney Hunter, James Tengatenga, Moses M'baya, Christopher Mwawa and Rodney Schofield. The latter became a Roman Catholic priest after his time at ZTC. In the exchange of ideas at ZTC, it is possible that these lecturers imparted Anglican sensitivities to their CCAP students.

### 2.2.2 *Congregationalism*

In Malawi, congregationalism (a form of church government in which final human authority rests with the local or particular congregation when it gathers for decision making) was introduced through the enterprises of Zambezi Industrial Mission, the Nyasa Industrial Mission, the Seventh Day Adventist Mission and Providence Industrial Mission. Most of these churches arrived on the Malawian scene in the person of Joseph Booth. The largest of these was the Zambezi Industrial Mission, founded in 1892 (see Phiri 2004, 153). The mission stations of these churches eventually attained the status of independent congregations. Each of these local congregations is autonomous, all the decisions are made with majority votes, and the church councils merely implement such decisions. In other words, the governing power rests exclusively with the members of the local church. Office-bearers, including missionaries, ministers and deacons are simply functionaries of the congregation. General meetings of all the congregations are organized not for making decisions or resolving matters in a way binding on all the congregations, but as conferences or general fellowship meetings for spiritual enrichment and consideration of matters they share in common. There has been no interaction between the congregational churches and the Nkhoma Synod. For this reason I cannot claim that congregational churches influenced the church polity discourse and practice of the Nkhoma Synod.

### 2.2.3 *Presbyterianism*

Presbyterian church polity or Presbyterianism is a system of church government by elders in their assemblies. It was introduced into Malawi by the missions of the Church of Scotland and the Free Church of Scotland. The two missions founded respectively the Blantyre Mission (later Blantyre Synod) and the Livingstonia Mission (later Livingstonia Synod). In 1924 they joined together to form the CCAP, a federated church which the CCAP — Nkhoma Synod joined in 1926. Retief describes the relationship between the theological traditions and the system of church government in the CCAP: "The name Presbyterian is added to indicate the system...which is followed by the Church. It is Reformed as to the Creed and Presbyterian to government as exactly the mother Church is" (Retief 1958, 157).

Retief's remark implies that the church government of the CCAP — Nkhoma Synod is Presbyterian, not Reformed. Presbyterian Church government, according to De Ridder, has the following characteristics: First, there is one basic office, the eldership, consisting of teaching or ordained elders, and ruling elders. Second, the ecclesiastical assemblies are arranged in a hierarchical order, with a church council as the lower court, a presbytery as the basic governmental unit, and a synod or general assembly as the highest court. These courts often function as judicatories. Third, these courts emphasize the ruling power (authority) of the elders. Fourth, the church council is in many ways responsible to the presbytery and under its control (see de Ridder 1983, 20). Below I will observe how these characteristics are retained and affirmed in all the churches that belong to the CCAP.

#### 2.2.3.1 *The Presbyterianism of the CCAP Livingstonia Synod*

The establishment of Scottish missions to Malawi followed the Anglican response to Livingstone's urgent appeal through letters, articles, and his address at the Senate house in Cambridge on 4 December 1857 (see Linden and Weller 1984, 39). The Church of Scotland and the Free Church of Scotland sent an expedition comprised of, among others, Robert Laws and Henry Henderson, the pioneer missionaries of the Blantyre Mission.

Efforts to expand the mission work resulted in the establishment of the following mission stations: Ekwendeni (1889), Loudon (1889), Njuyu (1900), Kaning'ina, etc. (see McCracken 2000, 109; Paas 2006, 189–193). These stations probably attained the status of congregations after they established Kirk sessions, which are comprised of ministers and elders. All the Kirk sessions were under an umbrella body, called the Livingstonia Mission Council, which consisted of all the ordained ministers and church elders representing every Kirk session. Organizationally the Livingstonia Mission did not exactly reflect the church order and church government of the Free Church of Scotland. McCracken notes: "It is one of the ironies of Livingstonia that a Presbyterian Free Church Mission should have been organized on highly centralized, autocratic lines. The Free Church of Scotland was a decentralized body with semi-autonomous parishes controlled by a minister supported and to some extent degree supervised, by a committee of lay elders" (McCracken 2000, 224).

The Livingstonia Mission has harbored strong tendencies toward hierarchicalism and clericalism, providing ministers with exclusive authority similar to that of the bishop in episcopal circles. The matter of parity among minister, elder and deacon did not receive any attention or consideration. The situation was also the same between the indigenous leaders and the ordained missionaries and among the office-bearers in general. Thompson quotes the remarks made by Rev. W.A. Elmslie who sharply said about his African colleague: "He is an assistant to me, working under my supervision. He has no congregation of his own. He lives on the station with me and takes his work according to my guiding" (Thompson 1995, 178).

Furthermore Thompson and McCracken both quote Donald Fraser who sharply emphasized, "Our native pastors are not equal with European ministers" (Thompson 1995, 178; McCracken 2000, 290). Although Fraser does not give details of what he means, this is an indication that from early times in the Livingstonia Synod church offices were viewed in terms of rank, dignity and status.

On the question regarding authority in the church, Sindima comments: "Livingstonia was slow in appointing Africans to positions of authority even when they had attained good educational qualifications and experience in mission work. Missionaries held all positions of authority, made all decisions without even consulting Malawians. In most cases, their decision was final since they considered it 'Law of Christ' The missionaries exercised major influence on all matters, including those of the Session, even when they were a minority" (Sindima 1992, 38).

One of the issues I want to comment on is the question concerning the seat of authority in the church. It seems the Livingstonia Mission held the idea that the point of departure in the church government is the rule of Christ through office-bearers. On this view the authority of the church is centered in the offices that constitute the highest assembly. Thus, the synod is the highest court of the church with the presbytery as the basic governmental unit and the church council as the lowest court. Van Wyk observes similar developments in the Church of Scotland: "The Presbytery was confirmed as the basic unit in the government of the church. Ministers were considered as first of all to be members of the Presbytery and only secondary related to the congregation. The replacement of the rule of

Christ through his Word and Spirit using office-bearers with representation of office-assembly as found in Scottish Presbyterian Ecclesiology was maintained" (Van Wyk 2004, 80–81).

Van Wyk also points out: "Episcopal related to individual was replaced by Episcopal exercised by Presbyters in hierarchical assemblies or courts" (Van Wyk 2004, 81). The hierarchical and clerical tendency in the Livingstonia Mission and (also later) the Livingstonia Synod was rooted in the fact that the eldership was a lifelong office as well as in the fact that the office of the pastors was separated from the congregation because it was believed that they represent and belong to the presbytery and synod and not to the local congregation (cf. Chilenje 2007, 156). It can be suggested that Livingstonia's hierarchical arrangements and attitudes influenced those involved in church polity discourses and church government in the Nkhoma Synod through their association in the General Synod of the CCAP and in ZTC.

#### *2.2.3.2 The Presbyterianism of the CCAP Blantyre Synod*

Presbyterianism similar to that of the CCAP — Livingstonia Synod is also harbored by the Blantyre Mission (later Blantyre Synod), a mission founded once again as a result of Livingstone's appeal through letters, articles and addresses (see Ross 1996, 23). It was the missionary organization of the (Established) Church of Scotland, which sent its pioneer Henry Henderson with the party of the Livingstonia Mission in 1875. The first mission station was established on 23 October 1876. By 1892 the Blantyre Mission had opened the following stations which by 1900 had attained status of congregations: Kapeni (1876), Zomba (1879), Domasi (1884), Chiladzulo (1884), Mulanje (1887). Ross describes the first stage in the training of African office-bearers: "The training of Africans took more shape in 1893 with the announcement that a deacon class of seven but representative of many more who will in like manner devote themselves to service, meets every morning at 7 o'clock.…All these successfully completed their training and were ordained as deacons on 4th November 1894" (Ross 1996, 112).

Together with the leading missionary David Clement Scott they formed a Kirk session as a body for exercising church discipline. In 1895 these deacons were ordained and given responsibility for the life and work of the mission, and for churches in certain groups in villages around Blantyre. Ross notes that this Malawian office of deacon is not familiar to Presbyterian churches in general (see Ross 1996, 112). It was a creation of D.C. Scott, who wanted to use the knowledge and wisdom of the Africans especially in the area of church discipline. Some missionaries opposed the ordination of natives because it implied a kind of equality between the white ministers and the indigenous leaders. They thought it utterly wrong to teach any native that he is as good as the white man, because he is not. If he were as good, he would be on a level with the white man, but it is because he is inferior that he is under the white man. Hierarchical tendencies among office-bearers and ecclesiastical courts of the Blantyre Mission were illustrated by Hetherwick: "The Presbytery recognized the order of deacons as an office preparatory to that of the eldership—their function being not merely to deal with the finances of the church but also to assist the elders in their office.... The deacons attended and took part in all meetings of session but had no vote. In practice after a few years on the deaconate they are advanced to the eldership" (Hetherwick 1931, 127).

The establishment of the Mission Council of the Blantyre Mission as the first governing assembly was followed by the founding of a Kirk session around 1900, a presbytery in 1904 and the synod in 1956. The Mission Council was responsible to the Home Committee in Scotland. Ross observes that, although in some areas indigenous structures were set up, "... the Mission Council was always the real source of both power and authority. This was because it controlled the larger resources usually including all the building, whether schools or churches....The local Session and Presbytery had little or no control over major elements in the staff and property of the churches in their area....The Mission Council, in effect a white oligarchy, controlled the major financial resources in the field, paying for African teachers and evangelists (that is for most of the full time staff) and controlling their posting and work. Neither the Kirk Sessions formed in 1900 nor the Presbytery founded in 1904 had any authority over these vital matters. Even the matter of directions in which the Church should expand appeared on the agenda of the Mission Council" (Ross 1996, 172, 177). Between 1904 and 1924, the Blantyre Presbytery was officially the highest ecclesiastical court for Europeans and Africans in all church matters, but in reality the Mission Council was responsible for everything. In 1924 the synod of the CCAP became the highest ecclesiastical court, although by this time the church had not yet received its autonomy from the Church of Scotland. In 1956 the Presbytery of Blantyre together with the Presbyteries of Livingstonia and Nkhoma attained status of synods, with a General Synod as Supreme Court of appeal. In 1958 the church received autonomy from the Church of Scotland.

Hierarchical tendencies were engrafted into the synod. Hetherwick recommended that the system of church government for the CCAP should resemble the civil government where the chief and the headman ruled over his council of elders—a system that according to Hetherwick might represent in the true rule of the church that of the bishop in his synod of presbyters, and of the minister in his session of elders (see Hetherwick 1932, 150). The system of church government operated by the Scottish missions, today the Synods of Blantyre and Livingstonia, has been characterized by a hierarchicalism similar to the system of episcopalianism in the sense that instead of a hierarchy of office-bearers summiting in a bishop, there has been a hierarchy of ecclesiastical assemblies in which the synod or the General Synod is the highest assembly and a church council or a session the lowest court. Van Wyk notes that in the Church of Scotland the office of minister was separated from the congregation, the office of elder was reduced to assistant to the minister, and the authority of Christ was transferred to the offices which govern the church through courts in an episcopal sense (see Van Wyk 2004, 166). He concludes: "The Presbyterian system of Church government became characteristic of the government of the Reformed churches in Central Africa. In these Churches, the emphasis falls on the maintenance of the institution through its executive functions in accordance with the comprehensive law book. The local church as a locus for the direct rule of Christ enjoys little or no attention" (Van Wyk 2004, 166).

Paas gives his personal comment on the problems of clericalism and authority in the CCAP: "The way how ministers are addressed, as *reverend* (exalted one), or *dominee* (lord) is indicative of their elevated position....The clericalist tendency is even strong in the churches that derive much of their Presbyterianism from the English scene. An example is the Church of Central Africa, Presbyterian in the countries of Malawi, Zambia, and Zimbabwe. External and internal authority in the Church is almost completely in the hand of ministers....The church is organized in a top-to bottom structure, leaving elders of the local congregation without significant influence at Presbytery and Synod levels. Practically, the ordained clergy take all the decisions in their respective Presbyteries and Synods. Full time clerical officials at Synod level are particularly powerful" (Paas 2007, 183).

The Presbyterian system of church government, which the CCAP of Blantyre and Livingstonia derived from the Scottish Missions, with its professionalism, hierarchicalism and clericalism, seems to be a compromise with the system of episcopalian church government. This compromise has not failed to influence the CCAP — Nkhoma Synod.

### 2.2.4 *The Reformed Church Polity: The Government of the Nkhoma Synod?*

The Reformed or Presbyterial church polity was introduced in Malawi (previously Nyasaland) through the missionary enterprise of the Dutch Reformed Church (DRC) of the Cape Synod in South Africa. The first missionary, Rev. Andrew Charles Murray, arrived in 1888 and a year later he was followed by Rev. Theunis Botha Vlok. They set up the first mission station, at Mvera in Dowa district, on

28 November 1889. From Mvera the mission work spread to many parts of the Central Region and to some parts of the Southern Region (see Pauw 1980, 174). Early expansion resulted in the establishments of mission stations at Kongwe (1894), and Nkhoma (1896). The stations of Livlezi (1886) and Malembo (1895) were taken over from the Livingstonia Mission because they were located south of the thirteenth degree latitude which was considered the boundary between the Scottish and Dutch mission fields (see Du Plessis 1929,307; Paas 2006, 195-197). The work of the DRC Mission (DRCM) was under the supervision of the Livingstonia Mission until 1897, when it became independent.

By 1899 each mission station became a congregation simultaneously with the institution of church councils. In 1903 a governing body, the Council of Congregations, was set up to be responsible for the practical functions of the Presbytery. The DRCM joined the Synod of the Presbyteries of Blantyre and Livingstonia in 1926. Thirty years later, it attained the status of synod together with the two Scottish Presbyteries. It became an autonomous church in 1962.

Although the church government of the Nkhoma Synod is said to be Reformed or Presbyterial, in which Jesus Christ alone exercises His rule and authority through His Word and the Holy Spirit using office-bearers who assemble in the formal ecclesiastical assemblies, it is characterized by hierarchicalism among office-bearers and assemblies, as well as clericalism, because the church is organized as a top-down system with clerical officials on committees and at synod level being particularly powerful (cf. Van Wyk 2004, 166-167; Zeze 2006, 8; Paas 2007, 183). The reason for this is that the church government of the Nkhoma Synod was developed in the context of its geographical landscape, and under social-political, economic, religious, and Christian-ecclesial conditions in which certain aspects of its contexts were able to influence negatively its polity discourse and practice. In addition to this Van Wyk has noted that the Nkhoma Synod uncritically imitated ruling systems of society, religious bodies, and other churches, such as those of the Malawian state, the Nyau Society and Scottish Presbyterianism (see Van Wyk 2004, 166f.).

Although my main intention is to investigate the impact of what is stated in the Preamble of the CO-CCAP, the most fundamental fact is that throughout history many churches have found it difficult to live under the reality of the direct rule of Christ. As a consequence they have come up with different theories to explain how Christ rules the church. The Roman Catholic Church takes its point of departure as the rule of Christ through Pope and bishops, whereas other episcopal churches take as their starting point rule through bishops (cf. Berkhof 1996, 580ff.). For some Lutheran and Anglican churches Christ's dominion takes place through the state (cf. Vorster 2003, 3). Congregational churches went further. For them Christ exercises his rule through every member, and the government of the church is transferred into the hands of the members of the congregations (see Coertzen 2004, 94). Collegial churches (including Scottish Presbyterians) stress that Christ executes his government through the representatives of church office-bearers associated in assemblies. In this regard, they are of the opinion that authority is centered in the ecclesiastical assemblies of presbyters (cf. Van Wyk 2004, 167; Berkhof 1996, 582).

### 3. *The Church Polity Sources of the Nkhoma Synod*

Founded in 1889, the CCAP — Nkhoma Synod is one of the churches with a direct or an indirect historical link to the Dutch Reformed Church in the Netherlands through the DRC of the Cape Synod in South Africa. Like the DRC in South Africa, the Nkhoma Synod subscribes to the so-called Three Reformed Symbols of Unity — the *Belgic Confession* (1561), the *Heidelberg Catechism* (1563), and the *Canons of Dordt* (1618–1619) — as its confessional formularies. Although the Bible is the primary source from which the Reformed churches have developed their polity, the three Symbols mentioned are also considered important church polity sources for Reformed churches. This section attempts to assess whether the three mentioned documents in addition to the Bible were really used as the sources from which the Nkhoma Synod developed its church order and church government. Special attention is paid to confessional articles that deal with church government, particularly with how the Word of God and the Holy Spirit are connected to church government.

In the *Belgic Confession* Jesus Christ is acknowledged as eternal King (art. 27), Lord, a universal Bishop (art. 30, 31), Head of the church (art. 29, 31), and Master (art. 32). These names indicate Christ's highest authority and sovereignty in the Church. They denote that not any other person should rule the church or ever assume the position of Head of the church (cf. Pauw 1980, 384). Article 30 of the *Confession* sees church polity, including its government, in the perspective of the Word of God: "We believe, that this true Church must be governed by that spiritual policy [polity -WZ] which our Lord hath taught us in his Word; namely, that there must be ministers or pastors to preach the Word of God, and to administer the sacraments; also elders and deacons, who, together with the pastors, form the council of the Church". This article indicates that church polity is something that is to be believed or confessed but not argued. In other words, the order and the government of the church is a matter of faith. There is a direct link between the Word of God and church government. It should be arranged according to the Bible, implying that the Bible contains guidelines for it. Beets comments: "The authority over this society [the Church] according to the Reformed conception rests with and is centered in Christ, the glorified Head of the Church (cf. Ephesians 1:22). He rules its members directly through His Spirit in applying the Word and the Sacraments. But indirectly the Church is governed by those who represent Christ, his deputies, the bearers of the offices existing in the church: minister or pastor, elders and deacons" (Beets 2002, 224).

For Beets the words 'policy' or 'polity' signify arrangement (see Beets 2002, 224). The word *spiritual* is prefixed to indicate that the government of the church is from God's Spirit and through God's Spirit. Church government is to be in keeping with the spiritual character of the church. It is not a hierarchy; neither should civil rulers be permitted to dominate the church's affairs, nor office-bearers lord it over each other. Article 30 also mentions four different purposes of spiritual church government: "[First] that by these means true religion may be preserved, [second] that the true doctrine everywhere propagated, [third] likewise transgressors punished and restrained by spiritual means, and [fourth] also that the poor and distressed may be relieved and comforted, according to their necessities. [Following this, a conclusion is drawn:] By these means everything will be carried on in the church with good order and decency, when faithful men are chosen, according to the rule prescribed by St. Paul in his Epistle to Timothy".

In the article above it is seen that the church does not consist of like-minded people nor can it be ruled according to the personal wishes of its individual members. It is not a democracy, where the people rule. It is not a social organization either, where the highest social rank rules. It is not a clerical aristocracy, where clerical aristocrats rule (governance is not by the clergy). It is a Christocracy, where Christ himself rules through his Word and Spirit using office-bearers (cf. Janssen 2000, 29).

Article 31 of the *Confession* stipulates that one is not permitted to rule the church in a self-chosen manner. When electing people to a particular office, the whole congregation is involved. The entire congregation is to beseech the Lord to show them for whom they should vote. Members are to implore the Lord to indicate who He wishes to use as office-bearers in his church.

The *Heidelberg Catechism* also contains important references to the concept of the headship of Christ. In question 50 we read, 'Why is added, and He sits at the Right hand of God?' The answer says that Christ ascended into heaven to manifest Himself there as Head of His church, through whom the Father governs all things. Question 51 asks, 'What profit is this glory of Christ, our Head, to us?' Answer: 'First, that by His Holy Spirit, He pours out heavenly gifts upon us, his members; and then that by his power He defends and preserves us against all his enemies'

Considering these articles, I wish to make two comments. First, the phrase 'He sits at the right hand of God' points to Christ's existence as well as to the conviction that the church is a heavenly work performed on earth, rather than merely an earthly society of like-minded people. In this understanding it is evident that office-bearers have no authority in and of themselves. Their authority is bestowed on them from heaven. Second, answer 51 asserts that the Holy Spirit is involved in all the activities in the church, including its government. As one school of thought stresses, this means office-bearers are not primarily representatives of the church members but of Christ.

The Reformed tradition developed a distinct understanding probably due to the profound influence of John Calvin, who writes: "*Why does God need men's service?* Now we must speak of the order by which the Lord willed his Church to be governed. He alone should rule and reign in the Church as well as has authority or pre-eminence in it....Nevertheless because He does not dwell among us in visible presence (Mt 26:11), we have said that he uses the ministry of men to declare openly his will as by mouth as sort of delegated work not by transferring to them his right and honor but only that through their mouths, he may do his work—just as a workman uses tools to do his work" (Calvin 1559, IV, 6, 1). Elsewhere Calvin writes: "Now it is Christ's right to preside over all councils and to have no man share his dignity. But I say that He presides only when the whole assembly is governed by His Word and Spirit" (Calvin 1559, IV, 9, 1).

Calvin's views on the way in which Christ rules the church is reworded by Van Wyk in his summary of the Reformed churches' view: 'The Presbyterial-synodical system of church government takes as its departure point the rule of Christ through His Word and Spirit using office-bearers in the visible church' (Van Wyk 2004, 165). Coertzen observes: "Reformed Church governments also confess that Jesus Christ is the Lord and Head of his Church. For example, article 31 of the *Dutch Confession of Faith* [*Belgic Confession*—Ed.] states that Jesus Christ is the universal Superintendent and the only Head of Church, while article 29 of the same confession of faith confesses that the true Church is where people behave themselves according to the Word of God, reject all that is in conflict and acknowledge Christ as the only Head" (Coertzen 2004, 95). He further states: "The way in which Christ practices his authority and sovereignty over the Church is through the ministry of the Word and through his Sprit. This takes place directly in the heart of each believer, but also through the ministry of people who apply for this" (Coertzen 2004, 95).

We conclude that the Reformed churches' understanding of the rule of Christ in the church is distinct in the sense that it maintains a well-balanced view of Christological, pneumatological and ecclesiological realities. This understanding demonstrates that the Reformed discourse on church polity has been the result of the work of the Holy Spirit in maintaining the rule of Christ through His

Word using office-bearers (cf. Van Wyk 2004, 165-166). In light of this, in the Nkhoma Synod's church order, particularly in its Preamble, it is seen that there is no connection between the Word of God and the Holy Spirit and the government of the church. What the Preamble fails to articulate can be considered a major theological shortfall which may have implications for church leadership and the organizational structure in the church. One wonders whether the Nkhoma Synod really used Reformed polity sources.

*4. Church Government through Office-Bearers: A Theological Deficiency*

We now turn to the question regarding the point of departure of the CO-CCAP with regard to the rule and reign of Christ in church government, and how it has impacted the exercise of authority, the development of leadership, and organizational structure within the Nkhoma Synod. The discussion revolves around the Preamble of the CO-CCAP. The history of the CO-CCAP is called-for first.

The history of the CO-CCAP dates back to 1903. The first edition is said to have been a translation of articles of the church order of the DRC together with revised resolutions and responses to some important overtures, i.e., questions sent to the church council or presbytery or synod (see Pauw 1980, 327). The first edition of the CO-CCAP probably appeared in 1904, soon after the first meetings of the first Council of Congregations in December 1903 (see Pauw 1980, 327). It contained stipulations regarding the minimum age of admission to catechumen classes, church discipline and the division of work between the Mission Council and the Council of Congregations. The current edition (2001) retains some elements of the DRC church order as well as some elements of resolutions of the Council of Congregations, the Presbytery of Nkhoma, and later of the Synod of Nkhoma. The Synod, in its assembly of 1970, resolved that after every Synod meeting the CO-CCAP would be supplemented with new regulations or amendments, and that after every ten years a new edition would be published incorporating all the supplements. At the same meeting it was also ruled that the book of *Zolamulira* would contain two types of laws: 'genuine laws' and 'ordinary decisions' Genuine laws are laws and regulations that cannot be speedily changed. Ordinary laws are regulations which can be changed or deleted at any meeting. They are provisional, relative, and temporal, subject to revision and correction.

The current edition of the CO-CCAP contains 813 articles which, *inter alia*, are laws and regulations. According to Mijoga, a good number of these laws and regulations are unbiblical (see Mijoga 2001, 32f.). On the contrary the Preamble of the CO-CCAP claims and defends itself by asserting that the laws and regulations are ecclesiastically-founded and scriptural. The preceding immediately brings to the fore the question whether it is right for a church order to contain numerous stipulations. One can respond to this question by saying that a church order may become a mere law book or a mere volume of regulations if it contains too detailed, numerous and less important stipulations. But too few stipulations or vagueness in church order may lead church members to consider a church order an unfair ruler. Coertzen quotes De Vries who argues that a church needs to be vigilant against turning its church order into a law book or a volume of regulations next to Scripture; adding that to regard and deal with church order in such a manner is detrimental to Christ's sovereignty and risks his church becoming the victim of human sovereignty (see Coertzen 2004, 192).

On the question regarding a link between the government of the church and Word of God and the Holy Spirit, as has already been noted above the Preamble of the CO-CCAP positively reflects the Reformed understanding of Christ's headship over the church, His rule, and the three-fold system of offices (the minister, elder and deacon) that constitutes a church council. But, negatively it is silent on the question whether Christ governs the church through His Word and the Holy Spirit using office-bearers.

Theologically speaking, the fact that the Preamble fails to say that Christ rules his church through the Word of God and the Holy Spirit implies that the CO-CCAP minimizes or ignores the sovereignty of the Holy Spirit, who though distinct with God the Father is fully God, co-exists and is co-equal, one God with the other two Persons of the Trinity. In stating only that Christ's government takes places through office-bearers, the CO-CCAP makes the authority of office-bearers equal to the authority of the Word of God and the Holy Spirit (cf. Coertzen 2004, 99). It seems the church polity discourse of the CO-CCAP separates Christocracy from pneumatocracy. Coertzen shows in various publications the serious consequences of separating the church from its foundation: "Christ makes use of the Word to govern his Church, and if the Church in any way was to abandon the Word, then it no longer has any foundation from which it can give witness to the world" (Coertzen 1998, 21). "However, it is by no means an imaginary danger that the church can emphasize its government to such an extent by means of the Word, that there is no room for the work of the Holy Spirit. Should this happen then the danger will be so great that dealing with Scripture can become a mere human event " (Coertzen 2004, 103). "We speak of the execution of Christ's government in the Church as something that takes place by means of the Word, the Holy Spirit and people's ministry" (Coertzen 2004, 99).

## 5. *Conclusion*

In conclusion, this essay clearly affirms that in founding its church order—in its attempt to develop a Reformed church polity discourse and church government—the Nkhoma Synod was in some ways aware of the church's context and the content of other church polity documents. That makes it even more mysterious why the Nkhoma Synod omitted that Christ's government takes place through his Word and Spirit. Apparently the Nkhoma Synod has not followed the Reformed tradition, where the Reformed confessions acknowledge that Christ exercises his reign and dominion through his Word and Spirit using office-bearers. By equating the authority of office-bearers to the Word of God and the Holy Spirit (cf. Coertzen 2004, 99), the Preamble has paved the way for other tendencies such as paternalism, patronage, hierarchicalism, autocracy, clerocracy and legalism as well as the problem of viewing church offices or ecclesiastical posts in terms of rank, status, and dignity. Ecclesiologically there has been a danger therefore that the leadership and authority of church office-bearers be identified too completely with the rule and authority of Christ because the office-bearers may claim unchallengeable possession of the power and authority of Christ. Consequently, they seem to claim the exclusive right to take the rule of Christ through His Word and Spirit into their own hands. Thus they tend to take Christ's place, by which they practically run the risk of excluding Christ's authority and rule from the church. Considering this danger, Dutch Reformed theologian Willie Jonker writes: "For this reason Reformers rejected the idea of identity between Christ and the office-bearers as well as the idea that the office-bearers possess any personal authority to govern the church. They contend that the Word of God alone should rule in the church and that office-bearers have no other duty than to administer the Word through which Christ rules. For this reason they see church government as simply making room for the rule of the Word of God alone" (Jonker 1965, 32).

Modestly speaking, this conclusion must not be viewed only as negative. On a positive note it should function as a point of departure toward understanding the church's discourse on church polity not only in Malawi but also in churches throughout the whole southern part of Africa. As such it is an invitation to further theological discussion, in order to grow nearer to biblical truth.

## *Abbreviations and bibliography*

CCAP: Church of Central Africa Presbyterian—Nkhoma Synod.

CO-CCAP: Church order of the CCAP (Zolamulira: Zopangana ndi Zolangiza. Vol. I. Lilongwe: Nkhoma Press. 2001).

DRC: Dutch Reformed Church (South Africa).
DRCM: Dutch Reformed Church Mission.
ZTC: Zomba Theological College.

Baker, Colin. 1971. Johnston's Administration 1891–1897. Zomba: Government Press.

Beets, Henry. 2002. A Commentary on the Belgic Confession. Grand Rapids: Christian Reformed Publishing House.

Berkhof, Louis. 1996. Systematic Theology. Grand Rapids: Banner of Truth.

Brown, Walter L. 2004. The Development in Self–Understanding of the CCAP – Nkhoma Synod during Forty Years of Autonomy: An Ecclesiological Study. PhD Diss., Stellenbosch University. Unpublished.

Calvin, John. 1559. Institutes of the Christian Religion. Two volumes. Edited by John T. McNeill. Translation Ford Lewis Battles 1960. Philadelphia: The Westminster Press — London: SCM.

Chilenje. Victor. 2007. The Origin and Development of the Church of Central Africa Presbyterian (CCAP) in Zambia. PhD diss., University of Stellenbosch. Unpublished.

Coertzen, Pieter. 1998. Church Order: A Reformed Perspective. Leuven/Dudley: Peeters.

Coertzen, Pieter. 2004. Decently and in Order: A Theological Reflection on the Order for, and the Order in, the Church. Leuven/Dudley: Peeters.

De Ridder, Richard R.1983. A Survey of the Sources of Reformed Church Polity and the Form of Church Government in America. Grand Rapids: Christian Reformed Publishing House.

Du Plessis, Johannes. 1929. The Evangelisation of Pagan Africa. Cape Town: Juta.

Hendriks, Jurgens (ed.). 2001. Reformed Encounters with Modernity: Perspectives from three Continents [Conference Proceedings of the International Society for the Study of Reformed Communities]. Stellenbosch: ISSRC.

Hetherwick, Alexander. 1931. The Romance of Blantyre: how Livingstone's Dream Came True. London: Clarke & Co.

Hetherwick, Alexander. 1932. The Gospel and the African: The Croall lectures for 1930–1931 on the impact of the Gospel on a Central African people. Edinburgh: Clark.

Janssen, Allan J. 2000. Constitutional Theology: Notes on the Book of Church Order of the Reformed Church in America. Grand Rapids: Eerdmans.

Joda-Mbewe, Osborne L. 2002. Urban Poverty as a Challenge for Ministry within the Malawian Context. PhD diss., University of Stellenbosch. Unpublished.

Jones, Griff. 1966. Britain and Nyasaland. London: Allen and Unwin.

Jonker, Willem D. 1965. Om die regering van Christus en sy kerk. Pretoria: Unisa.
Linden, Jane, and John Weller. 1984. Mainstream Christianity to 1980 in Malawi, Zambia and Zimbabwe. Gweru: Mambo Press.
McCracken, John. 2000. Politics and Christianity in Malawi 1875–1940: The Impact of the Livingstonia Mission in the Northern Province. Blantyre: Christian Literature Association in Malawi.
Mijoga, Hilary J. 2001. The Reformed Community in Malawi: legalism in the CCAP – Nkhoma Synod. In: Hendriks 2001. 32–39.
Msangaambe, Chatha. 2011. Laity Empowerment with Regard to the Missional Task of the CCAP. PhD diss., University of Stellenbosch. Unpublished.
Nation Newspaper, The. 30 October 2003. Blantyre Press.
Ott, Martin. 2000. African Theology in Images. Blantyre: Christian Literature Association in Malawi.
Paas, Steven. 2006. The Faith Moves South: A History of the Church in Africa. Zomba: Kachere.
Paas, Steven. 2007. Ministers and Elders: The Birth of Presbyterianism. Zomba: Kachere.
Pachai, Bridglal. 1972. The Early History of Malawi. London: Longman.
Pauw, Christoph M. 1980. Mission and Church: History of the Nkhoma Synod of the Church of Central Africa Presbyterian. PhD diss., University of Stellenbosch.
Phiri, Isabel A. 2000. Women, Presbyterianism and Patriarchy: Religious Experience of Chewa Women in Central Malawi. Blantyre: Christian Literature Association in Malawi.
Phiri, Desmond D. 2004. History of Malawi: From Earliest Times to the year 1915. Blantyre: Christian Literature Association in Malawi.
Pretorius, J.Lou. 1971.The Early Development of Education in the Dutch Reformed Church Mission in Nyasaland 1890–1940. Lilongwe: Nkhoma.
Reijnaerts, Hubert, Ann Nielson, and Jan-Mattijs Schoffeleers. 1997. Montifortians in Malawi: Their Spirituality and Pastoral Approach. Blantyre: Christian Literature Association in Malawi.
Retief. Malcolm W. 1958. William Murray of Nyasaland. Alice: Lovedale Press.
Ross, Andrew. 1996. Blantyre Mission and the Making of Modern Malawi. Blantyre: Christian Literature Association in Malawi.
Sindima, Harvey J. 1992. The Legacy of Scottish Missionaries in Malawi. Lewiston — New York: Edwin Mellen Press.
Thompson, T. Jack. 1995. Christianity in Northern Malawi: Donald Fraser's Missionary Methods and Ngoni Culture. Leiden — New York: Brill.
Veveau, Roland. 1989. The Apostolic Vicariate of Nyasa: Origins and First Developments 1889–1935. Rome: Historical Departments. Archives. Missionaries of Africa.

Vorster, Jakobus M. 2003. An Introduction to Reformed Church Polity. Potchefstroom: Potchefstroom Theological Publications.

Van Wyk, Jurgens J. 2004. The Historical Development of Church Offices According to the Tradition of Scotland. Zomba: Kachere.

Zeze, Willy. 2006. Confession of Faith and Church Order in the Church of Central Africa Presbyterian—Nkhoma Synod. Master Thesis. Stellenbosch University. Unpublished.

# DISTINCTLY FLEXIBLE

## On a Key Feature of Protestant Church Polity

Herman A. Speelman

A church is more than a congregation of believers. Greek Orthodox theologian John Zizioulas starts his well-known work *Being as Communion* by stating that: "The Church is not simply an institution. She is 'a mode of existence,' a way of being" (Zizioulas 1985, 15). Something similar could be said of a church order.

A church order is not just a compilation of rules. As Bram van de Beek argues, church polity is an expression of what the church is, "a reality that Christ has collected and keeps together" (Van de Beek 2012, 225). Both in the church and in its polity, there should be a space for God's Spirit to live and do its work. A church order should be able to breathe in its mission of directing those who trust in Christ for their lives and eternal salvation.

Whenever the Church, as an institution, gathers too much worldly power, it gets distorted. In canonical law, the divine law (*ius divinum*), primarily denotes loyalty to God rather than worldly power. However, the visible church is also a human, worldly institution. One of the changes that happened in the sixteenth century was a transition from a more divine order to a more human order, from theocracy to more democracy (see for example Calvin 1541/1561, 254, 266f.).

### *Does church polity have any typically Protestant features?*

Considering the question 'What are typically Protestant features of sixteenth-century church law? ', I arrive at the concept of 'flexibility'. During this period, the Protestant movement rebelled against all kinds of abuse going on within the established church. They articulated their new, evangelical ideas in a great number of writings, confessions, and church orders. The Protestants were especially critical of the existing, hierarchical power structure within the church. On a large scale, they abolished or creatively revised existing church law. This provided some very necessary space, without sacrificing any of the core aspects of Christian doctrine and practice.

In the sixteenth century two different Western visions of church law came into conflict. Roman Catholics considered the church a sacramental community (*communio sacramentorum*), while the Protestants spoke of a community of saints (*communio sanctorum*). From the perspective of church polity, in the former case God's graceful presence and mediation was guaranteed by the official hierarchy; the church had an independent authority, deserving of respect. In the latter, Protestant case, the church was placed under the authority of Scripture, so that, different from the Roman Catholic view, it had no authority of itself outside of Scripture.

Agitating against the hierarchical structure of the Catholic church, French protestants stated that "no one church should be able to make claims of superiority over another" (*Confessio Gallicana*, art. 1; hereafter CG). Two years later the Low Countries would follow the Huguenots in proclaiming that "wherever they might be, [all preachers] are equal in power and authority", and in recognizing Jesus Christ as the "only Head of the Church" (French: *seul Chef de l'Eglise*): "the only universal bishop" (*seul Evesque universel*) (*Confessio Belgica* 1561, art. 31; hereafter CB; very much comparable with CG, art. 30). According to the CB, the Bible, as God's Word, should be taken as the only criterion for resolving conflicts (CB, art. 5 and 7). But the interpretation of that same Holy Scripture has often been a cause of great division within the worldwide church, and that is true also concerning the criteria that constitute 'the true Church'. This is detrimental to the space and freedom Christians need in exercising their Christian identity in ever-changing contexts.

### *The church calls on all its members*

Within sixteenth-century Protestant churches, the position of the ordinary churchgoer was upgraded; that is to say, the rigid distinction between the ordained clergyman and the layman underwent a change: individual Christians were increasingly expected to actively participate in church life.

Luther introduced his doctrine of the priesthood of all believers, describing the church as a congregation of believers. The title of 'Christian' was no longer simply distributed on the basis of birth or baptism, instead it also required intrinsic motivation and a certain fear of the Lord. A Christian was supposed to have some knowledge of the Christian doctrines. Different from what was the case in the established church, individual believers were expected to read the Bible in their native tongue, to pray regularly, to faithfully attend church services and Holy Communion, and to regularly meet with their spiritual leader(s) to discuss their personal progress in the renewal and sanctification of their lives.

The pioneering Protestant leaders of the sixteenth-century church renewal also tried to bridge the gap between the internalization and externalization of religion. They were trying to purify and renew the church as it was, without losing sight of the good things of the ecclesiastical tradition, and with their eyes open to maintaining continuity with the church of all centuries.

*Two characteristics of the church*

The ecumenical symbols speak of the unity, the holiness, the catholicity and the apostolicity of the church. In addition, the Protestant churches asked for special attention to the sermon and proper administering of the sacraments. In one of the first official Lutheran confessions, the Augsburg Confession (CA), it is stated that God uses the teaching of the gospel and the administering the sacraments as tools (*institutum*) to give us the Holy Spirit (see CA, art. 5).

Article 7 of the same CA interestingly describes the church as a congregation of saints (*congregatio sanctorum*). In this way, these articulations try in an effort of redefining the church to denote the limits of the church while simultaneously giving it more space. As the confession continues in the Latin version: "It is however the church as the gathering of believers, in which the gospel is purely preached and the sacraments are properly administered. For true unity in the church, it is enough to agree about the teaching of the gospel and the use of the sacraments. It is not necessary that human traditions, that is, rituals or church ceremonies that have been set up by humans, should be identical in all places" (CA, art. 7).

More than a quarter of a century later, Théodore de Bèze, the successor to Calvin, wrote a confession in which he formulated several principles concerning church regulations within Protestantism. Most of the canonical rules are neither binding to our conscience nor valid in all times and places, he writes, because "while the doctrines, of which the sacraments are a part, concern our conscience and exist independent of human individuals...the canonical rules about behavior [within the church] only concern the external form....For that reason the canonical rules are mostly not universal and useful for all times and places" ("*La doctrine, sous laquelle aussi nous comprenons l'administration des Sacrements, touche la conscience, and ne depend point des homes...les ordonnances canoniques concernantes la façon and maniere de faire, est toute exterieure....à raison dequoy elles ne peuvent etre pour la pluspart ni universelles, ne perpetuelles sans exception*") (Beza 1561, ch. 5, § 18).

In Protestantism, church polity regulations are often 'subject to change' and 'the work of humans' (*muables and faites par les hommes*), said Beza. "A certain rule or practice can be useful in one situation, and useless in another. Something good at one time, might be harmful at another time" ("*Car tel ordre and façon se pourra tenir en un lieu, qui ne peut estres en aucun usage en un autre: telle chose aussi est bonne en un temps, qui seroit inutile ou dommageable en un autre*") (Beza 1561, ch. 5, § 18).

Local churches were free to decide on all kinds of aspects of church life: the liturgy, which of the many church holidays would be celebrated, specifications of obligated prayers, the use of church clocks, fasting, etc.

*Searching for a third characteristic*

In the famous church order and confession of 1552 (*Examen Ordinandorum*), German reformer Melanchthon describes obedience to the clergical office (*obedientia ministerio*) as the third characteristic of the church (a *notum ecclesiae*), next to the gospel and the proper administering of the sacraments (EO, LXXV and 37).

Ten years later, the Dutch reformer Guido de Brès called attention to the 'poor churchgoers', who, while being persecuted and scattered across the world, were also "united in the same Spirit through the power of their faith" (CB, art. 27).

In his search for a theoretical foundation for a more fluid understanding of the church, the contemporary Dutch theologian Maarten Wisse notes that in the CB, Article 29 refers not only to a correct understanding of the doctrines, but also to a correct way of living that enables one to recognize the true church. The Dutch confession assumes the true church to be recognizable, not only by what it preaches and the sacraments it administers, but also by the penitantial practices, 'punishing the sins' of the disobedient Christian. It also discusses the aspects that make an obedient Christian recognizable, namely the characteristics of the believer (*notae fidelium*) (Wisse 2010, 30f.)

For the members of the true church it was also clear what it meant to depend on Christ for their salvation and what fruits of the Spirit they would display: they would pursue justice, flee sin, love God above all and their neighbor as themselves. Here Guido de Brès goes beyond the formal aspects of the church in order to zoom in on its members ("*ceux que sont de l'Eglise*"). Church members and Christians can be recognized by their display of certain characteristics: their "faith and the fact that they had accepted (French: '*receu*') Jesus Christ as their one and only Savior, the ways in which they flee sin and pursue righteousness, their love of the true God as well as their neighbors, without turning to the left or the right, and that they crucify the flesh and its works" (CB, art. 29). Throughout the centuries, the confessions of the sixteenth century grew to be a genre in their own right, mostly dealing with matters of faith in God and the ways in which he communicates with his children through Scripture and the sacraments;

Protestant church polity especially emphasized the practical aspects of the religious life, such as the fruits of the Spirit manifest in the lives of believers.

After all, to be a Christian church is 'a mode of existence', and that is a reality Christ brought about. By focusing on the individual members of the church, the sixteenth century provides us with a less static, and relatively more open and variable and ecumenical view on the organization of church and religion, with considerably fewer church rules. This is made possible by a more flexible approach to church polity regulations and, above all, by the conviction that belonging to the body of Christ is a very special mode of existence.

*Question for further research*

The church is a way of being in communion with Christ and therefore a way of life. The church testifies to these aspects in various more or less solid forms and structures, sometimes contingent on local circumstances.

This raises a question as to which objective and subjective elements are indispensable as core aspects of the crucial practice of belonging to this holy communion — for instance, within a secularized environment in which many have given up on regular church attendance. Does active membership in a Christian church have radical implications for daily life? Can we learn something from the early church about being a church in a non-Christian world? What might a contemporary, ecumenical and outward-looking church polity look like if it aimed to actively address these rapid changes?

*Abbreviations and bibliography*

CA: Confessio Augustana (Augsburg Confession) (1530).
CB: Confessio Belgica (Belgic Confession) (1561).
CG: Confessio Gallicana (French Confession) (1559).
EO: Melanchthon, Philipp. Examen Ordinandorum. 1552. In: Corpus Reformatorum. 1859. Braunschweig: C.A. Schwetske. Vol. 23, 1–102.

Beza, Theodore. 1561. Confession de foy chrestienne, contenant la confirmation d'icelle, et la refutation des superstitions contraires. Quatrième edition, revüe sur la Latine, et augmentée avec un Abregé d'icelle. Caen. (1st edition 1559).
Calvin, John. 1541/1561. Ordonnances ecclésiastiques. In: Busch 1997, 236–279.
Busch, Eberhard, et al. (ed.). 1997. Calvin-Studienausgabe. Vol. 2. Neukirchen-Vluyn: Neukirchener Verlag.
Van de Beek, A. (Bram). 2012. Lichaam en Geest van Christus: De theologie van de kerk en de Heilige Geest. Meinema: Zoetermeer.

Wisse, P. Maarten. 2010. 'Hun heil verwachtend in Jezus Christus': Een andere fundering voor een fluïde kerkbegrip. In: Geestkracht 66(2010), 22–34.
Zizioulas, John D. 1985. Being as Communion: Studies in Personhood and the Church. Crestwood, NY: St Vladimir's Seminary Press.

# LIST OF AUTHORS

J. A. (Hans) de Waal M.A. is a PhD candidate in diaconal studies at the Protestant Theological University in the Netherlands (location Amsterdam).

Dr Wim Dreyer is senior lecturer of Church History and Church Polity at the University of Pretoria, South Africa.

Prof. A. (Dries) le R du Plooy is professor in Ecclesiology (in particular Church Polity) at the North-West University (Potchefstroomcampus), South Africa.

Prof. Allan J. Janssen is an affiliate professor of Theological Studies at New Brunswick Theological Seminary, New Brunswick, New Jersey, USA.

Prof. Leo J. Koffeman is professor of Church Law and Ecumenism at the Protestant Theological University in the Netherlands (location Amsterdam).

Rev. Godfrey Msiska is adjunct lecturer of Church History and Church Polity at the Centre for Christian Mission Seminary (location Kitwe), Zambia.

Dr Zakaria J. Ngelow is executive director of Yayasan Oase Intim, a foundation to promote contextual theology and empowerment of local ministry among churches in Eastern Indonesia.

Prof. Johannes Smit is extraordinary senior lecturer of Church Polity at the North-West University (Potchefstroomcampus), South Africa.

Dr Herman Speelman is a senior postdoctoral research fellow in the field of Early Modern Reformed Theology at the Theological University of Kampen, the Netherlands.

Rev. Roy Alexander Surjanegara is a minister of the Gereja Kristen Indonesia (Indonesia Christian Church), serving a congregation in Jl. Maulana Yusuf - Bandung, West Java.

Dr Helena van Coller is a senior lecturer at the Law Faculty of Rhodes, University in Grahamstown, South Africa.

**Church Polity and Ecumenism**
Global Perspectives
edited by Prof. Dr. Leo J. Koffeman (Amsterdam) and Prof. Dr. Allan J. Janssen (New Brunswick/USA)

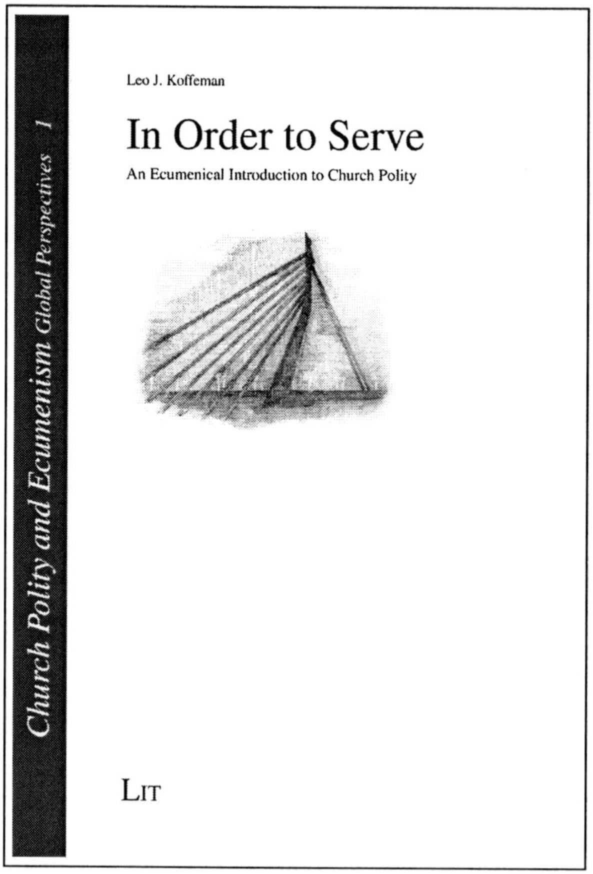


Leo J. Koffeman
**In Order to Serve**
An Ecumenical Introduction to Church Polity
Ecclesiology is in the center of current ecumenical dialogue. However, this hardly seems to influence theological reflection on church polity. This book explores new avenues in this respect, in an attempt to enhance a truly ecumenical and inter-cultural approach of the theological discipline of church polity, without neglecting its juridical character. Key issues like liturgy and ordained ministry are featured, as well as concepts like missional church, synodality, episcopacy, and many others. Examples from Roman Catholic and Anglican canon law as well as from a number of Protestant church orders clarify the issues at stake. Finally, its contextual approach stimulates new reflection on church – state relationships. Does a deeper ecumenical understanding of the nature and mission of the church foster a renewal of church polity?
Bd. 1, 2014, 288 S., 29,90 €, br., ISBN 978-3-643-90318-1